WHITE BUCKS
&
BLACK-EYED
PEAS

WHITE BUCKS
&
BLACK-EYED PEAS

Coming of Age Black
in White America

Marcus Mabry

MODERN TIMES

Library of Congress Cataloging-in-Publication Data

Mabry, Marcus
    White bucks and black-eyed peas : coming of age Black in white America / by Marcus Mabry.
        p.   cm.
    Originally published: New York : Scribner, c1995.
    ISBN–13 978–1–59486–820–7   paperback
    ISBN–10 1–59486–820–4   paperback
    1. Mabry, Marcus, date   2. African Americans—Biography.   3. United States—Race relations.   I. Title.
    E185.97.M117A3   2008
    305.896'0730092—dc22   2007046240

Distributed to the book trade by Macmillan

2   4   6   8   10   9   7   5   3   1   paperback

DEDICATION

For my mother and my grandmother

I envied and I loathed John McEnroe. I wanted to act that way; but, I couldn't.

I wanted to [get angry]. I couldn't afford myself that luxury.

Having to live as a black person in America has been infinitely more challenging [than dying of AIDS].

—ARTHUR ASHE

CONTENTS

ix

ACKNOWLEDGMENTS

This book would not have been possible without my mother and my grandmother—for obvious reasons. I thank them for their patience and their understanding as I "told our business."

I also thank the readers who made this book this book, the friends who anchored and steered me through the experience; my father and my brother, whose strength, humor and love are always inspirational; my editor for the first edition, Hamilton Cain, and my editors and friends at *Newsweek*.

I owe my current editor, Leigh Haber; my agent, Charlotte Sheedy; and Modern Times and Rodale my eternal gratitude for bringing this paperback to life.

And most of all, I thank my teachers, especially Joel Greenberg, who told me when I was a nappy-headed Second Former that there was no reason I could not paint my portrait of the artist as a young man, and Deborah McKay, whose rules I still try to live by: take risks, be honest, come into the room alone—and "a poem should not mean, but be."

NOTE ON THE
PAPERBACK EDITION

Twelve years have passed since *White Bucks and Black-Eyed Peas* first appeared in print. In revising the text for this edition, I tried to limit myself to correcting typographical errors that appeared in the hardcover edition. It was not an easy task. I was much younger when I wrote *White Bucks,* and while editing the text I often wanted to change it: to sandpaper overwritten prose or to further develop thoughts or feelings that had matured with me in the last decade. I resisted for the most part. My younger voice is the voice of this book, as it should be.

MM
October 5, 2007

PREFACE

I was born in 1967. The year before Martin Luther King was assassinated. One of the riot years. I started school in the post-civil rights era of the 1970s. For the eight years I was in high school, college and graduate school, Ronald Reagan was president of the United States. I belong to a class of African-Americans who came of age in the 1990s. I belong to that minority within a minority that is college-educated—and that minority within *that* minority that is male. We are almost a class unto ourselves: twenty-something, black, professional and bound for success.

We are both a testament to American opportunity and a bellwether of American turmoil. Our brief history has been one of contradictions and compromises. Individually, we have greater professional opportunities than any preceding generation of African-Americans. Yet, by many measures, black people collectively are worse off relative to white Americans today than they were before the civil rights "revolution."

Part of a famously nonactivist generation, we nonetheless helped push the United States "Out of South Africa" and pried open the canon of Great Works. Although we are the most assimilated and the most integrated black Americans ever, we seem to find true community only among ourselves. We seek to "make it," but we want to "stay black." We want white Americans to understand our culture, but not expect us to educate them: "It's a Black Thang, You Wouldn't Understand." We want to be judged by a colorless standard, but we proudly affirm our racial identity.

As we have been trying to unearth the men and women we are, America has been trying to figure out what to make of us. While we have been learning to play the white corporate game, the rules have been in flux. Poll after poll has shown that while white Americans say there should be equality between the races, they believe that today it is white Americans who have less opportunity to find a good job or attend a first-rate college.

By the time we "arrived," white Americans were already wondering if they had not given African-Americans too much. After college, companies hired us because of affirmative action, or merit. They promoted us because of quotas, or merit. And they resented us for being there.

Meanwhile, we have become increasingly separated from the masses of African-Americans, people who live in distant neighborhoods where we venture only for a haircut. Many of our parents had already worked their way into the middle, even upper-middle, class. Many had not. Most of us who trickled up from the ghetto and into the buppie (black urban professional) elite— through hard work, the remnants of government programs for the poor or a combination of both—left our mothers and fathers and brothers and sisters down there when we went off to good white schools and colleges.

We saw some of them slide deeper into the poverty pit as the post-industrial economy wiped out well-paying blue-collar jobs. We saw our old neighborhoods sink from being "poor, but proud" into a numb despair, brooding and violent by turn. We saw the cohesion and solidarity fade from Black America, as we broke into open class warfare between ourselves. Buppies loathing welfare mothers. Professionals crossing the street to avoid the brother on the sidewalk. And women wondering where all the men had gone.

Our generation never knew the America that had crafted a rough consensus on racial equality or how to achieve it. Never buoyed by the hopes and promise of the civil rights era, we were not disappointed when the dream was never realized. But the realization that, despite our individual opportunity, the dream would never come true for most black people made us cynical and pessimistic. While *I* was doing well, *we* were doing worse. And, yet, even the Talented Tenth had no abiding faith that tomorrow would be better.

My trek from AFDC to the Sorbonne is not meant to speak for all our experiences. No one person could; there are too many roads from there to here, even while there are too few. Each offers its own twists and turns, sacrifices, successes and sorrows. But like African-Americans of any generation when I speak of "me," I have to speak of "us." As much as blacks lament our unending travails in America, we, more than any others, are dependent on America for our very identity. This nation is not only the crucible of our suffering, it is the forge that made us.

I cannot understand my present without exploring our past. White people often ask me how I escaped poverty when so many poor black males do not. I usually answer *luck*. I might add Uncle Sam, with his Aid to Families with Dependent Children (AFDC), food stamps, Medicaid, Head Start, college grants and Perkins loans—all of which benefited me. But if reasons to explain why I am "an exception" are needed, then the first two are my grandmother and my mother. One planted me firmly in this world. The other taught me to reach for the heavens. My grandmother rooted me in reality, through her staunch loyalty to an unjust existence and her faith that life was its own reward. My mother taught me the power of dreams through her endless pursuit of experience and wonder. My story is only their story come to fruition, the seed of three generations of African-American promise that, until me, for myriad reasons, failed to germinate.

Policy wonks, social engineers and politicians—liberal and conservative—debate whether government aid or family values will elevate poor Americans from nihilism to productivity, from hopelessness to self-sufficiency. There is no magic formula, of course—three parts bootstrap and one part handout—that will guarantee a fair opportunity for the disadvantaged. I believe that without any grandmother and my mother's energetic involvement in my development, I would not be writing this book. Their determination that I succeed carried me far from poverty. At the same time, without taxpayers' dollars I would not have been empowered with the tools—knowledge, role models and a good diploma—to free myself from the cycle of low income and low achievement. If my mother and my grandmother were the heart and mind that propelled a poor black boy toward success, then that aid was the essential lifeblood that nourished them.

My journey took me from poverty to prep school; from New Jersey to Africa, Europe and Asia; and from assistant custodian on the government's now-defunct summer jobs program to *Newsweek*'s correspondent in Paris. The prep school from which I graduated with distinction is the same one where one of my grandmothers worked supervising the all-black cooks and waitstaff. I am proof that even today the clichéd American dream can come true for boys who start off in the world poor and black—even after crack,

Rodney King, Pat Buchanan; even for a member of "an endangered species."

The American ideal is meritocratic success through individual effort. But following that societal directive, instilled from our elite prep schools and our prestigious universities, is not easy. In order to achieve, we all make sacrifices. But for African-Americans, brothers in particular, this truism appears deceptively facile—especially for those of us who travel from poverty to success. While working-class Irish-Americans or Italian-Americans may face similar alienation from the families they leave behind, they do not hazard their group identification. In our quest for accomplishment, and in our success, poor African-Americans risk our families, our racial identity, our very selves.

In this book, I describe the events and people that shaped me. I was twenty-five years old when I began writing. I will be twenty-eight when the book is published. I do not intend to answer all the questions that my life to this point has raised; I am still unsure of many of the answers myself. And I find they change over time. Just as I have constantly grown in my ability to understand myself and the events and people that touched my life, so does my voice change in the course of this narrative: from passive observer to active participant, from self-centered to outwardly oriented, from naïve to contemplative. Do not read this memoir for conclusions. This is quite evidently not a life story, but the story of the beginning of a life.

The book deliberately begins and ends with my family because, at this early point in my journey, one important lesson I have learned is that more than the acceptance of any community of strangers, black or white, it must be in the support and acceptance of those I love that I find my sense of belonging, my place in the world.

I am ever grateful to my God, my family, my nation, my mentors and my teachers, and to the generations of African-Americans who died so that I might live free. Still, I must reckon the price I paid for the privilege of living in two worlds—one black and poor, one white and affluent—from the friction within my family to the questioning of my own personhood. The price of success seemed betrayal. I carry with me the scars of "making it": the uncomfortable and embarrassing dependency of my family, the feeling of "tomming" and the constant balancing act between everyone and everything, white and black.

CHAPTER 1

GOD MEANT FOR SOME PEOPLE TO BE POOR

We were a living contradiction: a tiny enclave of African-Americans—then, we were just black—wedged into a sprawling white suburb, ebbing over the Trenton city limits into the white oasis of Hamilton Township, New Jersey. Demographers and the men who ran the township government called our neighborhood Forest Valley. We called it White City. The first African-American pioneers named it that when they moved up and out of the crowded neighborhoods of Trenton.

In the 1970s and '80s, when I grew up there, White City was mostly poor and working-class families, with a marbling of middle class. Two-story houses huddled around green lawns that ran between them like alleys. By the 1990s, the 'hood would be laid waste, the blue-collar middle class barely surviving the twin scourges of the postindustrial economy and crack. Our homes never did look as picture-perfect as the white parts of Hamilton, with their split-levels and sprawling front lawns. But it was neat and clean and safe, and it was home.

I would sit on the rickety wooden porch for what seemed like hours after school. It had separated from the main structure years ago, sinking a foot below and away, making our house look like a broken toy. The slate gray paint flaked off everywhere. The tattered screens bulged out in some places and revealed huge holes in others. When it rained, we'd play *Star Trek* on the biggest section of screen. Pointing with a stick, I'd tell my uncle that an alien ship was approaching. Poking in a far-off quadrant, I'd designate a class-M planet on our trajectory.

On afternoons when my brother and uncles were out roaming, I'd sink deep into numbed boredom and dream of what I was going to do the next day at school. I'd molest the ants on our dusty front lawn, building earthen embankments to trap them. I'd watch them crawl over each other in a manic fury. Frustrated, they'd finally head up the stick. I'd shake them off and stab abysmal canyons in the ground, smashing their heads. We would start our game over until the myopic concentration that it required wore me out.

I'd lean back on the hulking, lopsided steps my uncle had poured and look up Field Avenue into the motionless distance. The gray pavement without sidewalks made me think of the South my family had left: still and tired. On one corner opposite ours sat the Tarvers' house, a three-story wooden monstrosity that would have been white if it wasn't for the brown cloud of dirt that had soaked into its surface. Disassembled cars and piles of spare parts littered their barren lawn.

On the other corner, Mr. and Mrs. Lewis owned a two-story cottage, painted a neat blue with shimmering white shutters. Mr. Lewis was a prison guard; his wife was a teacher. Grass ringed their house like a carpet, shining as if they sprayed it with Afro Sheen. Mr. Lewis mowed it every Saturday like it was a sacrament, his paunch stretching tight his white tank top, his light-skinned fat knees poking out below his baggy shorts. Their porch was solid, with a white balustrade and two tall white columns. They didn't have any screens.

Lida Street separated us. Our address, 723, was swirled on our aluminum mailbox with the leftover paint from somebody's home repair project. One end of Lida, after our yard, ran across a rag-gedy bridge to the cemetery and the roads that wound back to the white parts of Hamilton. The other end ran through the heart of White City (the neighborhood was only about a hundred blocks square). Up that way, crisp air hung under the tall trees before South Broad, the other border with the white neighborhoods—the lower-class ones, filled with Italians and row houses—that also bordered Trenton. But until you got there, the blocks were cozy and cool.

Some afternoons my grandmother would come into vision a few blocks up the street, weighed down by brown grocery bags. Pounding my feet into the black tar as hard as I could, I'd run to meet her, hardly able to contain my excitement.

"Hey, baby." A smile would lap over her tired yellow face. Dark fat bags anchored her lusterless red eyes, but her smile was all alabaster. I'd lift one of the sacks from under her thick arm.

"What's for dinner?" I'd ask, hungry more for something to think about than food.

Once inside, she'd heft her bag of groceries onto the kitchen table. Before she could pull her way up the narrow stairs, she would inevitably spot an uncle's sweater or books on the living room floor.

"Ronny? Ronny!" she'd bellow upstairs, her face scrunched tight with disgust. "Boy, you know you better get these here clothes off this floor!" she would yell. "Lord ha' mercy. I don't know what you think this is, boy, a pigsty?" Then she would make her way up the stairs and down the hallway, floorboards creaking under her heavy frame. First, she would take off her powder blue nurse's aid uniform and place it on a wire hanger. Then she would remove the stiff wig that lay flat on her head. Pushing the bobby pins in, she's adjust it on the pocked Styrofoam head on her dresser. Then, she would throw on "that ole housedress," as she called it, and her worn pink slippers.

I watched as she stood at the stove browning ground beef, then opening a can of Campbell's Cream of Mushroom soup. If I was lucky, she would decide to bake a cake—sometimes she baked even in the middle of the week—and I would sit at the kitchen table, spreading my warm arms over the cold formica top. She whipped the cake batter so violently, I was amazed it didn't splatter out of the bowl and onto the tattered linoleum. Her right arm was the size of a bodybuilder's. I'd clean the spoon and the bowl, straining my tongue not to miss a lick.

As dinner simmered, Grandmom would sit down with the paper, usually, the *Trentonian*, pulling on her glasses one arm at a time. If I felt like it, I would pick one of the books from the encyclopedia case. We had two sets, *World Book* and *Britannica*, that sat on a bookcase in the living room near the front door. Missing some screws, the shelves slumped to one side. The volumes were dated 1968, the year after I was born. It was already 1978. But reading was the only thing to do on an endless day—if I didn't have any homework or if the homework didn't take more than half an hour. Most days, one or the other condition was met.

"Baby, can you turn on the TV for Granmama? It's time for the news," she would prompt. After a few minutes, and an eerie high-pitched electrical buzz, the image would crackle onto the screen. The colors moved in and out like waves in the ocean, but the sound boomed clearly: "The *CBS Evening News* with Walter Cronkite."

My grandmother loved Walter Cronkite. I assumed he was one of those white people that all black people liked, like Billy Graham. The flashes of faraway places and fascinating people assaulted me. As I inevitably drifted off, I would think about how smart Mr. Cronkite sounded. So important. I'd listen to his soothing baritone while the smell of ground beef and mushroom soup filled the house. It felt good to fall asleep on the lumpy old couch.

At ten years old, my life seemed to be one long etherized dream, occasionally punctuated by happy instances and horrific nightmares. When the gaggle was at home—my mother, my brother and my two uncles—my grandmother's house brooded with potential conflict. Storms seemed to rise up suddenly out of nowhere to trouble my quiet boredom. Or sometimes they built slowly until they reached a thunderous crescendo.

My mother hated the way my grandmother raised me and my brother. She didn't match our clothes the way Mom wanted. On one school picture day she had us go to school "looking like uncoordinated as Biafrans," Mom said. My mother thought her brothers, just a few years older than Charles and me, took advantage of us.

Sometimes the fights would erupt when my mother came home and discovered we had not eaten, even if no one else had eaten either.

"I go away to work and pay you people to take care of my children," she would yell, directing her anger over the heads of my grandmother and her sister Corrine as they sat talking. "And you can't even feed them at a decent hour? My God! Come on Markie and Chuckie. Get your coats. We're going to McDonald's." Embarrassed, I would slide into my coat and shuffle behind my mother out the door, unable to turn to look at Grandmom. My brother would bound down the steps and out the front door.

Sometimes my mother and my grandmother fought about how our hair wasn't well combed. Sometimes they fought about money or bills or where my mother had been the night before. But the underlying theme was always the same: my mother hated having to leave us with her relatives while she worked. She alternated between jobs as a Red Cross disaster assistant, a social worker and, most often, a home health aide. Sometimes she worked twenty-four-hour cases, living with her patients; sometimes she came home every night. To me, it seemed like she never kept the same job for more than a year. Either the patient died or my mother grew tired of dealing with whatever nursing agency had hired her.

Every argument between my mother and grandmother would become an argument about the past. My grandmother would get so hot that she would fire back, spitting vitriol, "Well, I don't think I did *so* bad. You turned out alright. And you're staying here, aren't ya?" Often the fights ended with my mother snatching us and fleeing—up Field Avenue to Old Man Clait's house or to a motel on Route 206 if she had the money.

It was worse if we had nowhere to go. Then, my mother and my grandmother would yell from one floor to the other for what felt like hours, going to the stairwell to vent their rage.

"I don't need a goddamn thing from you," my mother would stomp over to the stairs and yell up. "You can have your damn house. You never did a thing for me anyway," she would cry.

"No. No. No. Unn-uuhhnn. Now, hold on, Miss Lady," my

grandmother would say in a clinched, constricted voice. The floorboards would creak. "You don't curse in my house. You hear me? Don't you curse in *this* house. You can do what you want out there in the streets, but don't you bring it up in here."

She would make her way down the stairs, her face twisted into a terrifying scowl, her eyes burning. Then, with her hand on one hip, her other arm extended as far as it would go with a pointed finger hammering her every word, "Now . . . let me tell you something . . . "

It was a tradition in our family, as in so many others. My grandmother raised my brother and me as much as my mother did—like my grandmother's mother had raised my mother. It was a quasi-Amazonian society where men occupied a secondary position. They either left at some point after a child's birth or, if they were around, they were scarcely present. Which was just as well, since their presence often brought more sorrow than security.

The scariest confrontations in my life pitted my uncle Bobby, the "man" of the house, against either my mother or my grandmother. When he was young, he would erupt like a volcano.

Whenever he and my mother clashed, it looked like they would kill each other. Often the fights erupted because Bobby, a varsity football player and wrestler, had eaten food that my mother had bought. Once it was because he had broken her car window. I remember watching the storm rising that time, my stomach knotted. I felt nauseous. Their voices pitched the house. Curse words sliced through the air. They stood eye to eye (or eye to chest), screaming into each other's face. Their arms and fingers and lips flailed so wildly that the slightest miscalculation would have caused them to touch. Physical contact, I knew, would bring tragedy.

"Come on, big man," my mother said, rolling up the sleeves

of her bulky sweater. "Hit me, then, motherfucker. You so bad. Hit me."

"If you got any sense, you better get out of my face before I smack you, girl," he said, towering over her, glaring. "You better not touch me. You better not touch me, bitch." He pushed himself up against my mother.

She stomped into the kitchen and retrieved a butcher's knife. "I am not scared of your fat ass." She swung the blade, slicing through the air around her to punctuate her sentences. "You are not going to throw your weight around in here."

He ran upstairs and grabbed a baseball bat. "I'm ready. Come on," he ran down the stairs, swinging it through the air.

My grandmother tried to stand between them. "Now listen. This is *my* house. And nobody is going to kill anybody. Why don't y'all stop this nonsense?"

I tried to call my mother away. My brother was ready to scrap if my uncle touched her. My younger uncle, Ronny, stood silently nearby.

"Marcus, get out of here. Get Chuckie and get out here," my mother shrieked, not turning to look in my direction.

"Marcus, baby, call the police," my grandmother said calmly.

I ran to the phone and dialed 911.

My uncle left before they came. They took my mother's statement on the car window.

It was the second time a squad car had rushed to our house, sirens wailing and lights flashing. I remembered the other fight, when my mother and my uncle had both stayed after Grandmom called the police, yelling obscenities at each other past the officers. I was embarrassed to see my family behaving that way in front of white people. I thought about what they were going to tell their children and their wives.

But, I was relieved that no one would die that night. Usually calm returned without police intervention, as tempers failed. No one could sustain such intense rage for long. Still, sometimes, even in happy moments, the unsettling thought would seize me, from nowhere, that something might go wrong—some comment, some action, some mishap—and bring the storm again, out of the blue.

....

White City was indistinguishable from my lonely adolescence. They were the same. I didn't seem to fit in outside—no good at basketball and a bookworm—so I spent most of my time inside. I was rarely teased about the fact that I liked school. Once in a while my friends called me "professor." Still, it didn't seem normal. Standing around with the other kids in the neighborhood, I quickly grew bored; I was different. Looking back, the loneliness may have been caused by a lack of intellectual stimulation, or the result of my aspiring to do the exciting things I saw on the nightly news, or maybe I was just a geek. Whatever the reason, the isolation led to reading and the reading led to learning, and the more I learned the more I wanted to learn. My mother and my cousin Beverly had read with me as early as I could remember. When they stopped, as I got older, I read the books on hand: the encyclopedias. It never occurred to me to ask for a library card; besides, the library was on the other side of the township.

I seemed to be the only kid who believed my grandmother when she said the streets had nothing to offer us and that we should stay in the house.

My grandmother and my encyclopedias were my best friends. My mother was always working or out with her girlfriends. My brother, one of the most popular kids in the neighborhood, was always playing. My grandmother, though, was always there. Our schedules were almost identical. In the winter, she piddled around the house, reading her paper or cooking dinner. In the spring and summer, she tilled her backyard garden.

She would stand between the rows of tomato plants, her sturdy legs glistening under her pale greenish blue house dress as it waved in the late spring air. She wore a red and white head rag (what white boys called a "bandana"). It kept the sun off her head and held down her short brownish red hair, only a shade darker than her body. Leaning slightly forward, she'd absentmindedly brush down her dress with her heavy forearm.

"Baby, run in the house and get Granmama a brown paper bag to put these tomatoes in," she'd say, reaching down to balance one of the ripe red Jersey tomatoes in her hand.

She spent hours in the garden. Going from plant to plant, she'd lay thin green beans across the width of her palm and pluck them from their stems with a quick jerk of her wrist, up and out. Eventually, she would call into the house and ask me to bring her a chair. She'd lay the pile of beans in her lap, spreading her legs apart and letting the housedress flap over the tattered plastic seat cushion. Pulling a bucket beside her, she would face the garden or the creek behind the house, snapping the beans in two or three places, throwing the midsections into the bucket and leaving the ends in a paper bag. She snapped so fast she could prepare a dinner's worth of beans in minutes. Working with her older sister Corrine, they could snap a Thanksgiving's worth of vegetables in less than an hour.

It was when working in the yard that my grandmother looked most satisfied. She was very beautiful when a smile came over her face—you could see how she must have been a "fine woman" growing up in Georgia. I imagined one of those oily black men out of the movies trying to sweet-talk her. She would have resisted, telling that fool to stop wasting his time and hers. I conjured up good-for-nothing Negroes coming around looking to see Merle, hoping to melt her still formidable resistance.

Our tranquil backyard recalled what I imagined to be the South. My only experience with the region was what I had seen on TV or heard relatives say. I had been the first northerner born in my family and took great pride in the fact. Maybe because my family always put down southern people, southern accents and southern ways. Just like on TV, all the things they associated with the South were bad: the Ku Klux Klan, lynchings, the word "nigga" (a much more virulent formulation than the northern "nigger"). The most present southern remnant in my life was that word that my grandmother and her sisters always used for white people, "cracker." They said it was because white people were the color of soda crackers—a foreign concept itself, since I said "saltines." But the southern appellation more closely matched reality: every white person I knew looked more like a soda cracker than the Crayola crayon smugly named "flesh."

The electric spring and summer days only emphasized my loneliness. Every minute of the weekend would float by for hours, suspended on the dense air. My mind would wander emptily through the unbearable quiet, following a bird or a butterfly or a bee. By the time I was twelve, a stillness had settled into my soul, more intense than boredom. I thought that this was the way I would always feel when my hands were idle, when no thought occupied my mind. I'd sit on the front porch and look up Field Avenue into the static distance, dreading the passing of time, but wanting desperately to see it through so it would be over. I'd turn images around and around in my head, losing all sense that the world was moving.

My redemption came with the waning sunlight: I'd walk into

the cool house and click on the TV. At seven o'clock on Sundays, *Battlestar Galactica* came on. On Saturday night, I would watch *The Love Boat*, straight through *Three's Company*, all the way to *Fantasy Island*. (Mr. Cronkite didn't read the weekend news so I didn't watch it.) On weeknights, after dinner and my news-induced nap, my life became exciting on Tuesdays with *Happy Days* and *Laverne and Shirley* and on Thursdays *Starsky and Hutch*. Colonial warrior Captain Apollo of the *Battlestar Galactica* was my first male role model. Samantha Stevens, my first boyhood crush. Frank Hardy was the big brother I never had. And the Jeffersons (some of the rare black characters in my world) were like family. As I laughed the hours away, communing with my very real fictional community, I could forget about my other life.

Monday night during football season was dismal for me. Even before it came on, I could hear that theme song in my head . . . Then, the real music, the graphics and the sportscaster's booming: "*Monday Night Football*." Boredom seeped back. No one had ever explained to me how this game was played and I had never asked. But I knew it took all the time from dinner to bed, and it was dull, dull, dull. I would wander over to the encyclopedia case or flip through a textbook upstairs, but there was no escape from Howard Cosell's resonating baritone and the shrill referee whistles.

Other times, I couldn't get my TV fix because the electricity was cut off. For a few days we would live by candles and kerosene lamps, until my grandmother or my mother found the money to pay the bill. It was embarrassing, but it was better than when the phone was disconnected. Then, anybody who happened to call would know, including my white classmates. In school the next day, they would ask me what was wrong with my phone, though I think they knew.

The only hours on this side of the small screen that rivaled the television world came on holidays, when our whole family gathered together. My grandmother, the matriarch, was the middle of the three sisters whose offspring represented "the whole family." Everybody would drive to our house for Thanksgiving, Christmas, the Fourth of July, Memorial Day, Easter. Then, we feasted.

My grandmother would rise just after the sun and fill the first pots on the stove with cold water and long strips of fatback or big chunks of ham hocks. When steam plumed from the pots and the water inside filled with shiny, flavorful pools of oil, my grandmother would scoop up the heap of collard greens she had stemmed and chopped and plunge the leaves into the boiling water. Her face would flush red. You got the feeling she was doing God's work. With a slight heave, she would send a bowl of soaked black-eyed peas rushing into the other tall, midnight blue pot.

By the time we woke up, the house would be filled with the smell. Grandmom would still take the time "to beat up some pancake batter," as she said, and serve us stacks of hotcakes with Alaga syrup and Land O'Lakes butter dripping over the golden edges. By the time we dressed, our cousins, aunts and uncles would have launched their invasion, wave after wave of relatives plowing into the living room.

"*Oo-woo*, something smells good!" my Uncle Charlie (we pronouced it "Cholly") would howl as he came through the front door. He'd carry a couple of the cakes my mother's sister Bettye had baked. Coconut, chocolate, rainbow. Behind him would follow my aunt with a few pies. Sweet potato, apple, coconut crème. My cousin Moonie, Charles Junior, pulled up the rear. My great aunt Corrine would arrive with her brood: my other uncle, Estine, and two of their kids, Beverly and Glenn. Sonny, their oldest, usually snuck in later to avoid any scenes with his parents. Finally, the Allens, my grandmother's younger sister, Janie Lillian (which we pronounced "Jane-lee-en"), and her six children would make their entrance. Her group was the largest and the loudest. Janice was the only girl; Terry, Apple, Gerald, Danny and Corey were the boys. They were my favorite cousins and our only relatives who lived in Trenton proper. When I went to their house, we did the same things that I did alone most days—only when we would plop down on their porch, eventually the whole neighborhood strolled by and stopped to sit on the stoop and play cards or just talk and laugh. (Life in the urban jungle had its advantages.)

When everyone had arrived and my grandmother had shooed my uncles out of the kitchen, the food would be spread over the kitchen table, the stove and the TV trays and spilled into the dining room, where we kept the television. The spread would feature a twenty-five-pound turkey or two, a baked ham, mountains of potato salad and platters of dressing. Green beans, and candied yams swimming in a syrupy brown sauce, complemented the greens and black-eyed peas. Pies and cakes would be piled on a table in the corner.

Laughter bounded off the peeling wallpaper. The loud, boastful voices of men; the sarcastic, judgmental voices of women, black women, would resonate throughout the house. While the men and children convened in the dining room, plates laden with food, to watch football, the ladies would gather around the still-full pots in the kitchen and gossip. Miss So-and-So was supposedly seeing Miss Ann's husband. The deacon had done this, that and the other thing. And you-know-who was going into therapy, like the white folks.

White folks were always a source of entertainment. Sometimes they served as a positive example: Look at the white folks, they don't throw away their money, they don't stab each other in the back, et cetera. Other times, they provided a negative analogy: Boy, don't you put on that holey old T-shirt . . . like white folks be wearing. Mostly, they represented a powerful, dangerous force against which to be cautioned: Don't you children be going back to that McGalliard School to play basketball, you hear. Don't be going in them white folks' neighborhood. My grandmother was always a racist, but never malicious—an apparent contradiction that would help me deal with my own racism and that of other "good people" later in life.

On a daily basis, she generalized about white people. She talked as if they had caused black people only grief and pain. But she praised the good men and women she knew—Miss Wentworth; Ed, "the fish man"; Mr. Schwartz, the oil man—and she never supported any vindictive plan to pay the others back. And if I asked her to explain a prejudiced remark, she would backtrack: "Well, son, I don't mean to say all white folks . . ." But it was clear that she saw a difference between them and us. Not because of genetics or evolution or IQ, but because that was the way life was.

She said there had been days when she resented the white families she worked for in Georgia, when she "would have done back to them what they did to me," but as she got older those feelings softened. Instead, she spoke with pity about what 1990's politically correct types would call the "oppressor class": "They couldn't help it. They didn't know that you can't mistreat people and have life be good to you."

On holidays, my grandmother held court in the kitchen, sitting quietly to the side of the roast, resting her head on one arm or laying her hands in her lap, bathing in the joy her family brought. Occasionally, she would goad someone forward or dispute a fact in a gentle but persuasive manner that demanded a reply. "Chile, gone . . . Now, you know that ain't the truth," she would cackle as the room erupted in laughter.

I was happy to watch their spectacle from the dining room where the men sat. After two helpings and three desserts, I would drift from one room to the next, listening to the two separate worlds, until I was finally bored. Then I would go out into the yard and watch my cousins kick around a ball or toss one back and forth. If it was kick ball I would join in. I avoided catch. I threw like a girl and didn't want to embarrass myself. The older kids would walk up Field Avenue to play basketball at the park. It felt good to be a family.

My grandmother and her sisters had trekked to New Jersey from Quitman, Georgia—by way of West Palm Beach, Florida. My grandmother and Corrine, Betty Mae Copeland's eldest children, grew up sharing the role of oldest sibling, both of them responsible for their three younger brothers, their sister Janie Lillian and their father, who had a drinking problem. Although she only had marginal control over her husband, Betty Mae Copeland, a Methodist minister's daughter, governed her children with a kind of tough love that rarely spoke in adoring terms or soft gestures. She demanded the strictest discipline and explained little to them. When they transgressed they were beaten with a switch.

Merle Thomas, my grandmother, was born on a plantation twenty miles outside the dusty rural town of Quitman. As a girl, she lived with her sister and parents in a two-room wooden shack, with a wood-burning stove and glassless windows. "We never lived in a one-room shack," my grandmother still says proudly. Her parents worked the fields from sunrise to sunset.

When Merle was about ten, her family quit the plantation for a farm and sawmill closer to town. Life improved. My grand-mother worked in one of the owner's daughters' houses. Even if they saw her as an ageless servant, the daughter and her two little girls, who were about the same age as Grandmom, treated her kindly. She even wore their hand-me-down clothes. Her only uncomfortable moments came when she cooked the family's meals in the summertime. They would open only the rooms they used, using ceiling fans to circulate the air. To keep out the heat, they closed off the kitchen where my grandmother boiled huge caul-drons of water for canning preserves and vegetables. Along with the heat from the stove, the steam filled the kitchen and puckered her face, soaking her clothes in sweat.

Betty Mae Copeland wanted something better for her girls. She had heard about a black woman who taught school to colored children. Miss Ollie Reed, a strict woman whose breath always smelled of garlic, was preparing black children for life in the seg-regated South. She had only a handful of students and Betty Mae had to pay tuition for the girls. There they learned how to print their letters and say their multiplication tables and read.

After a year or so at Miss Ollie's school, Merle and Corrine graduated to the black grammar school in Quitman. A fast learner, my grandmother was often at the head of her class. But, by this time, Betty Mae Copeland was taking care of two toddlers, as well as her husband. She told the girls that one of them would have to stay home to help.

Since they both wanted to continue their education, Merle and Corrine decided to trade off weeks, and they fell further and further behind in school. Eventually, they both stopped going. They went to work full-time and tended to the younger children. They were fifteen and sixteen years old. They had a fifth-grade education.

Their only world outside of work was the occasional trip to the sanctified Baptist church in Quitman, which they managed only when Betty Mae, who normally worked seven days a week, took a day off. Today we might call it a Pentecostal church; then everybody just called the parishioners the "Holy Rollers," because, taken by the Spirit, they would often break into a fevered sweat and roll around on the church floor speaking in tongues.

Merle was always very light-skinned, far up on the southern tone hierarchy. Many fair blacks growing up in the South in the 1920s and '30s used their light skin to "pass." My grandmother could have, but didn't. She was almost ashamed of the privilege that a high-yellow complexion conferred on her. Her own grandmother had treated her father and his brown-skinned brothers and sisters differently from the light-skinned ones (who'd been fathered by a white plantation owner), serving tea to the white children from one pot and to the blacks from another. Detesting the shade bar, my grandmother went out of her way to treat all black people with dignity, respect and solidarity. She sought out relationships with dark-skinned men. She said she never understood why black men would look to white women for love, when black women had so much to give.

My grandmother gave birth to her first child when she was seventeen years old. She worked until the day she went into labor and she paid for the delivery with her own money. She would have her last child at thirty-six. Seven children in all. She was also mother to her mother until she died—not to mention to most of her grandchildren at some point in their lives. She transmitted a seemingly infinite supply of love to those around her. (After one of my uncles had argued with her and frightened her into calling the police to escort him out of the house, she let him back in a few weeks later. He would sleep at the foot of her bed.)

She eventually moved her family from Quitman to be closer to a hospital. Her third husband, Walter Thomas—the first "good man" in my grandmother's life and the last—was a World War II veteran afflicted with leukemia. There were no VA hospitals near Quitman, but Mr. Thomas found one in Coral Gables, Florida. Merle's sister Corrine was already living in relatively nearby West Palm Beach with her husband.

In 1959, West Palm Beach was an upscale Garden of Eden, at least to my family. There was the Atlantic Ocean. There were black people with big cars and big houses. There were rich white people across the intracoastal waterway who needed their homes cleaned. The city was downright cosmopolitan compared to Quitman, with its unpaved roads, dirt-poor black folks and clapboard houses.

At first, my grandmother cleaned house in the sprawling estates of Palm Beach for "good money." Then, she realized she could work eighteen-hour days in restaurants and earn even more. She added waitressing to her curriculum vitae. Soon the family moved out of Corrine's tiny house into a small bungalow on Third Street.

Eight people—my grandmother, her mother, her two daughters and four sons—lived in the two-bedroom house, another luxury by Quitman standards. When they needed to, my grandmother's sisters would move their clans into my grandmother's house too. To my family, this involved no sacrifice. My relatives do not have such solidarity today; but, in the olden days, my grandmother and her sisters pooled their resources and their energies. When one woman needed help the other two sacrificed to give it to her.

After only seven years, the family left West Palm Beach. My grandmother's two oldest children and her sister Corrine had already relocated to the North, that Promised Land where life was rumored to be even better than in South Florida. Her oldest daughter Bettye had married and moved to Trenton. Her oldest son Frederick was in the U.S. Army. He had enlisted at Fort Dix, New Jersey, and been shipped off to Vietnam. Her husband had died and Merle's mother was growing ill. In 1966, Frederick sent a thousand dollars south to move the whole family north. After a twenty-four-hour train ride, they arrived in Trenton and started over. The strange land of New Jersey would be as close to a personal paradise as my grandmother would ever know on earth. She still worked long days as a home health aide, but she bought land in the white suburb of Hamilton Township and owned her own home (thanks to a generous landlord dying and willing it to her). She accomplished more than she had ever anticipated, simply by living the only way she knew how. She realized her version of the American dream.

By the time I knew her, my grandmother was a middle-aged woman in her forties, strong, with vigor etched in her pale yellow skin and in the furrows on the backs of her hands. Whether she was wracked with anger, lashing out to backslap one of my uncles, or sitting coiled in a chair, massaging her aching arms, she was as solid as the trees from which she cut her switches and as gritty as the dirt where she planted her garden. She was immovable. She taught me the importance of hard work and constancy, not because it was moral or because it was noble, but because it was all she knew. She never preached to me; her sermons were the life she led; her pedagogical tools, her hands, her feet and her back.

She had no time for excuses or lassitude. When my uncle Ronald complained about a racist teacher giving him a poor grade, she told him to work harder. Annoyed at his naïveté, she scolded, "Boy, don't you know that to get half the credit, a colored person has got to work twice as hard?" When my uncle Bobby protested that he had not gotten a lead in the play or a spot on the starting team, she asked, "Well, do you want to enjoy yourself or are you looking for personal glory?" She spit "personal glory" out of her mouth like it was an obscenity. She expected nothing from life, except hard work. She took everything as an article of faith: when she went to her room at night, she would say, "I'll see you in the morning, son, God willing."

As I got older, Grandmom and I would talk about her life, her arguments with my mother and her belief in God. We spent long Sunday afternoons during my winter vacations from school discussing questions of faith and destiny. She would hunch over the heater, rubbing her thick hands over her wide shoulders, and look into the distance. "Well, son, I don't know . . . Some people with this education say God doesn't exist. But, I say, if He doesn't, then this is a sad, sad life we living . . . and for what?"

CHAPTER 2

TILLIE IS NOT MY NAME

I was so excited I couldn't sleep. All the other kids were snuggling up in the blankets on their cots, but I couldn't shut my eyes. I wouldn't really be five years old until the weekend, but my party was today. I had been telling all the other kids at nursery school that we were going to celebrate, and our teacher made an announcement. Just after nap time, my mom was bringing the cake, the huge white creation from Emil's Bakery on Broad Street, with buttercream frosting spread smoothly over the top in deep, straight furrows. Swirls looped one over the other along the edges, and yellow and blue icing blossomed flowers in the corners. My name was scripted perfectly under the words "Happy Birthday," with an exclamation point.

By three o'clock, my mother still hadn't shown up. My classmates stole glances at me, trying not to point. My teacher said that something must have come up.

"No," I replied, looking her sternly in the eyes. "She's always late." I went to lie down on my cot, tears racing down my cheeks.

Throughout my childhood, my mother *was* always late. Once, before a second-grade field trip, my teacher held up our bus as long as she could, but my mother never showed. Looking out the window as we pulled away from the school, I prayed that she would flow into view. The lump was so heavy in my throat that I had to hold my breath. When we arrived at our destination, my mom was waiting for us. Running late, she had just missed our bus, so she had taken a cab. But my disappointment had already hardened. Over time, it would become so firm and the layers so deep that it would seal my sense of hope under a protective skepticism. Eventually, I wouldn't trust anyone—even my mother, who actually met every need I had as a boy—to give me anything. To guard against disappointment, I convinced myself that every promise was empty, every dream impossible. Even as I worked tirelessly to win, I was preparing to lose.

What she lacked in punctuality, my mother more than made up for in passion. She protected my brother and me voraciously. One winter day in 1974, she stormed into the brick school building, her eyes sharp with anger, her steps heavy and deliberate.

"Where is Mr. Moody?" she asked the fat white lady behind the front desk.

"Do you have an appointment?" the secretary asked.

"I don't need a damn appointment," she said, striding through the door marked PRINCIPAL.

Someone had ripped my new leather raincoat while it was hanging in the cloakroom of Miss Skokos's first-grade class. My mother demanded to know the culprit's identity. She was hot: she did not send her children to school to be terrorized. She would not tolerate it.

As Mr. Moody interrogated the class, my mother stood fuming, one hand on her hip, cutting her eyes from him to the children and back again. When he finished she gave her own lecture on responsibility and courtesy to the petrified children. "Your parents work very hard to give you the things you have," she said in a measured, condescending tone I knew. "You would not want someone to destroy your things, your toys, your clothing."

I was a proud six-year-old.

She pointed her finger at my classmates. "Remember, do unto others as you would have them do unto you." It sounded more like a threat than a moral. She and Mr. Moody thanked Miss Skokos, turned smartly and left the room, the principal following my mother.

I watched and listened, amazed at her strength. She would loose her strength time and time again, defending her children whenever she thought we had been wronged—an opinion my mother often held. She confronted cousins, uncles, grandparents when someone had spanked us or nabbed a toy. She took on teachers, principals and guidance counselors when she thought we were being mistaught or neglected. When it came to my brother and me, things were black and white: either we were being treated properly or we were suffering abuse. Period.

Growing up, my brother and I had no idea we were poor. That would have been a limitation, and my mother didn't discuss those. For my yearly science projects, the only bounds were my imagination: If I could conjure up the invention, she would find a way to buy the materials. If I saw a chemistry set, a microscope or a telescope that got my mind to reeling, "I wonder if . . . ," she purchased it the next day. When I wanted to be school president in junior high and the whole campaign consisted of putting up one poster in the main hall, she suggested a two-feet-by-three-feet format the likes of which Grice Middle School had never seen. (I conceived the glitter motif.) When I won reelection as Jimmy Carter in a mock election in 1980, she made sure I had a presidential overcoat when my ersatz motorcade roared onto campus. When I got an itch to make movies, she found a secondhand

Super 8 camera and projector. When I wanted to write plays, she unearthed an acquaintance's prehistoric typewriter.

When she was working, she used her salary to finance my dreams; when she was not, she used welfare money. Under no circumstances was she going to let being poor cramp our development— or our style. We were as good as any other children, only better, she told us. While some children wore no-name skippies, we started the school year with new Pro-Keds or Converses. While kids with two working parents who owned their own home had to settle for "Sears specials," we wore Levi's or Lee's. "Just because you're poor doesn't mean you have to look it," my mother once told me, an inversion of Grandmom's dictum.

She was less circumspect in her own life. She had dreams. She began countless projects: careers in show business, direct marketing, social work. She rarely finished them. But she did provide my brother and me with the ability to imagine ourselves anew. My brother, Charles, all five feet six inches and 140 pounds of him, thought he *could* be an NFL superstar. When it became clear that that was a virtual impossibility, my brother decided he wanted to be a carpenter. (Despite the realities of union nepotism and racism, he still longs to build his own carpentry business.) I dreamed of being a lawyer, maybe the first black president, maybe an actor. My mother told me I could do any of it, all of it; and she believed it. She never paid any mind to the obstacles or the doubts. She cared only about the possibilities.

Growing up with her—she was a teen mother—I would find her optimism both frustrating and intimidating: frustrating because she naively believed in our power to make the world right; intimidating because it demanded so much of me—the way a Brahmin banker father expected his son to excel in sports and scholarship. If I ever failed, I could blame only myself.

When I reached adolescence, thinking I had come to know the world, I would disparage her naïveté, her lack of understanding that the universe was malicious and unfair. She would fire back that I was young, that I didn't know everything, however smart I might be.

Actually, I was no smarter than she, just more realistic. And I was endowed with greater perseverance and patience. She was a survivor. I was a planner. She was a dreamer. I was a doer. And as much as we loved, admired and respected each other, both of us loathed the other's opposing personality. I resented her wasting her life away and, later, my money. She resented my telling her what to do: "You are not my father."

....

The small brown girl leaned close to the iron grill. "Come home, Uncle Stan. I'll take care of you. You'll never go to jail again." The wiry, handsome young man on the other side smiled back. Then, the girl's grandmother took her hand and led her out of the correctional facility. Even at six, my mother was invested with an uncanny ability to try to will into reality wishes that could never come true. She believed things so mightily that you got to believing them too—even if, objectively speaking, they weren't 100 percent correct. (Caught in my mother's spell, no jury would have convicted you.)

Folks called her Tillie, the nickname her mother had given her. (Merle meant it as a term of endearment, after a comic-strip character who was always keeping busy—but to my mother it was plain, plain as an old rag.) She was drawn to experience; she made friends with all the old people in Quitman (they were the only ones willing to answer her incessant questions), even old Miss Mary Jane, who was supposed to be crazy. Maybe that's why Tillie thought Miss Mary Jane was the woman to know. Tillie had big eyes and hand-me-down dresses. And to her, Miss Mary Jane looked like a queen, with her soft skin, high cheekbones and woolly mass of hair. She wore hats and she walked tall and upright. Nobody in Tillie's family walked that way.

She didn't find it strange that royalty lived alone in a one-room shack at the edge of the woods, two houses down from her. Or that Miss Mary Jane cooked her food on stones in an open fireplace. Tillie's grandmother forbade her to call on the old woman, and for a while the family nicknamed her "Miss Mary Jane." Undaunted, she visited the recluse most days after school and every day she could sneak there in the summer, just to sit and talk and listen.

Tillie loved the world of grown-ups. She could sit and watch it work forever. Nothing was too mundane. Breaking the social dictum that one should never stare, and a child especially, she would sprawl on the open porch and watch Big Fat Marey Watts chew tobacco for hours. Tillie was fascinated by the way saliva kept dribbling out of Marey's mouth, all day long, like there was an endless supply. The little girl was looking for something to do, to feel; somewhere to be. She seemed like an alien that had fallen from some distant star, not at home with these strange people, her alleged family. All Tillie had were questions and these people never communicated. They didn't tell you why things were and they didn't much like to be probed, thank you very much. Children were meant to be seen and not heard.

"Why is the Earth round?" she would ask her mother. Not looking up from the stove Merle would reply, "Because the Lord made it that way."

Tillie couldn't stand her mother's small-mindedness. She, especially, couldn't stand being called Tillie. Her name was Jerilynn.

Not Jerri-Lynn, in that 'Bamified country way, but Jerilynn, in that sophisticated New York City way of speaking. She talked proper and held her head high. But her mother had saddled her with that horrible nickname, and it stuck.

Only Uncle Stan would answer her questions—and if he didn't know an answer, he would make one up. He would entertain her when she was punished—and her inquisitiveness was always getting her punished—by singing one of the songs he had learned on the chain gang. He stood to his full six feet and braced his legs, spreading them apart as if he were about to launch into a soft-shoe.

"Sixteen tons and what'd ya get? Another day older and deeper in debt . . ." he crooned in a raspy baritone. "Saint Peter don't ya call me 'cause I cain't go, I owe my soul to the company store." Maybe that's why Stan and Tillie were confidants; they were the family's fringe.

Of course, Stan, Merle's youngest brother, brought greater flare to his oddity than did his niece to hers, sauntering or swaggering as the mood struck him. He was a macho vet one minute, a limp-wristed candy ass the next. Of course, the family never discussed his run-ins with the law. And Tillie couldn't protect him. Wherever they lived, the pattern was always the same—first the local lockup and then "the big house," a sprawling state penitentiary. Only the offenses changed. In Georgia and Florida he was busted for robbery. In the North, for solicitation as a gay street hustler.

Until then, Stan was a queen, a hustler, an aesthete, an intellectual, an entertainer, a comedian, a fool—whatever it took to get over. When he worked in ShopRite's produce department, he would take whole hams and stuff them inside a bag of vegetables and scribble "beans/59 cents" on the outside. And like his father, he had a drinking problem. But Tillie found in him a soul mate because he, too, was adventurous and open. He had seen the world with the army and he knew all kinds of people and was always willing to meet new ones.

Every two or three years the only other man in Tillie's life, her father, would sail into Quitman from Jacksonville, Florida, showing up unannounced in a brand-new car. Tillie adored his stylish clothes and fancy automobiles. But in a few days Jerry Mitchell would leave as suddenly as he had blown in; he wasn't the stayin' kind.

Despite his four-foot-ten stature, he thought he was a big man. His gilded mouth glittered brilliantly between his thick dark lips. His automobiles, like his teeth and his skin, shimmered with extra shine. It was said that he would buy a car that was nothin' but chrome from hood ornament to tailpipe if they made one. He never missed a fashion shift—sporting his broad-rimmed hats and wide lapels or a subdued fedora and black overcoat, as style dictated. He earned his money at a post office job, a privileged profession for black men in the 1950s. He worked hard because he wanted to live well; he saw no higher merit in the work itself.

To Tillie, days seemed to last forever, stretching out for weeks at a time, as if she had been exiled to this dull and lifeless family on a dull and lifeless planet to do penance for whatever sins she had committed in her home world. She felt her older brother and sister hated her because she was so foreign to them. She was annoying and intrusive. She so craved experience that she would run to the front when their grandmother lined them up for their weekly dose of cod liver oil. Worse than that, she got away with everything. Their normally strict mother was putty in her hands from her siblings' perspective. They took their jealousy out on the little menace when their mother wasn't around. All of them would argue, but Tillie and Frederick, the eldest, would really scrap, until he finally pinned her.

The children united only when faced with a common enemy. Every morning they had to walk from the outskirts through town and across the railroad tracks to reach the black school in the colored part of Quitman. A "po' white trash" family lived on the black side of town and had to pass over the tracks to get to their school in the white section. Because they were so ugly, Tillie, Bettye and Frederick named them the Dog Family. Most mornings they battled the Dog Family at the train tracks. The confrontation was rarely violent, consisting mostly of observations about one another's ethnic heritage, and, having performed their duty dance, each troop continued on its way.

In the 1950s Georgia was, in many ways, still the Old South. Schools, drinking fountains and playgrounds were segregated. Black children like Tillie didn't question it. It was a law of nature, like water flowing downhill. Rural blacks were still dirt poor. In the early 1950s, Tillie's family didn't have indoor running water or electricity. Some of the girls' panties were stitched from cotton flour sacks. Tillie's grandmother had sewn her a rag doll out of burlap croker sacks and cotton scraps. Their store-bought paper dolls came two in a pack. Since the cut-out clothes wore quickly, Tillie and Bettye would trace dresses out of grocery bags and color them with crayons. Although their house at 517 North Quincy Street had a kitchen, a tall, dark green wooden shack in the back with a hole in the earthen floor served as their bathroom.

Betty Mae Copeland, Tillie's grandmother, kept a chicken coop in the backyard where Tillie fed the chicks. When one grew to a hefty size, though, her grandmother would go out and wring its neck, then pick up her small axe and with a thoughtless downward stroke chop off its head. Each time she witnessed the execution, Tillie cried, but still she watched, obsessed with the happening. Most of the family's meat, vegetables and fruit came from that yard, where there were trees bearing pecans, pears, plums and figs. The children and their grandmother also picked blackberries in the thicket behind the white school. Betty Mae canned preserves from the fruits. When the adults went to pick cotton, Betty Mae would give Tillie a straw hat and a book and sit her under a tree. It was too late for her to save her own daughters, but she wanted her youngest granddaughter to go to school. She did not want her to know cotton. Betty Mae always tended to her grandchildren, and until the day she died, all of them called her Mama. They called their mother Merle.

To Tillie, Mama was always old, the backbone of the family, "pecan tan," tall and thin, with fine hair she let her granddaughters braid. She was generous to her neighbors and to any black folks who needed help. The best cook around for several counties, she could take air and water, it seemed, and bake a pound cake that melted on your tongue like butter in the summer sun.

The adults announced to the children that they were moving to Florida. On the day the family was supposed to leave, Mr. Isiah "Ike" Ponder came to pick up Daddy, Tillie's grandfather, to take him to Slab Town, the seedy part of Quitman to cash one of his paychecks from doing day work. Daddy told Betty Mae and his daughters that he would return directly. Tillie insisted that her grandfather bring her along. After a lot of whining, begging and threatening, he agreed. Sitting in the car outside the bar where he cashed his checks—and where you could buy fish and chicken sandwiches and moonshine—Tillie was amazed at all the adults that revolved through the streets, staggering men, women in clothes fancier than any she'd ever seen.

After a long wait, the bar belched Daddy out into the afternoon, drunk. Crying, Tillie sensed that that meant he would never reach Florida. Mr. Ike drove Tillie home. Merle declared that the family would move on, leaving Daddy and his demons behind.

....

By adolescence the dreamy, talkative child with the big, round eyes was already a woman—skinny with high, round breasts and full, thick lips. Her cocoa brown sensuality frightened her mother. Merle raised her children with an iron fist and a heavy hand, the only kind of rearing she knew. And yet, Tillie considered her an absentee parent. She never forgave her long work hours. The irony was that Merle spoiled Tillie, her favorite. She wasn't like her brothers or sister, Merle thought. She wasn't like any of the other children in West Palm Beach or in Quitman. She was even more restless than the preteens coming of age in the early sixties: endlessly bored, always dreaming.

Merle didn't know what to do with her. She was always out in the street, always up to something, going somewhere. She went on and on and on about all the things she wanted to do, all the things she wanted to be, all the places she wanted to go. "Chile, stop talking that foolishness," Merle would snort. "Don't you know, God meant for some people to be poor?" (My grandmother denies ever believing this—or saying it.)

Tillie didn't care what her mother said. After all, her mother wasn't glamorous, like her idols, the all-girl singing groups of the '50s and '60s. For as long as she could remember, Tillie wanted to be a star. Her family mocked her bulbous lips and huge eyes, but she told herself she was beautiful, that she musta been adopted. She sang in the Glee Club after school, she read poetry aloud and she acted. She tried to tell herself that, after all, she really wasn't *that* different from other black girls coming of age in the South. A girlfriend pierced her ears with a safety pin, a match and a clothes-pin in the Girls' Room. She mimicked the girl groups with her gang and they discussed boys in very serious low tones.

Since Merle didn't allow party-going, Tillie would crawl out a window to sneak off. To Merle, it was all foolishness. *She* had been a teen mother, and she wanted better for her children—at least for them to finish high school.

In one of the after-school activities that she had joined without her mother's permission, Tillie first spied Maurice Hall. His class was near the Always Ready Club, the school's honor society. They didn't start going together until the sixth grade, but as soon as Tillie saw the light-skinned boy with the pink bottom lip, she was in love. The lips fascinated her. More alluring than that, though, he was smart. The smartest in the class, and the most arrogant. Tillie liked that.

Their puppy love lasted through high school, on and off. One night, in the backseat of Maurice's mother's car (a brand-new light blue Ford Fairlane 500 with a royal blue interior), he introduced Tillie to sex. He had to talk her into it, and she bled and hurt. After the first time, though, the lovers went wild. They did it on the living room couch while Maurice's mother corrected her second-grade class's papers. They did it standing up on the porch.

Just about the only place they didn't do it was in a bed. They never saw each other's bodies completely nude. Tillie was look-ing forward to that most, once they were married—one of the many visions even my mother would not be able to will into taste and touch.

In some ways it seemed like she and Maurice were already married. Once he earned his driver's license he would pick her up in the mornings, drive to his house where she fixed him breakfast and then chauffeur her to school. In the afternoons, he would take her home after Glee Club.

Singing at a school assembly one day, Tillie caught the ear of Miss Ada Davis Stecker, a local white eccentric with a lot of money. Miss Ada decided the colored girl had talent, told her she wanted to sponsor her career and took her to audition for a traveling teenage goodwill troupe called Up With People. Tillie was selected to attend the group's camp that summer in Estes Park, Colorado. They were supposed to be trained and then taken on a world tour. The white woman convinced Merle to let her child wander so far, and Miss Ada Davis Stecker gave Jerilynn an armful of secondhand sweaters and an airline ticket.

Maurice and Tillie's sister, Bettye, escorted her to the airport. It was the first time she had ever been on a plane. In Colorado, she saw snow and mountains. She met children from all over the world. For the first time, she made white friends. The Up With People members woke up at five in the morning to do calisthenics, hiked in the Rockies and rode horses. They rehearsed song and dance routines. They ate together in one huge dining room called the Ponderosa. They read the Bible. They even flew to Monterey, California, to perform. When Merle's letters arrived, pleading for her to come back—Mama was getting sicker and sicker—Tillie begrudgingly returned to West Palm Beach. She would blame her mother for the next twenty-five years, denying how much her rapidly expanding universe—her first draught of the experience she had so craved—had left her frightened and dizzy. Longing for experience was easier than living it.

Thirsting for each other even more after two months apart, she and Maurice—the only person in her world who called her Jerilynn—dove into sex. When she was in Colorado they talked on the phone for hours, running up his mother's phone bill. That summer, she felt the strongest emotions she had ever experienced for anyone. That summer I was conceived. Maurice would be the only man my mother would ever love.

....

Tillie had wanted to go North for so long. She imagined sparkling high-rises, fancy sophisticated women and broad boulevards with mammoth cars. As the Silver Meteor streaked into Trenton station, her heart sank. There were no high-rises or broad boulevards. The cramped, squat buildings outside her window were shoved so tightly together that no light penetrated them. *I came all this way for this?* she thought.

Driving from the station to their new neighborhood, White City, she kept looking for white people. There were few. The deal on their prospective house had fallen through, so Merle, her children and her mother moved in with Corrine. Twelve people crowded into two tiny bedrooms, a dining room and a living room. It was worse than the South.

Only seventeen, Tillie gave birth to her first child, Marcus Bernard Mitchell, at 9:24 a.m. on May 31, 1967, at St. Francis Hospital in Trenton. She named me after Maurice's mother, Margaret Bernice. Tillie and Maurice had had a falling out just before she left; out of spite, she did not tell him she was pregnant. When she finally did, up North, he denied paternity. He would never support his son. But my mother would still love him for years to come.

Since she was anemic the birth was difficult. The pain of the baby's feet pressing into her spinal cord had been so terrible that she had tried to jump the bed's rails. As she held her newborn son, she cried again; partly for the high school graduation she would miss, partly for the love that she thought she would finally receive.

Soon after, leaving her newborn in the care of her mother on the weekends and aunt Corrine on the weekdays (whom she paid), she went to work, first at Neihman-Vorhees department store—wrapping gifts, operating an elevator—and then as a cashier at a five-and-dime. Later, she landed a job as a waitress. At night she attended classes to get her GED.

New Jersey might as well have been another country for my mother. As a teenager in Florida she didn't even know what birth control was, but in the space of two years up North, she was experimenting with recreational drugs.

She met Charles Mabry at a Trenton cabaret. Because he seemed like a kind man, and because he respected her (he called her Jeri), but most of all to get out of that crowded house, she married him on April 14, 1968, just two months after they met. She was already pregnant. Charles was working as a waiter and busboy at a nearby private school called Lawrenceville, where his mother ran a dining hall in one of the Victorian-style houses. Marcus in tow, they moved into a little basement apartment up Lida Street from Merle.

My mother gave birth to her second child, Charles Henry Mabry III, on November 12, 1968. After her husband lost his job, the newlyweds and their two children moved back in with Merle. They argued more than they made love: Charles kept losing jobs and Jeri believed he was running around. She kicked him out of the house. They had lived together for nine months as husband and wife. She wasn't sad about the end. Eventually, she told herself, she would be with Maurice Hall anyway.

Her odd jobs paid minimum wage, not enough to feed and clothe her children. My mother went on welfare. She kept her jobs and received what the welfare administrators called "partial payment," less than a hundred dollars a month and about two hundred dollars in food stamps. "Full" welfare was $283 a month, plus food stamps, for two children—when my mother was not working at all.

It was the first time anyone in our family had ever been on AFDC. My grandmother and my great-grandmother, as poor as they had been all their lives, refused to take "government money," preferring to make a way on their own without depending on white people, as they saw it. But the monthly check gave my mother a sense of independence. She didn't have to ask Merle for money so we could eat or go to a movie. More important, being on Medicaid meant my brother and I would receive dental exams twice a year and regular doctor visits. (No one in the family had ever had those either.) I was three years old.

Shortly after the breakup with Charles Mabry, my mother met Brandy Alexander (not his real name). He thought she was still very much a country girl from Quitman and set about educating her—how to deal with people, how to be proud of being black, the importance of education, the secrets of the "erogenous zones" and 1970s high-fashion style. He urged her to complete her associate's degree at Mercer County Community College, which she had started after getting her GED. Their relationship would last five times longer than her life with Charles Mabry and would be both literally and figuratively richer.

Brandy was a drug dealer—not really a dealer, a lieutenant. A big-time supplier would deliver the "stuff" to him. He would cut it, then distribute it to small-time dealers all over Trenton. Afterward he would collect the profits, not always an easy task since a good number of the dealers were addicts too.

For me, my mother and my brother, Brandy was the mother lode. In my youthful snobbery, I resented him personally because he dressed so loud and flashy; he was another reason for my mother to dump us for days at my grandmother's, while she went away with him to a show in New York or Atlantic City. My grandmother held her nose aloft at him and his "drug money," as she called it. But, neither my brother nor I refused the gifts it bought. At Christmas we received thousands of dollars in toys and clothes. Once we got matching electric cars that you sat in and drove, with a gas pedal and brakes. We wore real fur coats and, at Easter, three-piece suits and white bucks.

My mother was generous with her new wealth. She treated ten cousins to a one-day spending spree at Great Adventure amusement park. She paid for my cousin Janice to chaperone all us kids to the movies when we stayed at their house in Trenton: *Super Fly*, *Shaft*, *Cotton Comes to Harlem*. As a result, my mother was considered the hip adult in the family—and the neighborhood. She was no longer skinny, but she was younger and prettier than most moms. She would drive up while our friends played in my grandmother's yard and come over and laugh and talk. My girl friends especially loved her. "Your mother is so glamorous," they would coo, the lightness of heroine worship in their voices.

"That's your mother?" my boy friends would ask, eyeing her shapely legs and her outta-sight clothes.

I was so proud of her youth and her energy that I wanted to show her off. She talked "proper" and held her head high. She was as perfect as a TV mom. For me, her star power distinguished our threesome from the rest of our plodding, extended family.

Brandy spoiled us because he loved her. She was finally living in the style to which she thought she should become accustomed. She had her hair and her nails done once a week, at least. She and Brandy bought a huge beige Cadillac. They became one of Trenton's celebrated couples: my mother was buxom with big, beautiful dark eyes; Brandy was tall, handsome and bearded, with a deep Barry White baritone. When my mother was granted an apartment in the Donnelly Homes housing project in Trenton, Brandy moved with us.

My mother fought far less with him than she had with my stepfather, Charles, and when they did battle, it was psychological rather than physical. After a particularly bitter argument, she donned a suede micro-miniskirt, a halter top and a silver fox coat, put ten one-hundred-dollar bills in her evening bag, and drove the Cadillac to Trenton's hottest night spot, the Tuxedo Club. She sat at the bar in a room filled with men, the only woman in the joint. She amused herself by crossing her legs and ignoring the men, refusing drink after drink with a wave of her hand. When the story got back to Brandy of his woman alone flirting with a room full of men, he was furious, but powerless.

This was the crushed velvet early seventies. Our apartment was draped in Day-Glo posters, strong African fists clenched the air all over the place, in posters and in the form of wooden sculptures, and the air was thick and sweet with incense. At the time, I, and the millions of adults who were wearing loud shirts and bell-bottom pants, did not think it strange that our world looked like an exploded tempera paint factory.

My favorite weekends were when my mother wasn't working or was skipping classes at Mercer County Community College and she would take us shopping downtown. One of her best friends, a Black Muslim, owned a store called Ira Blackman's Right-On Boutique. Dashikis hung in the front window and collections of the green, black and red signs of the time were displayed inside, like the one hanging in my mother and Brandy's bedroom. I still remember the last lines of the funky, Black Power love poem: "I am not in this world to live up to your expectations and you are not in this world to live up to mine. And if by chance we find each other, it's beautiful." I'd lay on their bed reading the psychedelic lettering over and over again, my first poetry.

My mother didn't believe children should be completely shielded from the world. She wasn't going to be like her mother. "You can't keep things from children," she always said. That's why my brother and I knew from as long ago as we could remember that we had different fathers. As four- and five-year-olds, we took the knowledge the way we took everything my mother said, like grains of wisdom from a guardian angel.

Despite her frankness (she told us about sex before we ever asked. A man and a woman, who should love each other, have sex. He puts his penis in her vagina and if the sperm fertilizes the egg, nine months later she has a baby) my mother did protect us from some of the deeper "shit" of the soulful seventies. We could see *Super Fly* and *Shaft*, but were clueless about the real-life crime and drugs that thrived in our home.

Even Richard Pryor was off-limits. Whenever my mother and Brandy listened to one of the many tapes Brandy had, we had to go to bed. Lying in the darkness, I would hear them laughing and talking in low tones as I fell asleep. It was a comfortable, secure sleep—as tranquil as that of any four-year-old in the suburbs, I imagine. I got the same feeling being lulled to sleep in the back of the Cadillac as we drove from my grandmother's house home to the projects, the smell of the Corinthian leather and my mother's perfume enveloping me while the smooth vibration of the road traveled my body.

In spite of their countercultural lifestyle, my mother and her man had decidedly middle-class aspirations. She worked part-time as a teacher's assistant at the Trenton Adult Learning Center; for his day job, he worked in an auto factory. They planned to move out of the projects. They bought an apartment in middle-class Morristown, Pennsylvania, and furnished it with custom-made drapes and wall-to-wall carpeting. It would be just a stopover, until they could afford a house in truly upscale Princeton.

Although Brandy dealt heroin, they never used it. They smoked marijuana; my mother barred other drugs from the apartment when my brother and I were there, including the crank. A couple of hoods didn't know that when they ransacked the apartment one day while she attended class. They knocked in the door and ripped open cushions and cupboards. They nabbed some quinine, which Brandy kept in a sugar container and used to cut the heroin. They missed the seven thousand dollars in cash that was stashed in a pillow in the living room.

The experience led my young mother (she was twenty-three years old; I was five) to think about breaking up with Brandy. Though she loved him—and trusted him like a father—life had been getting tougher lately. When his supplier was busted, the whole operation withered. We lost our subsidized apartment because we couldn't pay the rent with my mother's part-time job. Brandy had been laid off from his factory job as the company cut back. Neither he nor my mother had ever thought to save any of the hundred-dollar bills that had slipped through their hands. Their instant cash evaporated as quickly as it had come. In 1974, we moved back to White City.

Soon my mother found another dream. A friend told her about a woman in New York who was a talent agent and could make her a star. My mother left us at my grandmother's and set off with a round-trip train ticket and two dollars. She moved in with the "agent" and told us she would send for us later. She instructed my grandmother to keep the welfare check for food and clothing, but to give some to Corrine for babysitting us after school.

She found work, first at Macy's, then at a city mental institution. In the meantime, the agent enrolled her in voice classes and set about recasting her image with new clothes, shoes, manicures and pedicures. The big lights of New York City had thrilled my mother when Brandy first took her to visit, and living there was like a movie. Finally, she would be a star.

But her agent, Penelope Jenkins, turned out to be ineffectual. After six months, my mother had not attended a single audition or casting. Every time Penelope advised her to buy a new dress or shoes "to enhance her image," she had to buy one for Penelope too. She blindly adopted Penelope as her mother—and told Merle so. Whereas Merle hailed from small-town Georgia, Penelope was a sophisticated New Yorker, tall and broad-shouldered with a fawning black bourgeois accent, not uncommon in her generation of New York's artistic community. My grandmother told my mother to be wary of her new mentor. My mother thought Merle was insanely jealous of their relationship. When my brother and I went to live with my mother, Grandmom hated the fact that we were in "that New York City," as she called it, so far from her and so dangerous.

My mother had not been making enough money to support us, so she decided to marry a Trinidadian who had fallen in love with her. We all lived in the middle-class Stuyvesant Town development. I started the second grade at P.S. 40. But once we were there my mother and her fiancé broke up. He returned to the islands; we kept the apartment.

My brother missed Trenton. I loved New York. I was seven years old. Stuyvesant Town had nineteen playgrounds. I had a beautiful girlfriend named Jamar and friends who were Korean, Jewish, Egyptian, Indian and just plain white. Sharing a fascination with our city, my mother and I were closer than ever. For the first time she was independent from her mother and from men. She was supporting us on her own, working as a mental hygiene health assistant at Gouverner's State School. She earned less than ten dollars an hour, but it was enough to hire a housekeeper to watch us after school. We rarely talked to anyone in White City; first because we had everything we needed in New York, and secondly because my mother had had a falling out with our family just before we moved.

During an argument, my grandmother had grabbed her arm. When my mother snatched it away, her long manicured nails scratched my grandmother's face. When my oldest uncle Frederick showed up and saw my grandmother's scarred face, he decided that if Tillie was going to assault his mother then she could get out of the house alright—all the way out. He summoned the entire family to my grandmother's house, where, in Carnival-like revelry, they retrieved our stored belongings from the attic and tossed them in the yard, the expensive booty of my mother's life with Brandy: furniture, clothes, appliances, toys. Days later it rained, a torrential downpour. As my mother cried, my brother and I huddled around her in our Manhattan apartment.

"It's okay, Mommy. Don't cry. We don't need that stuff anyway," I said, patting her shoulder, "as long as we're all together."

"I'ma kill 'em," my six-year-old brother said.

I hated my extended family, but the three of us were independent and autonomous, and wonderfully together, forever. Then New York City went broke. They reduced the staff at Gouverner's State School and eventually closed it. My mother was laid off. At the end of the school year we moved back to New Jersey, back to my grandmother's house, back to White City.

My mother started working as a home health aide at Princeton Homemakers. Since she earned half of what she had made in New York and couldn't pay for medical benefits for Charles and me, she went back on "partial payment" welfare benefits. She would go from case to case, helping rich, sick white people live with their pain and watching them die, losing a piece of herself each time. She would devise endless schemes, classes, partnerships to get out of the "shit-cleaning business," as she called it. She would start training programs and quit because she got bored, or they would lead to empty certificates. She would eventually settle into the maddening existence of a perpetual procrastinator, taking most of her joy from the small victories in her sons' lives.

One of her patients, Helen Houston, was so impressed with my essays and grades, which my mother showed her constantly, that Mrs. Houston offered to pay for my education at a private day school in Princeton. The catch was that I had to go live with her; she would take charge of my upbringing. She had no children and would adopt me. Dazzled by the possibilities that I would have— the opportunity for experience that she herself had missed—my mother offered me the choice.

I was eleven. I was aghast that she would even suggest it. A private school. Leaving home to live with a white lady. "This could be a great opportunity for you, Marcus," she said.

And at that moment, I saw a powerlessness in her eyes that I had never seen before. Through all the pains and challenges that she had lived, she was always invincible to me. But now I understood that she thought there was something I could get from a stranger that she could not give me. It was reflected in gray whirlpools at the center of her pupils, gyres of despair and fear that sucked light endlessly down into them until it vanished. It must have taken a Herculean effort to keep them hidden from me all those years, I thought, or maybe they had only recently appeared there. I didn't know which, but they frightened me.

I said no. I felt at once too protective of her and my brother to leave them, and too dependent to live without them. Mrs. Houston died a few years later and her lawyer contacted my mother. She had inherited a small sum from the estate. I would have been her sole heir if I had taken her offer.

When my junior high school principal Mrs. Sigafoos suggested two years later that I go to a private school instead of Hamilton High, this time I conceded. The principal's own kids attended private school. She had picked me from the masses because I had "leadership ability"; despite being a social wallflower in White City, I was president of the school, editor of the newspaper, the only mock President Carter elected in Hamilton Township public schools and a straight A student. Mrs. Sigafoos thought that leadership ability would be best cultivated in an environment with fewer intellectual limits and greater challenges.

She suggested the idea to my mother, and my mother told me she wanted me to go. She wanted me to escape the fights at home, the worrying over bills and money. "It's your decision, but I want you to reach your potential," she pleaded. "There is nothing you cannot do." I was tired of the arguing at home, too. I was sick of being thirteen and bored, and I was ready for a change, any change. I felt cramped in the house and even in White City. And, besides, with Mom only twenty minutes away, what was I risking? I could come home anytime.

My guidance counselor, Mr. Mackenzie, drove me to Lawrenceville, the best school in the state. After he walked me through the tour and the admissions interview (my mom was working), he told me he thought I would definitely get in. As we headed back to Grice Middle School, this tall, broad black man turned to me and said, "You'll be successful, Marcus. You'll be able to have anything you want. But remember where you came from."

"I will," I said, not really knowing how I could forget, after all.

On the day of the Secondary School Admissions Test, my mother's temperamental car wouldn't start. The night before, a severe storm had dumped a foot of snow on Central Jersey and it was still snowing heavily. My bright new future was over before it even began. I wanted to cry. But my mother told me to get dressed. She left the house. My stomach making gurgling noises as I waited, I finally heard a car horn. My mother rushed through the front door in her big brown coat.

It was the greatest paradox of her life: as incapable as she seemed of making her own plans jibe, she was amazingly efficient at making the lives of others run smoothly when it truly mattered. Infirm patients would beg her to stay if she was planning on leaving a case. She had an uncommon effect on people, however old, however sick, however rich or white. She was the one to whom everyone in our family turned when they needed a lift or assistance. She saw that people were receiving the correct attention when they were in the hospital; she harassed doctors and nurses, speaking their medical language. She helped everyone except herself.

Between her own procrastination, her chronic lack of planning and her abundant bad luck, she seemed constantly dogged by hard times. When she finally put her mind to something, someone died and she had to abandon her project to attend to their funeral preparations. Or someone needed her. Or she got sick. Or she was in an accident that was the other driver's fault. It was one tragedy after another. I obsessed endlessly about her pain.

Now, as she swept through the front door into the living room on SSAT day, she commanded, "Okay, Marcus, let's go."

A man I had never met sat behind the wheel. Dr. Wendell Price had known my family since they moved from Florida. My mother hadn't talked to him in years. His family had been the first black people to settle White City, back when blacks first started calling it "white," after the majority of its inhabitants. Their house had been smeared with graffiti, swastikas and "KKK."

In the middle of a snowstorm, she had tracked down a ride for me. As I climbed into the back seat, Dr. Price greeted me. "Hello, young man." I thanked him for the lift. He said he wouldn't miss taking me to the SSAT for the world; he wanted me to get into Lawrenceville. The man who had had the courage to integrate the white suburb I called home for most of my life was escorting me, literally, to our people's next advancement: entry into one of the last bastions of white WASP privilege. Placing myself in the African-American family tree of progress put a weighty responsibility on my shoulders as I went into the exam. But mostly the sense of heritage—what this old man had bequeathed to all us White City kids (the yards, the safe streets, the one-family homes)—and the debt I owed him and everyone who had gone before, gave me a sense of pride and confidence.

....

Six months later I enrolled at the Lawrenceville School as a boarding student on full financial aid, $6,800. My mother wanted me to go there more than anyone; indeed, more than I wanted to myself. She was afraid that by staying in White City and in my grandmother's house, my promise would somehow be wasted— like hers. She felt that her family had held her back. Her own life had been ruined, so she sent me away—twenty miles up I-95 to Lawrenceville. She could not have known that our relationship would be transformed in ways that seemed beyond our control. We would still love each other more than all the world, but I would also eventually become another of those men in her life that helped her make ends meet.

CHAPTER 3

THE WAY OF THE WASP

It had to be a dream. The sky was so blue, the sun was so bright. You could actually smell the flowers. Jesus, you could even smell the grass. On the other side of the black wrought-iron fence this sanctuary had looked so forbidding. But, inside . . . peace. Comfort. As my mother drove her pale green Chevy Nova onto campus, I thought, "Even the air in this place smells different than the ordinary oxygen outside," which was stifling and impure. I was fourteen years old. My stomach was whirling; my head was light. I felt like I might vomit any minute.

Boys in long shorts and Lacoste shirts tossed lacrosse balls back and forth on the huge circular lawn. (Good thing I'd read the catalog, otherwise I wouldn't have known what they were playing.) Other boys, in bright pants and T-shirts, ran in and out of the Victorian-style brick buildings that surrounded The Circle. There were so many buildings.

I had told my mother to take the Lawrenceville/Princeton exit off I-95. I knew it wasn't the shortest route to my new dorm, but the first time I drove onto campus as a student, I wanted to pass through the main gate. This was a special day; it required ceremony. So we entered campus from Route 206, which was called Main Street over the small stretch that ran through Lawrenceville. On one side sprawled the school's 360 verdant acres. On the other clustered "the village," a collection of small stores, houses and apartment buildings.

In the middle of the semicircular brick entrance stood an inlaid white marble fountain with a lion's head spilling water from its mouth into a basin below. Above the head was engraved LAWRENCEVILLE SCHOOL, along with the school seal, a Corinthian column in front of a sprig of laurel. On one side of the column was etched the year of Lawrenceville's founding: 1810. On the other side, a burning lamp. Around the edge of the seal ran the school motto: *Virtus Semper Viridis.*

The driveways on either side of the fountain led to The Circle, an immaculate circular lawn designed by Frederick Law Olmsted, the landscape architect who had also planned Central Park. Memorial Hall, constructed with huge, rust brown stones, with entrances at either end and a grand stairway in the middle that fronted onto the lawn, dominated The Circle. The stairs rose to a circular well. I imagined that if you stood there you would feel like a king surveying his realm. The Chapel rose next door, a matched set with Mem Hall, but more supple and spiny, with its tower and ivy-smothered facade.

Rounding the circle, five Victorian buildings majestically framed the lawn: Cleve, Griswold, Woodhull, Dickinson and Kennedy, The Circle Houses. The houses were united by geography, but distinguished by architecture, each taking a different form: some had a turret, some a bay window, some had two. Off The Circle sat Hamill, the sixth and oldest house, constructed of gray stone. This was the heart of the school, where Lawrenceville broke boys into small pebbles with the hope of rebuilding them into men.

Leaving behind The Circle, my mother and I drove past Mem Hall toward Lower School.

I had never seen so many rich white people. Outside the houses, station wagons and luxury sedans, piled high with clothes, stereos and more lacrosse sticks, crammed the narrow blacktop roadways. Mothers in cotton-knit shirts and skirts walked arm in arm with their sons. Fathers stood in casual conference with other men. Many of them wore the same outfit as the women—long shorts with polo shirts, the flaccid collars turned up in back— some wore green blazers, or red ones or yellow ones, with loud plaid pants. If we were back home we would have said they were 'Rican (as in the flamboyant taste black folks attributed to Puerto Ricans). Here, we called them preppy.

We officially registered at the Kirby Arts Center. Overwhelmed by sensory stimulation, I walked up the stairs to the second floor where boys divided themselves between two tables. Although my mother followed me, I was almost unaware of her presence. I stood before the M table and the old man behind it handed me my folder. He directed me toward the photographer.

We couldn't find my dorm. The first person who happened by was a muscular black student—to our unstated but mutual amazement. He looked like a football player.

"Excuse me, dear," Mom said in that voice I hated, it sounded so falsely snooty and condescending. She asked him if he could point us toward Cromwell.

Beaming, he replied, "Yes, ma'am," and told us we were standing right in front of it.

It felt so good to see him, like somehow I was protected now, but I tried not to show it. Then my mother asked him if he would look out for me. I wanted to die.

Mom left as though she were in a hurry to get off campus and back to the known universe. I didn't miss her for long. I had to unpack and order my new existence. It was my first beginning, the first one I was conscious enough to appreciate, anyway. I already sensed a surging current of freedom. I threw open my window and let the sweet air of the waning New Jersey summer drift in. It mingled with an old, comfortable musk. I would discover it time and again in later years—in elite clubs and fancy restaurants where elderly white men gathered.

It was all so new to me, I couldn't imagine a more alien world. It felt like paradise—clean and bright and green and blue. I wanted to dance around and yell, "Woohoo, woohoo!" but I figured that would definitely betray me as a newcomer. They might think I was undignified. Instead, I ran my hand over the faded wallpaper. I put my nose close to it, to suck in the smell of tradition. I ran my hand along the hard wooden desk and sat gingerly on the bed. Then I laid on it and laughed a ridiculous laugh. I couldn't believe I was going to live here; I clearly didn't belong. Awed by the miracle, I stopped laughing and stared at the ceiling above me. *Whoa*, I thought solemnly, stillness settling over me.

I had seen boarding schools on TV: *The Facts of Life*, NBC, Thursday nights at nine. Now I would be able to live the drama and the sitcom myself. Lawrenceville would provide the happy endings and be a surrogate father to boot. Settling instantly into a rhythm that put me in sync with the community around me for the first time in my life (we were all busily constructing our individual selves), I had no way of knowing that I could never fully belong here—or that belonging was not the greatest reward this enchanted place had to offer.

I arranged my clothes in the chest of drawers, then tuned my radio to a good station. I unfurled the posters we had bought at Quaker Bridge Mall. I was figuring out where to place them, standing back and spinning around the four walls as if I was about to hang an important acquisition, when an Asian kid came bouncing in to introduce himself.

"Hi, I'm Steve," he said with a huge smile, extending his right hand.

"Hi, I'm Marcus. I mean Marc," I stuttered, trying to mirror his beaming self-confidence. Only I had forgotten I was trying out this new name. You could be whomever you wanted to be in prep school and I wanted to be Marc. Then Steve's mother called him from across the hall, and soon they were in a yelling match over how Steve should decorate his room. I couldn't help but giggle.

As other boys filtered in they stopped by to introduce themselves. The most impressive was Matt Bernstein, good-looking, smart, witty. The way you were supposed to be at Lawrenceville. Almost everybody in the house was a second former (ninth grader) except for a couple of first formers. Matt had been a first former last year. So at just fourteen, he was called an "Old Boy." I admired him right away. We all did. Matt would teach me to tie a tie before the end of the year—and one day sitting in his room, listening to Squeeze, Matt would look over at me and say, "You know, you really fit in here." His comment would hit me like a punch to the gut. I wouldn't know whether to be angry or hurt. I would be hurt. Later, I would learn to be angry.

I don't remember whom I ate dinner with that first night. But I learned later that it was always important to eat with someone cool; it indicated your social standing. After all, other boys saw you walking the quarter-mile from Cromwell to the dining center—and they saw who walked with you. It would take me months to learn how popularity was determined. When I first arrived on campus, I was lucky enough to know nothing—absolutely zero—about the way of the WASP. By the time I left Lawrenceville, I knew so much about it that I would joke with Asian friends about WASP customs and mores, making buzzing sounds between our silly riddles.

But in early September 1981, Boy George was big, the Police were hot and I was as green as a "rhinie" could be. Maybe I was a caricature. I lacked the wit and, above all, the cynicism that most of my fourteen-year-old prep school peers were armed with. As I lay in bed, with the window open so I could smell the grass and feel the warm air tickle my face, I felt like I was living at the summer camp of my dreams.

The next day, I woke up two hours before class was supposed to start. I figured I had to wait for a shower, dress and eat breakfast first. (The catalog stipulated that Lower Schoolers were required to attend every meal.) I had noticed that the shower included two heads behind one curtain. I definitely didn't want to shower with anyone else, but I figured if that was the way things were done here, I'd have to rise to the challenge.

The still campus in the soft morning light radiated a reassuring calm, and a sweet sense of privilege. I pulled on my new velour blue robe and gathered my instruments. Toothpaste, soap, towel and washcloth, the razor that I used once a week, and the shaving cream. I was relieved to discover that no other fourteen-year-old wanted to shower next to another boy either. The pounding hot water blasted off layers of dead skin and lifted the red film from my eyes. Breathing in the fresh scent of soap, I toweled off, dressed, grabbed my books and hurried down the marble steps of Cromwell into my new life, almost running.

Behind the counter, the black woman in her starched white uniform and hairnet nodded at me. "Well, it's good to see *you* here, young man," she said.

Proud of myself and of the relationship that I could have with a total stranger on the basis of our skin color, I smiled broadly. I realized that I had already started to miss an indescribable deep brown warmth from back home.

"Good morning, ma'am."

"What can I get for you this morning?" she asked.

"I guess I'll have some scrambled eggs and sausage," I shrugged, elated at the thought of free food, with a *choice*.

"Yes, sir," she said, and she dished them out. "Now you have a good day."

"Thank you, ma'am. You, too."

It was a great breakfast. Looking through the glass walls onto the sloping green lawn of the dining center and to The Circle beyond, I thought how important it was that I succeed here, for everyone back home.

....

My first Lawrenceville class—where I would learn if I was intelligent or just looked that way because I was in public school—was French, starring Edmund Megna. As we sat motionless around the immense oval table, he paced the room, staring at us, sizing us up one by one. He was not a tall man, and he had a small wart on his nose, but he was intimidating. I had been warned by Old Boys: he had a reputation for devouring his students, especially Lower Schoolers.

Shutting the door, Mr. Megna slowly walked to his place at the head of the table. With his gelled hair glistening black and gray, his face fixed in a scowl, he said sternly, "*Bonjour.* This is French Two. If you are not supposed to be in this class, leave."

And with that he slipped into French. Today, I can say publicly that his accent was closer to Brooklyn than Paris, but as a Lower

Schooler I sat petrified at the prospect that he might call on me. The only time he broke his French was to insult someone.

The pattern was always the same. He would ask a question: "Monsieur Mabry . . ."

I would look up from my notes.

"Monsieur Mabry . . . ?" he would ask again. Sensing doubt, he would escalate my agony. "Monsieur Mabry . . . *oui*," he would say, shaking his head from side to side. Then, "*Non*," he'd say, nodding up and down.

Forced to blurt out something, I would spit out the wrong article, "*le*" when it should have been "*la*," or "*de*" when it should have been "*des*."

A silence hung oppressively in the air. He'd pounce: "They shot Lincoln," he intoned in feigned disgust, drawing out each word with a deep bellow and a piercing stare, "they hang pictures, and yet, they let *you* walk around the Lawrenceville campus."

You could see it coming from miles away—and each of us, when it wasn't him being crucified, would silently relish the pain inflicted on our classmates, a sickly adolescent pleasure. Mr. Megna loved it, too. Terror was not considered politically correct pedagogy in late twentieth-century teaching, but terror may have been the only way to force American teenage males to learn French grammar.

For all his intestinal bellowing, Mr. Megna was fair; diligent students received As. Not all classes were that easy. We used to joke that "Shakespeare would have gotten a B-plus in a Lawrenceville English class . . . on a good day." English teachers took particular delight in the saying. My personal hell, though, was Lower School biology. It was supposed to be "a challenging course for Lower Schoolers with a demonstrated aptitude in science." Since I had loved science in public school and had earned straight

As, I enrolled in the course. It proved more nightmarish than challenging. We read a chapter a week and memorized whole schematics of muscles and skeletons. I had to study two hours a night just to stay prepped for the quizzes Mr. Graham sprang on us unannounced.

I had bio just before lunch and Mr. Graham would comment on how the orange juice from breakfast was starting to come back as the gasses in our empty stomachs built up.

"Ahh, it always tastes better the second time around," he'd say, rubbing his belly.

From the beginning of the year, I felt a special bond with him. Almost all the teachers at Lawrenceville were like parents and mentors; it seemed their lives were devoted to us. But Mr. Graham was particularly down-to-earth, almost fatherly to me.

I figured he must have spent time with black people at some point in his life. I remember the day that he brought in the maple syrup that he bottled at his Vermont cabin. He took a swig and swallowed it down.

"Yuck," I gasped loudly.

"Try it," he said, holding out the container.

"No way."

"But it's not like Alaga," he said, trying to entice me.

"No thanks."

I tried to keep my adolescent cool, but what I really wanted to ask was, "How in the hell do you know that I eat Alaga syrup?" It was true; until boarding school, the viscous, sugary cane syrup had been my favorite brand. I had never even tasted maple syrup, but I was not going to admit that to Mr. Graham. Besides, it seemed he already knew.

I reveled in the orderliness of school, not just classes (A period at 8:15, B period at 9:00, C period at 9:45), but meals (breakfast, lunch, dinner). Sports from 3:30 to 6:00, study hall from 7:30 to 9:30, lights out at 10:30. As students grew older the school gave them more freedom, but in Lower almost every minute was committed to study or athletics. My life had order—beautiful, secure and dependable. I was able to think about far-off great ideas, like democracy and archetypes, and distant places, like Greece and Rome, without terrifying eruptions from my family or neighbors. Everything that I needed was contained in this perfect little microcosm—in adequate quantity and in appropriate measure. I would later learn that that luxuriant comfort came at a price, but for now, Lawrenceville furnished me with the one thing my mother could not: tranquility.

The school even provided positive role models; only one was black, Mr. Maxwell. But the teaching masters and intramural coaches became surrogate fathers to me. Only rarely did I wonder if my real father would have been proud to see me at Lawrenceville. For what felt like the first time, I was truly content. Being so happy made me nervous that something could go wrong, since it always had before.

I worked hard—mostly because learning was exciting and my teachers were enthusiastic—and made the honor roll. My classmates were visibly amazed at my success: "You take *those* classes and you get *those* grades? Wow." I don't know who was more surprised, my white classmates or my black ones. About four percent of Lawrenceville's six hundred and fifty students were black. (Less than two percent were Hispanic.) About half of the black students came from poor families in cities like Trenton, Newark or New York, but a few hailed from upper-middle-class backgrounds, the sons of doctors or foreign-service officers, and had gone to better schools.

It was a year of fantastic discovery on the athletic field and in the house as well. I had never learned to play sports, but here athletics were mandatory, and we exercised on the most beautiful grounds I had ever seen. In public school, the very word "grounds" had meant a prohibition, as in "You are not allowed to bring candy on to school grounds." But at Lawrenceville, it signified privilege and splendor: "The Board of Trustees decided yesterday to invest $100,000 in the upkeep of the grounds." At Lawrenceville, the grounds were the plush lawns, the ivy imported from famous heroes' graves that crept up the Chapel, the paths that wound from Foundation House back to the Music House, past the soccer fields and the library toward the Science Building and all the way around the Kirby Arts Center past the football and lacrosse fields and back toward the pond, the Field House and the hockey rink.

Only in quick mental blossoms did I sense that I had walked these paths before. When I was two or three years old I had lived at Lawrenceville for several months. When each Circle House had its own dining room and the boys were served by white-coated waiters, Charles Mabry's mother had supervised the all-black staff in Griswold and was granted a small apartment at the back of the house.

Once in a while during my four years at Lawrenceville, as I walked from the dining center to my Circle House, for instance, I would catch a familiar perspective of the Victorian lampposts that guarded The Circle, then experience a bloom of memory: the way the lights looked like a string of pearls dotting the dusk, or Dickinson's slated roof against the reddening sky. The flashes of memory came when I least expected them, and each time they sent waves of recognition rippling through me. It made me feel secure to remember that my people had been here before. They had been domestic workers, like the majority of black people on campus now; but, hey, my people had been here before.

....

Maybe it was that comfort, left over from early childhood, or maybe it was adolescent naïveté and ego, that allowed me to integrate myself so successfully during my first year at boarding school. I was as surprised as Matt Bernstein.

We were both stunned when I beat him in the election for president of Cromwell House. Like every election at Lawrenceville, like every election in every high school in America, it was a test of popularity, not merit. So how could a poor black kid from Trenton trump a popular white Old Boy? (Still beats the shit outta me.) As we sat nervously in Matt's room, waiting to be summoned back into Mr. Schiel's apartment where the dorm was voting, I don't remember what we talked about . . . something, anything. When Nick Gwyn, a lanky blond kid filled with the confidence and the disarming smile of a New Orleans gentleman, meandered down the hall and extended his hand to me—"Congrats, Mabes . . ."—I grew suddenly dizzy. Every step from there into the housemaster's quarters was dreamlike.

Accepted, I thought to myself. *Scholarship, black and all. Accepted. By all these white boys. To be their president.* Suddenly, everything I had been told about America—the good parts—seemed true. Anyone could become anything he or she wanted. Race was no longer a factor in life. My grandmother's and my mother's worlds now evaporated—and, in a sense, their roles in my life with them. I no longer needed their protection. I belonged. I had traveled from White City to Lawrenceville, from a black community to a white one, and it was here that I found acceptance. It was as if I had never been an outsider at all; it was my former world that had been out of whack, not me. I had discovered my lost tribe; I had been reclaimed. As I entered the Schiels' apartment to thunderous howls, I fought back tears.

Matt was elected vice president. Nick Roegner (also a New Jerseyan, with whom I'd form a bond that would cement a lasting friendship) and the only other Old Boy in the dorm, Mark Cohen, rounded out the Cromwell House Council. I took my job very seriously. We met in my room every week to discuss dorm business, which consisted mostly of figuring out if and when we could hold dances with other dorms and invite girls' schools to come, and how many boxes of Snickers to buy for house concessions the next week. I had only been in this magnificent place for four weeks and already I was king of the mountain. Not because I was house president. No, that wasn't the real measure of popularity. In the real plebiscite to be a cool boy, the public voted with their feet. And my room was always packed. Boys clamored over the small twin bed and my desk. They scrunched into the Naugahyde armchair. They leaned against the walls and sprawled across the floor. I didn't hold court as much as provide a forum. The spontaneous town meetings could happen in any room, or in the long straight hallway that ran through Cromwell, at any time— between classes, after sports period, before evening study hall. It was a great honor for the gatherings to erupt in your room.

We discussed politics, or school, or girls, or sports, or foreign countries. I performed well in politics and school and could fake my way through girls or sports. But I had never traveled to a foreign country. Hell, I had never even been to Connecticut— and a good number of Lawrentians started out there. So when the conversation turned to the comparative merits of foreign cultures,

I should have shut up. Only, no self-respecting fourteen-year-old Lawrentian would voluntarily bow out of a verbal pissing match, and I had self-respect. Unfortunately, I also had an unnatural affinity for France, a favorite prey of the Lawrenceville jet set. A pattern was born.

Nick Roegner or Nick Gwyn would sound the debate with "And, of course, the French are the biggest assholes in all of Europe . . ." The other would refine the generalization with details from his last trip. I, unable to hold my Francophile offense, would accept the dusty glove.

"No way, the French are the greatest . . ." My limp assertion would have the scent of easy victory for the Nicks.

They eyed each other, almost licking their chops: "*What, Mabry?*"

I would confidently stride into the fray with some remark about how neat the food was or the literature . . . my only knowledge derived from second-year French class: *la ferme, la vache, la poule*. But sword drawn, I could not retreat.

"The books, the food," I'd repeat like an idiot.

"*Whaaaaat?*" one of the Nicks would whine in disgusted astonishment. Then they would lunge, one after the other, with anecdote after vivid anecdote of French snobbery, rudeness and general grotesquery. Then, always when I was most vulnerable and out of "buts" to stammer, the *coup de grace*.

"Have you ever been there?"

I'd stumble backward onto my sword. My vertebrae would curve and I'd shrivel into a small, uneducated insect, unworthy of Lawrenceville. Somehow, having never been to France, I felt, made me lesser than the Nicks.

But those arguments were the exception. On lazy weekend

afternoons, especially Sundays, we would sit in my room in Cromwell for hours in raucous community. During the week—when our free time was measured in minutes—a handful of us would gather between classes to schmooze or shoot the shit, depending on where you grew up. Since Dan D'Agostino and I had the same free periods, we became fast friends. Dan was good-looking, smart, an Old Boy like Matt. And he was a day student, free to go home after classes, free from mandatory study halls from 7:30 to 9:30 p.m., free to see girls whenever he wanted—at least as far as any of us knew. From the first day I met Dan in Matt's room, cracking jokes, his backpack slung over one shoulder, I knew he was cool.

Cool was the paramount concern of our lives: more important than family, more crucial than grades. To be cool, the whole point was to lose the green: act like an Old Boy, talk about women like an Upper Schooler, beat up your fifth-former prefect (the big-brother types who lived in Lower School houses to watch over and counsel the kids). And Dan could do two of the three. He never tangled with our senior prefect, a tough guy from a working-class family in Brooklyn.

Dan became my "hanging partner," as my brother and his friends called it back home. We would have never met if I had not gone to Lawrenceville. He was from a respectable upper-middle-class family in the affluent suburbs nearby; my family was still on and off welfare and food stamps. Somehow, though, I seemed to be the more conservative of our duo. He would cut up, drink, thrash around the hall. I had a big mouth and an earth-shaking laugh that seemed very disturbing to my friends' mothers, but never the balls to break a rule. Overcoming my fear, I only drank twice freshman year. But playing straight man to

Dan's shenanigans and sex talk made me feel cool too. We were like characters in an S. E. Hinton novel (Hinton being Dan's favorite writer of the moment). Outsiders, all youthful rebellion and disdain for society—at least that was the way we talked.

I didn't know that Dan was also someone to fear, that in insecure adolescence, I would want to be him. Not necessarily Dan, in particular, but like him. To be all the things that he was, to have all the things he had, all the possibilities, all the confidence. No doubt many black kids harbor such feelings in our racist society, where we are feared and loathed, even sometimes by ourselves, and where whites may have to struggle for material success or high position but are accorded, by virtue of their skin, the fundamental attributes of humanity: respect, dignity, honor. For African-Americans—marooned by history in a land that is not our home, but knowing no other—it was the ultimate taboo: wanting to be white.

No black person could ever admit he or she had actually felt the twinge, the pang of self-hatred. But, being with Dan, being at Lawrenceville, brought it into sharp, terrifying solidity inside me: at times, I wanted to be a white boy, or at least to have all the privileges they did. Never consciously and never, ever vocally. To speak that horrible, forbidden desire, more humiliating than the fear of white racism or personal failure, would shame me and my ancestors. I wouldn't admit it until sometime after college. And if ever accused, I denied it vehemently. As a fourteen-year-old, I managed to deny it even to myself.

Dan hung out in my room between classes instead of in the day-student ghetto, the library. Most of the time we bitched about biology, prepping each other for Mr. Graham's quizzes.

"Where is glucose reabsorbed into the capillaries through active transport?" I would query.

"In the collecting duct? The loop of Henle?" Dan would venture timidly.

"No, fag, in the proximal convoluted tubule," I'd say, chucking the book at him.

Fag was a common Lawrenceville word. We often used it instead of commas to punctuate sentences, the way kids in the Valley used *like*. Or we used it for emphasis (as in, "An A in computer biochem? You fag!") or just because you liked someone ("Hey, fag, wanna go for a pizza at TJ's?") I often called Dan "F'Agostino," or just "F'Ag" for short, a real test of friendship since all of us were the biggest bunch of homophobes imaginable. Of course, who would be more homophobic than six hundred horny adolescents stuck in an all-boys boarding school? It would be hard to imagine an environment more scary for a boy having to confront burgeoning homosexual desire.

Behind biology came our second favorite topic of conversation, only loosely related to our rampant homophobia: girls. We spent long hours talking about sex. How far we had gone, who would go all the way first. Once we had both lost our virginity, we debated the virtues of oral sex over vaginal intercourse. Dan thought getting a blow job was better. I was on the fence. In the ninth grade I didn't have any basis for judgment until after spring break. Naturally, I couldn't tell Dan that; he already knew how to perform cunnilingus. Of course, I told him, black girls didn't like that nasty stuff anyway, yet another racial myth.

Of course, girls—or the absence thereof—was Lawrenceville's major drawback. My worst hours slinked by during that dreaded single-sex-school institution, the "mixer," most horrific for black boys. If it was a schoolwide dance, there was simply no hope. There were three of us for every black girl. If it was a house dance, between one or two Lawrenceville dorms and an entire girls' school, there were better odds. Of course, that didn't mean you would like the black girl or vice versa, but you would obligatorily dance at least once with her.

I didn't know that by sophomore year, most black guys would no longer even bother to go anymore. The white girls were afraid to dance with us and we were afraid to ask. White guys danced with black girls though. And even if we managed to find a partner, the music was all white and all rock. AC/DC. Pat Benatar. The Doors. Stuff nobody was meant to dance to in the first place. Get drunk to, get high to, maybe, but not dance. We hauled girls in from as far away as Maryland (The Holton Arms School) and Virginia (Madeira and Foxcroft). Every girls' school had a reputation and a corresponding nickname. Kent Place in North Jersey was a regular at Lawrenceville dances, and it was genteelly labeled "Kennel Place," or worse. Brearley and Chapin, New York City day schools, were known for their attractive and well-bred girls.

Despite the unending frustration of wandering back through pine woods, lonely and depressed, I would persevere even after my first year at Lawrenceville. The only positive experience I ever had at a mixer was in the horse country of Virginia years later. I had trekked down to Foxcroft for a meeting of African-American independent-school students. The weekend was meant to allow us to talk about our collective problems at our different schools. Of course, we really came to dance. The ratio was amazing.

I had been eying a beautiful, cocoa-skinned girl with long hair—one of the Foxcroft organizers—all day. Every time she spoke, her big eyes sparkled with intelligence. Every time I talked, I tried to impress her with some profound reflection. With the sophistication of a college woman, she nodded softly, affirming my thoughts. As soon as we broke for lunch, I worked my way over to her. She was even prettier up close. At the dance that night, we were inseparable.

I had never seen such refined beauty up close—except in ads in *Ebony* and *Essence*. I had seen plenty of preppy white girls, but they never seemed sophisticated and never looked as elegant as she did. She even spoke French. Her father was in the foreign service and she had grown up in Africa. I spent most of the night wondering if I would ever kiss her.

As the dance wound down we stepped into the chilly Virginia night and held hands. I wanted to turn my head toward her so I could look into her eyes, but the thought couldn't travel from my brain to my muscles. Finally she said something in French. It gave me the courage to *ask* if I could kiss her. *I'll do it in French*, I thought. Only, I knew there were two words in French that were really close in pronunciation. One meant *kiss*. One meant *fuck*. Suppose I chose the wrong one?

"*Est-ce que je peux te baiser?*"

"*Oui.*"

It was the best kiss I had ever had. (Actually, I had asked her if I could fuck her, but I didn't learn that until I studied at the Sorbonne.) I took the train back to New Jersey madly in love.

My new girl Sylvie and I talked on the phone for a few weeks, made plans to get together at an L'ville dance some day. But as the weeks drifted on we realized the futility of a long-distance relationship and we stopped calling. My first love affair was over.

It would be at another minority student weekend—at Exeter, in my senior year—that I met Edmund Perry. Out-of-town guests were hosted by Exeter students the night we stayed over. As soon as we all got back from the dance, Perry and his friends lit up a joint. He invited the other Lawrenceville representative, John Atwater, and me to join in, but we decided not to risk it so far from home and so close to graduation. We talked for about ten minutes before John and I went to sleep. Like everyone during senior year, we discussed colleges. Perry asked me where I wanted to go. I told him I had been accepted to Yale early, but I was waiting to see what Stanford would say. He said he would love to go to Stanford: "It would be a dream come true." But he doubted that he could get in. He said he might have to settle for Harvard. We both grimaced and laughed.

As it turned out, Perry did get into Stanford. He would have been in my class there, only he was killed by a New York City undercover cop later that summer while allegedly trying to mug him. His death made national headlines, not to mention a book, and ignited a debate—short-sighted and ill-informed—over whether "inner city" black kids profited from prep school.

The gist of the articles seemed to be that the black students were almost all poor waifs, confronting the challenge of smarter and richer white kids. Upset by Perry's death, I felt somehow personally implicated. The vapid debate enraged me; it was at best paternal, at worst racist. How could having a shot at success *not* be better than not having a shot at success? Of course, many of us would fail, but many white kids from privileged backgrounds failed too. Most news articles failed to mention that in the 1980s the dropout rate for black kids at prep schools was lower—yes, lower—than the overall dropout rate. Perry's tragic end became just another excuse to condemn black males to the dungeon of low expectations.

Race was the one issue that D'Agostino and I never discussed. It didn't seem important. Maybe it was because Dan, an affluent Italian-American from Princeton Junction, thought of himself as much as a Puerto Rican as a white boy. (He had lived in Puerto Rico growing up and spoke Spanish flawlessly.) By my first January at Lawrenceville, my having a different skin color than everybody else in Cromwell was merely a slight annoyance. That first year at Lawrenceville, I had more friends, real friends, than I had ever had. In place of the isolation I had felt in White City was acceptance and encouragement. I was at home here. Other than Matt's solitary comment pointing out my uniqueness, no one seemed to care much that I was black.

Then, as the year passed, they started to. Or I started to.

The worst experiences stabbed me out of thin air, as if to say *"Yo! Nigger! Wake up!"* Like the time the house had congregated in Mr. Schiel's apartment for a "feed," the weekly revelry where we ate junk food and watched movies with the housemaster and his wife. It was a spring night in the third trimester and we were sprawled over the TV room. We had been living together for so many months that their TV room felt like home to us.

During a break in the program, a Kentucky Fried Chicken commercial bounced onto the screen. I got a queasy feeling. Amidst the black-folks-getting-down-greazin'-on-some-Kentucky-Fried-Chicken rhythm, Nick Gwyn suddenly chimed, "Hey, Mabes. You gettin' homesick?" The room pitched with laughter. I rose wobbly from the sofa and walked out of the apartment, down the hall to my room. The comment had picked me out and divided me from my classmates, holding me and all black people—my people—up for ridicule. Few of these guys would ever get to know a black person outside of TV images and strangers on the street. And to them, all we were, all *I* was, were cartoonish caricatures.

I sat at my desk and opened a textbook, remembering all the cautions that my grandmother and my mother had issued before I left home. I could attend that school, but I would never be one of "them." They could act like my friends, but they would never really be my friends. Race would always divide us like a penitentiary wall, always make them different from me.

I wanted to cry like a baby. "Stupid. Stupid. Stupid. What the fuck do you think you are? Nigger. Who the fuck do you take yourself to *be* . . . boy?" I hammered it into my head, over and over again, "Stupid, stupid." Some of my friends wandered down the hall to console me, saying Gwyn had meant no harm. He stopped by himself after the feed was over, as boys streamed out of the Schiels' apartment. I think it was his own embarrassment that delayed him, but I didn't know that then.

"Hey, Mabes . . ." He said he was sorry.

Only Steve Wong came in and said, "Geez, what a racist." And Steve and I broke into one of our first "fucking WASPs" conversations. We had no idea that lonely night in Cromwell how many more would follow.

Most of what I learned about race from white kids at Lawrenceville was what I learned from southerners, like Nick Gwyn, or Jefferson Davis Bennett from Charleston. At first, Jefferson's accent, combined with my own prejudices about the South, made me intensely wary of him; but, as we ran into each other over the years in classes and through mutual friends, I grew to respect him. A quick wit, he talked about race as openly as any black person I knew. He talked about America's and Lawrenceville's racial ironies and stereotypes as much as any of us did. And, unlike the other white kids, if he had a question about black people, he didn't hesitate to pose it. Eventually we joked freely, sometimes wryly, about race and prejudice. Other white students, even friends of mine, would stare in astonishment as they heard J.B. (as I came to call him) say things I never would have tolerated from them—not without launching into an impassioned lecture. But they failed to realize that honesty gave us license.

As fate would have it, there would a boy from Louisiana in my house every year. Gwyn in second form, Carter Mills from Monroe in third, Chris Lauricella from New Orleans in fourth and Charles LeBourgeois, one of the freshman I was prefect to during my senior year, from Metairie. The first week of school in my third form year, Carter observed that my roommate, Hal O'Kelley, was white.

I said, "Yeah, Carter. And not only that, he's from Texas, too."

Carter was undaunted. "Well, is that normal here? They put black kids and white kids together in a room?"

A little amazed myself, I became as grave as Carter. "Well, actually at the end of Lower School, we asked to be roommates in Circle, being friends and all."

"Wow, that's great," said Carter, genuinely enthused. "That would never happen at home."

He went on to tell me about racial conditions in Monroe, how blacks and whites deliberately segregated themselves. You could work with someone of a different race in the office, have lunch with him every day, but you would never go over to each other's house for dinner. You wouldn't think of inviting the other guy, and he wouldn't expect it. In fact, you would probably live on different sides of town.

Charles LeBourgeois told me how most every lodge in Mardi Gras was segregated: some for whites, some for blacks and some for Jews, who were also considered a minority in the South. (In fact, some racists hated them more than they disliked blacks.)

The southerners taught me a frankness about race that no

northerner had ever expressed—at least not to me, unless he was yelling his frankness from a car speeding through my neighborhood. They told me what ideas they held themselves that they considered racist. They told me how they thought northerners, and Lawrentians, were at least as racist as anybody back home. They told me how racism was passed down from one generation to another, how some things had changed, and how some things would never change. Some things were just the way they were.

Most important, they taught me that people could hold incongruous thoughts simultaneously. Through the anecdotes from "back home" about the decent, kind people who committed unspeakable acts or who thought indecent thoughts, they illustrated how "good" people could be racist. Before Lawrenceville, I had thought that racism and prejudice were evil and anyone that succumbed to either was irredeemably wicked. I came to understand that I too had prejudices; that we are all creatures of race, even the best of us. That's when I first acknowledged that my grandmother, the most righteous person I knew, was prejudiced. The basic understanding that good people can have evil intentions allowed me to understand the political turns that the country was taking in the early 1980s, turns that seemed so utterly unfair to the poor and working-class black Americans I knew.

During the long New Jersey winter of second form, my popularity gradually ebbed away. I didn't know why. My door was still permanently open, but only my closest friends ventured in: D'Agostino, Roegner, Wong, O'Kelley. The overflow crowds never materialized. Perhaps the novelty of living with a black person had worn off for them, perhaps I had grown smug since I became house president. For whatever reasons, it happened. I felt isolated and alone—in a house of fifty boys. Finding more and more differences between my dormmates and me, I became increasingly hostile. My idyllic beginning had ended.

Our rap sessions always lurched to politics now, as I yelled about social injustices and rich people. My peers relished my fury. They would parrot the conventional conservative wisdom of the day—condemning welfare queens and wimpy liberals—because they believed it and because it sent me orbiting, wild-eyed and out of control. Storming into my room, I would slam the door behind me, shaking the old walls. I'd blast Diana Ross, pop queen of the early eighties, but the symbol of black Revolution to me then. If I was really feeling funky, I'd pump up Rick James. "Shake it up my baby . . . Pretty little thing . . . I wish that you were mine." The notes, distorted and shrill, would screech from my cheap boombox, an impenetrable barricade separating me from "them." Trying to stretch out on my bed to the point of ripping my torso from my waist, to leave sinewy red nerves and blood vessels dangling freely, I shifted uncomfortably between ethnic rage and racial pride.

I told myself that I was better than them because I was poor and had come to this place not because my parents forced me, but because I chose it. I tried to convince myself that I was here for the folks in the 'hood and not for my own glory. Because if I were here for selfish reasons, then I deserved to be ostracized for my differences. I *was* different. But, if I were here to advance The Struggle, I could assume a martyr's stance. In that case, I was just the most recent in a long line of pioneers who had paid the price of challenging white society in aching isolation.

I sank into a deep depression. Even my earlier popularity became a source of pain. I started to think, *Why did these preppie white boys like me to begin with?* Everyone told me that they would be racist. My mother, my grandmother, everybody said they would treat me coldly because I was black. They wouldn't like me unless I acted white. Well, they loved me at first. They elected me house president.

Clearly, I had screwed up. I *had* acted white.

They had never really liked me. They liked the novelty, the oddity, of living next door to someone who put grease in his hair every morning, on purpose.

I searched for reasons. But I had no idea what had changed, or why. Looking back with friends, I've grown to understand the reasons for my fall from grace. To a large extent, it was a typical adolescent tale. Everyone was more popular at the beginning of the year. Cliques had not yet been formed. Once they were, I didn't belong to any, so I was suspect. That was exacerbated by my not joining in the bonding rituals of male adolescence. I didn't go drinking on weekends or play "hall ball" (where one group of guys would whip a tennis ball down the corridor with alarming speed, trying to sting the guys at the other end). I didn't play the requisite pranks to belong, like pushing garbage cans full of water against someone's door, so when he opened it, water flooded his room. I was a Goody Two-shoes, a housemaster's pet.

Other reasons were linked to race and class. I raised my voice in arguments, I slammed the door after bitter disputes. In upper-class WASP culture, such displays of emotion meant you were out of control. The other boys were frightened by my rage; they weren't used to violent outbursts in public. They didn't know how to deal with my anger. Mostly, understandably, they didn't *want* to deal with my anger. Meanwhile, their calm (which to me meant every issue was merely academic to them) only made me more hostile. Eventually, people just steered clear of me. Another race-based reason was jealousy, some of my white friends say today. Many rich kids didn't like the fact that I got better grades than they did. They resented my success.

At any rate, I decided I would hang black. I had been going to the sporadic black student organization meetings since the beginning of the year, but I had always confined my social activities to the residents of Cromwell. They were closer. Now, I decided I would cultivate friends during the hour-long black student meetings. In the Dining Center lobby or Mr. Maxwell's living room, the school's only black faculty member, older boys ranked on each other's clothes, grades, girlfriends and haircuts, laughing up a storm. The younger boys followed suit. They all spoke "black English" effortlessly, they all knew what was supposed to be funny and what was serious.

Sitting in the meetings, I felt like a white-boy exchange student. One of the other Lower Schoolers asked me why I had never come to BSU earlier in the year. I told him I hung in my house. Silence. Everyone understood that that meant I hung white, but no one seemed to bust on me for it. Maybe because L.T., the president of the club, who seemed to do less code-shifting than most of the guys, intervened. "You can hang out with whoever you want, Marc. Don't listen to these Negroes."

I felt better that he made a joke of it, but I knew that this was not my community. These were supposed to be my boys, but I didn't feel like we had anything to say to each other, other than to complain about white people. And even that seemed empty, since at least Steve Wong and I complained about white people we both knew.

These brothers were strangers.

My isolation increased from all sides. It would last through my sophomore year. I performed perfunctorily in my classes, my sports, my clubs. My friendship with D'Agostino, like many high school "best friends" relationships, dried up and blew away. He found a niche in the jock clique. The chief connection between myself and this magnificent place was disintegrating after just six months. The only thing that made me feel like I was actually alive was my poetry, over-emotive works like "*Les Pensées de Suicide*" ("Thoughts of Suicide"). I wrote prodigiously, often using words like "prodigiously" when "a lot" would have done just fine.

Freshman year ended and my mother drove me home. I was exhausted; in three trimesters, I had covered more material than public school students had a year and a half to learn.

I was also relieved. The summer would be my savior.

As the Nova sputtered back onto I-95 and I freed my brain to choose its own course, the Robert Frost poem I had read in one of Dan's S. E. Hinton novels whispered through my mind, settling there:

> *Nature's first green is gold,*
> *Her hardest hue to hold.*
> *Her early leaf's a flower;*
> *But only so an hour.*
> *Then leaf subsides to leaf.*
> *So Eden sank to grief,*
> *So dawn goes down to day.*
> *Nothing gold can stay.*

Lawrenceville's motto was a poetic exploration of the connection between green and gold: *Virtus Semper Viridis*, Latin for "Virtue is always green" or "Youth is always virtuous." The little poem was the best epilogue to my first, breathless year of what the catalog had called "the Lawrenceville Experience."

CHAPTER 4

YOU CAN'T GO HOME AGAIN

Outside of vacations, I had gone home only once during my freshman year. Boarders could spend two or three weekends a term off campus; I just didn't want to. Going back frightened me more than pushing onward. When the novelty of weekend dorm life wore off, I opted to stay because Lawrenceville had become my home. I was more comfortable there, both materially and socially, than in the place I had come from. Other than long talks with my grandmother, White City promised only boredom. My mother was always working or running around with her friends. My brother and I barely spoke to each other, and I had drifted away from the few friends I had. I felt great divides widening between myself, my family and my old community.

From the first time I returned to the 'hood, I felt different, transformed. When I ventured outside I risked encountering a group of neighborhood kids who would mock my "accent."

"Why you talk so white?" they would ask, giggling.

God forbid I went to a house party. The few times I did, a void would develop around me and my dance partner, and the other revelers. Whispering or pointing, they would sneak glances at us.

The whole dance floor revolved around us. Ignorant of the latest steps, I danced white too—too animated to be a black male, too inhibited to be talented. I even walked white, according to some of the b-boys in the neighborhood—lacking the rhythmic bump to my stride that announced I was a proud black man.

Even before I went away to school, I had been suspect because I spent so much time in the house, reading instead of shooting hoops at the park. Too much into books and not enough into hanging. Back then, I had sat with white people in the junior high school cafeteria, where all White City could see me. My white friends had turned me on to white music. But, now that I was *living* with rich white boys, it was certain: I was an Uncle Tom, a traitor to my race. Just as I was seen as a novel guest in a white universe at Lawrenceville, at home I was as an Oreo on leave. My brother fit in so well that I imagine my outsider status made him uncomfortable despite his pride at my success. Even during vacations we lived separate lives, never socializing with each other and rarely having any substantive conversations.

Before I started school old people like Mr. Clait had told me, "Booooy, you go to that there white folks' school and you do yo' mama and yo' grandmama proud, you hear? You do us all proud," he'd said, thwacking me on the shoulder with his heavy, calloused hand. It seemed like all the old folks and all the parents in White City had wished me success when they heard I was leaving for "Lawrence Prep." Even some of my peers had expressed admiration, usually the girls: "You so smart. You going be president one day, ain't you?"

But when I returned home, I felt all of Black America had turned on me; like they had made common cause with white society to convince me that I couldn't, or I shouldn't, succeed. Success meant somehow losing my blackness. Speaking Standard

English, liking school, getting good grades—all indicated whiteness. As if because I spoke differently I thought I was better than
poor black folks.

I had left the community because my mother thought it would
be best, not because I wanted to escape being black. No one
seemed to remember that. It was like leaving the Earth to live on
the Moon and coming home only to be crushed under the weight
of the gravity I was no longer accustomed to. I had no defense, no
explanation for my apparent whiteness. I did listen to *their* music.
I did use their words, like "excellent" and "awesome."

Feeling like a freak, I spent my fall and winter vacation days
in a cocoon of boredom and food. I slept till noon, got dressed in
the afternoon and watched reruns and talk shows until time
for the news. *The Beverly Hillbillies. My Favorite Martian. Bewitched.
The Brady Bunch. The Flintstones.* I was miserable. I hated White
City with its stark, desolate streets and its thick, lifeless air.

At school I had cherished the thought of vacation—especially of
sleeping more than five hours a night—and emptying my brain of
all worthwhile pursuits. Each time I returned to my grandmother's
house though, life there seemed more ragged. Grandmom's health
was deteriorating, and with it her ability to discipline my uncles.

Even something as basic as taking a bath was an ordeal there—
and one that I'd avoid for days at a time. The bathroom was dank
and smelly, and in winter, as frigid as the outdoors. The tub was
rusted and mildewy, filthy. Since the hot water heater was broken, I had to boil tap water in a big pot and lug it upstairs until I
filled the tub. Since it took so long for the water to boil, I usually
used one pot's worth and bathed in a stingy puddle at the bottom
of the tub. With water not even up to my ankles, it was impossible
to get wet. Naked and embarrassed, I dreamed of the scalding
showers on winter mornings at Lawrenceville.

At Grandmom's, my mother, my brother and I all crammed into a six-by-twelve-foot room with all our possessions. I slept downstairs on a pull-out bed. I'd think about my classmates' whining about the old wallpaper at Lawrenceville and the hyperactive heating system that kept our rooms boiling from November to March.

....

By spring break of my first year at Lawrenceville, we had moved again, from Grandmom's back to inner-city Trenton, a Lawrentian's archetypal example of everything I didn't want to be associated with: destitute blacks, housing projects, crime, delinquency and ignorance (which was why I insisted I was from Hamilton and not Trenton). Over my four years at Lawrenceville, I would live in three different homes during breaks: first, one in a middle-class neighborhood in Trenton; then, back at my grandmother's; and, finally, one in Trenton's decaying downtown shopping district. We moved whenever my mother found a house or apartment that, for some reason, did not require two months' rent as a deposit. She never had any savings. My mother always claimed that we lived in the suburbs so my brother could go to Hamilton schools. It was illegal and if we were busted, Charles would have been expelled from the school system, but it was worth the risk. He suffered learning disabilities and received attention in Hamilton that he would not have gotten in Trenton.

For the time being, we resided with a bitter Jamaican man named Roderick. He and my mother had met while she was nursing someone he knew. I never discerned the exact nature of their relationship; I suppose I didn't want to. He was a small, crumpled man with a bald head and an infinite Caribbean ego. Despite his unimpressive physical appearance, he would give long lectures on life, work and women as he sat at the head of the dinner table, presiding over our make-believe family. After just two trimesters at prep school, I had become sufficiently snobby to resent Roderick—with his crass jokes and his Jamaican patois—not just because he was ugly and uneducated, but because my family was so obviously dependent on him for shelter—a beautiful house in West Trenton off Cadwalder Park. ("Cat Water Park," as most black folks called it.) Brick with a white wooden porch, it had a tiny overgrown backyard and a pantry. We each got our own room: me, my mother, my brother and Roderick.

I only talked to two or three friends from White City, and I communicated with them the same way I talked to the ones from Lawrenceville: by phone.

I came home from school exhausted at the end of my first year. After describing my excruciating final exams to my mother and updating her on the state of my relationships in Cromwell—who was cool, who was a loser and who was turning out to be cooler than expected—I fell asleep in the car before we even drove the fifteen minutes to Trenton. At home, my mother nursed me back from exhaustion with Halo Farms Orange Drink and Fruit Punch, my favorites. For my first dinner back, she made fried chicken with macaroni and cheese. The next night she grilled lamp chops. She demanded that everyone, even Roderick, the Jamaican, treat me reverentially. My brother had to be silent while I slept and no one could touch the Entenmann's chocolate doughnuts she had stocked in the fridge for me. (Nothing improves the relationship between a mother and her teenage son like three months apart.)

Roderick contracted diabetes-related gangrene. His foot had to be amputated. The gangrene continued to spread and both legs were eventually cut off. I would hear him sitting alone in his bedroom or in the dining room whimpering. My mother quit her regular home health aide job to nurse him full-time.

Her life had been moving smoothly. She had a regular case with a good agency in Princeton—and now, once again, she was leaving stability and prosperity to help someone else. I despised the way she brought her life to a halt every time someone needed her.

She became Roderick's will. She changed his dressing, gave him his medications. She carried him up the stairs on her back until he could pull himself up. She administered his physical therapy exercises once he received his prosthetic legs. She made him as whole as he could be.

She also ran the house. Although he had cried on her shoulder when he thought he would never walk again, once Roderick got his strength back, his male ego would no longer support his dependency on a woman. He and my mother had a falling out. He told us to leave. We moved back to White City.

We always ended up in White City. I figured that it was some kind of cursed placed that its inhabitants could not escape from; it always drew them back. With dread I thought, We were all doomed to return there sooner or later; I knew that to stay was the death of ambition and hope.

Thank God in the summer there was CETA, the federal jobs program for poor kids. Most of the teenagers in White City qualified. The middle-class kids, whose parents made too much money, actually felt left out. As soon as I was of age, fourteen, I applied. With the minimum-wage checks that arrived every two weeks, I opened a bank account. My mother refused to take any of the money. That first summer I worked as a custodial assistant at a public school. The irony was not lost on the elderly janitors at

Robinson Elementary that a preppy was cleaning their toilets. Once they stopped laughing about it, they told me the hard work would deflate my swelled head.

I rode my bike into one of the nearby white neighborhoods every morning to work. I had to be there by nine. We met in the janitor's room, a dark cubical barely larger than a closet, near the boiler. We talked while they had coffee and I drank orange juice. Then the head custodian, the white guy who supervised a black man and woman, gave us the day's orders. I usually had light duty, cleaning classrooms or scrubbing tile floors. The hard labor, cutting the lawn and cleaning the boiler, was reserved for the older male custodians.

We all met back at "the office" at noon. Under a naked light bulb, we ate our brown-bag lunches on our laps, and my co-workers quizzed me on academics, the world and Lawrenceville. I quizzed them on life. Through nine years of public school education, I had never talked to custodians, until I got to Lawrenceville and it became an act of racial solidarity. They were the hardest-working people I had ever met, next to my grandmother.

My second summer on the program, I worked as a janitor's assistant at Hamilton High School–West. It was the first time I had ever been inside the school I would have attended if Mrs. Sigafoos had not suggested prep school. It was mammoth and brown and institutional. The familial kidding I shared with the old janitors at Robinson vanished; here, a younger ten-man crew worked just to get through the long crappy day.

After two summers I was still grateful to have something to do for forty hours a week, but I was tiring of the monotonous routine of a custodial existence. The real purpose of CETA, I thought, must be to teach poor kids why we should stay in school; otherwise we'd really have to work these depressing jobs.

At the beginning of my third CETA summer, I set up an appointment with the program coordinator to request another assignment. A lot of the kids in White City didn't take Lori Carmignani, a pretty, petite white woman with fluffy brown curls, seriously. She smiled all the time and seemed excessively chipper. Your typical silly white girl, everyone thought, until someone didn't show up for his job or slacked off in his resume-writing workshop. Then Lori got tough. She'd ball up her fists and scrunch up her face and yell as loud as any homegirl trying to cop an attitude in the street. Just about the only thing she didn't do was curse or roll her head around on her neck.

I came in to see her while she was setting job assignments the week before CETA started. She was in a little side office at our neighborhood center. As soon as I walked in, I could see she was having a hard time dealing with my fellow ghetto youth. The frustration of having to be overly solicitous, to ask questions three times before getting a reply, to decode "uhn-uhn, I don't know," was written all over her face. She was obviously a good-hearted liberal; but she couldn't figure out why so many of us acted like we didn't want or need her help.

As soon as I saw her nameplate, I asked if she was related to a Bob Carmignani, a classmate of mine and one of the best soccer players at Lawrenceville. The question knocked her off her tough-girl, all-business posture. She let her body relax into the orange plastic chair.

"He's my brother," she smiled. "You know Bobby?"

"I go to Lawrenceville," I said flatly. How many Lawrentians qualified for CETA? And how many CETA counselors had Lawrenceville students walk into their office?

Shocked to find out that I had been an assistant janitor for two summers, Lori told me she would find me something more challenging. Only the CETA program didn't offer much in the way of "challenging" assignments. After a monotonous two-week stint as a file clerk at the Board of Education, I asked Lori if I could be reassigned as a summer camp counselor at the Center. The Center—or the "Cinner" as we all pronounced it—was not just our government-subsidized neighborhood service center; in the summer, it transformed into a day camp for underprivileged kids under fourteen. The rest of the year, it catered mostly to elderly white people in the neighborhoods around ours.

The Cinner was run by another White City institution, Uncle Bubba, who was rumored to have a lot of problems. Some people charged that he gave out jobs and free cheese (the surplus variety that the USDA distributed to poor folks in ten-pound cardboard boxes in the '80s) chiefly to his relatives. Others alleged he was ignorant and self-promoting. There was no disputing that he was extremely sloppy and overweight.

Still, he was loved. He knew how to deal with "the white folks" who controlled the township and how to bring some of that government money back to our side of town. The Cinner was his fiefdom. He hired and fired everybody. He made all the rules. He also kept neighborhood hoodlums from pestering the good kids who just wanted a place to play air hockey and foosball.

In the summer, the Cinner became the hub of White City social life. Kids from five to thirteen attended the camp, and all the older kids wanted to be counselors. As Reagan phased CETA back and then out, camp went from being an educational experience meant to broaden the kids' world to a babysitting business. The average field trip became a walk to the park up the street, instead of an excursion to the Philadelphia Zoo or the Franklin Institute.

I counseled the ten- and eleven-year-olds. They were old enough to be smart and inquisitive, but young enough to be natural and accepting—including accepting of me. They didn't know that I talked white, unless they heard one of my fellow counselors mention it.

I had asked for the Cinner job because I wanted to transcend my fear of being dissed by my peers. I did. I was hazed, mainly at staff meetings or while the counselors congregated at the park, watching the kids from a distance—either for my blue-and-white-striped polo knits, my pressed and starched consonants or just my general stick-up-the-butt white mannerisms.

The brothers interrogated me on the white boys at Lawrenceville . . . and what about the white girls? "Hamilton wasn't good enough for you, man? What's up with that?"

My close relationship with Lori Carmignani, the white center of power in opposition to Uncle Bubba's rule, didn't help. Everyone wanted to know why we were so chummy. They often saw us talking outside the Cinner, laughing as if we were sharing some inside joke. But the same people that so wittily castigated me for socializing with the boss white lady, and liking it, grew tongue-tied around her. As uneasy as I felt in the jiving give-and-take around the hoop, they were as uncomfortable at the prospect of speaking with Lori—the tension of clashing cultures was too much for them. I didn't understand then that their hazing echoed their suspicions of their own inferiority before a white authority figure more than disapproval over whom I hung with. Only later in life would I recognize that camouflaged insecurity—that unacknowledged, smoldering self-hatred—was more destructive to the African-American community than the most conspicuous Uncle Tom. It ate black American men up from the inside, like moths do wool, leaving hollow, business-suited corpses that move through the corporate world. Zombies in blackface.

But there, in the hazy summer, no reply could have saved my face; the question was the condemnation. Usually, one of the female counselors would eventually defend me against the implicit accusation of tomming. Some of the girls were good in school too. It was okay for a sister to be smart, as long as she didn't talk white or act uppity. Any brother who was into books, though, had better be able to prove he was down in some other ways: like hanging with the boys or knocking boots (having sex). Studying was not considered manly.

Some counselors cut me slack because they respected the way I handled my kids, firm but understanding.

When one of our girls experienced her first menstrual period while our group was stuck inside the Cinner on a rainy day, the room broke into pandemonium. Girls and boys started screaming and running in every direction, climbing on top of one another. Apparently, the little girl had no idea what was happening to her. Some counselors hurried her out of the room, then one of the female counselors and I gave an impromptu lecture on puberty and adulthood, followed by a question-and-answer period. The kids were entranced.

Despite being consistently dissed during my first summer at the Cinner, counseling pint-size African-Americans was so fulfilling that I decided to do it again the next year.

Outside work, I was surprised to find that I still felt alienated from White City. These were my people. This was my home— the only one I had spent more than eighteen months in anyway. But it was like being at a never-ending church picnic where none of the congregation members invited you to come sit down. Many of the young people in White City thought I thought I was better than them. Or they thought they were less than me. It produced the same net effect.

TV still offered my chief escape, but I had picked up another tool for survival: music. I toted my little radio with me from home to school and back, the one constant in my Jekyll-and-Hyde existence. Some songs bound my two worlds in a seamless familiarity. The "black music" that was my refuge at Lawrenceville—Earth, Wind & Fire, The Sugar Hill Gang, Rick James—was my only key to acceptance at home. The "white music" that I had discovered at school—the Go-Gos, the Police, Billy Idol, Huey Lewis and the News—salved my growing homesickness for L'ville.

Coming home made real the suspicion I had not faced—hadn't really even formed clearly in my own mind yet—that my closest connections were with the white boys I had left behind. I called my Lawrenceville friends more and more and shared their vacation stories. The more moneyed ones would be off skiing or touring Europe. The others would be sitting at home like me, bored and willing to talk for hours.

CHAPTER 5

ANGRY BLACK BOY
IN AN IZOD

The center snapped the ball, the helmeted players scattered and the line of scrimmage disappeared. It looked nothing like the diagram. The X with the ball wasn't going through the hole and the Os were piled over to the right side of the field—on top of the X that was supposed to be coming through the opening. Or was it the O? I was so pitiful that after a week of preseason training the coach asked if I would mind terribly not playing JV football. "We just don't want anybody to get hurt," he said, placing his hand on my shoulder. He told me I should play in the very competitive house intramural league and come back out for JV next year. Only two of us didn't make the team.

I had returned to campus in September 1982 an Old Boy, and nothing had changed. Dedicated to becoming a decent athlete and thinking that maybe that would end my enduring depression, I had arrived early to try out for football. I had never put on a shoulder pad in my life. But, I thought, team sports would make me feel something: comradery, pain, agony, victory. Anything would be better than my constant numbness. Only it backfired. I didn't even understand the game. Another failure. I grew increasingly moody.

"Marc, people see you as an angry black man," Takuo Kata-yama told me one night while we pasted up galleys for the student literary magazine.

While I still excelled in the toughest classes I could take, the work no longer fascinated me. I saw no meaning in my life. I felt no sense of belonging. I just was. Much of my alienation was typi-cal teenage angst, only exacerbated by my chameleon existence. My friendships languished; my walls grew higher.

One goal did excite me as the year wore on: I wanted to be president of Kennedy House. It gave me, literally, a *raison d'être*. Throwing a sheet over my isolation and depression, I played best friend to every member of my dorm. I buddied up to each clique, feigning interest in their classes and their jokes, smoking the pot they smoked and watching the sports they followed. Jon Bronner, the only black fourth former in Kennedy—the muscular football player my mother had asked to "look out for" me that first day at Lawrenceville—saw me trying to kiss up to somebody he knew I disliked.

"That's all right, Marc," he yelled across the Kennedy dining room. "You'll get a position on the house council. You don't have to try so hard." The room went silent. My heart sank.

It was a sorrowful year—the symptoms grew old and familiar like good friends or a musty couch, but I still could not diagnose the disease. I can remember only one joyful night early sopho-more year: the eve before Christmas break, Lawrenceville's most magical moment. In the frost of the New Jersey December, the campus became an elegant decoration. Students gathered from every house at the Chapel. Two flawless evergreens stood on either side of the altar, each dressed in tiny white lights. Every pew was crowned by candelabra of long, white candles that illu-minated the soft dusty air.

The pipe organ vibrated through the candlelight, as boys whispered to friends from other dorms. Teachers, seated at the sides in their academic regalia, chatted among themselves. Dr. Fish, our ebullient and unconventional chaplain, and Dr. Sipple, his cerebral second-in-command, followed the colorful procession of the school and house flags, and took their places up front. In his magnificent baritone, Dr. Fish launched into an ecumenical sermon about humanity and knowledge and love and passion and forgiveness.

"Make a joyful noise," he enthused in a loud final flourish.

On Mr. Lauffer's cue, the Glee Club roared from behind the altar, "Jesu, joy of man's desiring..."

The sound bellowed, above, beyond and under us, sending its tremulous tones rumbling through our bodies and out, audaciously, into the heavens.

"Soar to un-created light..."

We sang a medley of classical masses and traditional carols. "The Gloria." "The Magnificat." "Silent Night." It seemed that on this night the adolescent male's famously impervious armor against sentimentality was pierced. Mr. Williams, a tall and imposing math master, housemaster of Hamill and the varsity tennis coach, sang a tenor solo.

"... the weary world rejoices ... Fall! On your knees," he boomed. "Oh, hear, the angel's voooooooices. Oh niiiiight deviiiiiine, oh niiiiight, oh niiiiight deviiiiiine." Turning a scarlet red, he hit notes that I didn't think anybody could reach. The Chapel erupted into applause (not a common occurrence). Religious diversity notwithstanding, this was one of the few times when the Lawrenceville School truly felt like one community. Our voices, exuberant and unified, rang against the cold night outside.

The Dining Center was draped in Christmas finery, each table covered with a white linen tablecloth and candles. Even the normally ragged Lawrentians came in coat and tie. Our appearance, fresh and clean, added to the wonderment of the occasion. After dinner, sated by the prime rib and dessert, we closed the sliding glass doors that led to each house dining room and lit up cigars. Big fat stogies, thin little erudite numbers, smuggled Havanas. We had all bought at least a box at the pharmacy across Main Street earlier that day. The seniors came back to the Circle House where they had spent their third- and fourth-form years.

In no time, each glass-encased room was filled with smoke. From the outside, they looked like banks of fog. Inside, we all suffocated. Any other time, you needed parental permission to smoke and you could only do it in a few selected areas on campus. Now, we were thrilled to be smoking with our friends, teachers and housemasters. Through the dizzying haze, we would wander back to our dorms, many of us to begin the unofficially sponsored part of the night's festivities, the drinking of alcohol.

At the end of sophomore year, I lost the election. Jon Bronner was wrong; I failed even to get a position on the Kennedy House council. The popularity contest was over and I had been declared a loser, an unbearable title at Lawrenceville.

It was the most fortunate catastrophe to thrash my teenage world. After just two years, I had become so obsessed with being liked that my ego depended solely on the titles and awards I accumulated. Losing the election wrecked my value system, and I decided to explore other parts of my life for a sense of accomplishment: the Glee Club, the literary magazine, the newspaper, the drama club. Duty and ambition be damned, I was free from the overwhelming demands of overachieverdom. I would do all the things at Lawrenceville that I wanted to do, including taking the classes that I liked. No more chemistry. Ever. My junior year, I took college-level courses in biology (with Mr. Graham) and American history. Senior year, I took college-level English, French and calculus (the last one because I had to know if I could do it—I could, but not very well, it turned out). I didn't need anyone's vote anymore. I didn't have to be liked. I didn't have to create an identity that would please everyone I met. I was finally free.

English was my love, and Lawrenceville's strongest department, with unconventional and relentless teachers who probed your limits. They were nothing like the stern masters of classical prep school lore. There was Mr. Maxwell, an intelligent and handsome man who spoke with a distinguished blend of British and Jamaican accents. When a student made a gaffe that vividly illustrated the fact that he had not read the previous night's assignment, Mr. Maxwell would shout, "My God, man . . ." And if, in fact, you had not read last night's assignment, the best strategy was to ask Max a question about cricket, his other passion. This would inspire him to place his copy of *Invisible Man* on the table and go to the chalkboard, diagramming the cricket pitch and the players. Forgetting the assignment, he would draw in the batter running between the two bases, tracing the line over and over again. With one hand in his back pocket and the other holding the chalk, he would extol the virtues of the game as a palpable sense of relief settled around the Harkness table and the clock sped toward the end of the period.

Mr. Waugh was the opposite. He couldn't care less if you had read the assignment, as long as you had something interesting to say in class . . . about anything. Sporting a graying scruffy beard and the same blue jean jacket every day, he taught the most sought-after English course at the school: The Wasteland. His students read T. S. Eliot, *One Flew Over the Cuckoo's Nest, Trout Fishing in America, The Crying of Lot 49* and *The Lime Twig,* and listened to gritty recordings of Ginsburg reading "Howl"—"I have seen the best minds of my generation . . ." We left every class feeling like our minds had been deflowered, swimming in newfound knowledge we knew we had absorbed, although it wasn't quite organized yet.

One day we were puzzling over the relationship between Randall Patrick McMurphy and Nurse Ratched. "That's . . . hum, hum . . . R . . . P . . . M," Mr. Waugh said, with a grunt, "and . . . Nurse . . . ummm . . . Ratched . . . ummmmm . . . Ratched." He clenched the air, as if each hand were a vise grip. (Outside the class, we imitated his habit of humming and gurgling between words but we still thought he was the greatest genius that would ever teach us.)

"Why is McMurphy in the asylum? What brings him there?" he asked, finally formulating a question.

Walter Jean raised his hand, a show of politesse Waugh detested. He wanted us to call out our answers. In his hallmark green tie and red sweater, Walter (later our class valedictorian) piped up, "He tells Billy Babbitt that he is there because he fights, drinks and ummm ummm's too much." Smelling an intellectual untruth, Waugh stopped his perpetual pacing around the big wooden table.

"What, Walter?" he said, straightening up from his usual slouch. He looked almost offended. "What? What does he do too much?"

"Uhm-hum," Walter said, clearing his throat. "He fights, drinks and . . . you know, too much," Walter hurried out.

Knowing the ignoble verb that Walter avoided, the class's attention piqued.

"No, Walter, I don't know. *You* tell *me* . . . uhm-hum, Walter."

Now perspiring slightly, Walter sat even more erect in his chair, touched his glasses and said softly, "Fucks, fights and drinks too much."

"*What, Walter?*" Waugh said, hammering every consonant and elongating every vowel. "I can't hear you."

Determined, Walter sat up even straighter and said clearly, "He fucks, fights and drinks too much."

"Oh," said Waugh. "Fucks. He fucks, fights and drinks too much, Walter." He said it with great flourish. "Repeat after me Walter, fuck, fuck, fuck, fuck, fuck, fuck, fuck, fuck, fuck, fuck," he ranted in an insane staccato as the class erupted in laughter and Walter, turning a bright red, chortled in his chair. Despite his bourgeois Hong Kong Chinese upbringing, half-suppressed laughter wracked Walter's body.

But what conscientious students like Walter did not like about Mr. Waugh's class, indeed none of us did, was that he refused to give us grades. Instead, he would hand our papers back with a page of handwritten comments and stickers of flowers, insects or fruit. We would sit around after class trying to figure out what a ladybug meant as opposed to a grasshopper. We thought that since praying mantises were so rare, they had to be an A. He laughed at our consternation and told us to chill out: "Hey, man, relax."

He was all Beat Generation. He assigned a spontaneous exercise where we had to choose an object, sit in front of it, contemplate it for ten minutes, then write in a stream of consciousness whatever came into our heads. I chose an award I had been given for excellence in AP biology: The Aldo Leopold Environmental Sciences Award. It was a stainless steel and pewter cup of typical prep school-prize design. I wrote:

Shining distortion hard against the smooth black desk looking searching across the hall looking dying in the mall—
Come to stay be alone with me—Come to stay and wonder
free—It came upon a midnight clear bearing myrrh—and if
I do call you that will they elope through the side window
carrying berry-berry in a car—moving station wagon along
the suburban farm to where the grass lies shy and dew-cov-
ered on heads of deaths and mounds of shit—Away go don't
see the sun stop and catch the pot run run stop no not here
not to see the green grass die—to when the Earth is young
Elizabeth sees her child die in the gutter and smashes the
house to bits—yes, It's not Allentown to see the foresight
wash over reason and trickle through my head and glisten in
the midnight sun not to wander over and in but to rest and
smile and turn a spin—not too sick if I may inquire just to
sit and parler sire—but, don't you like my williwacks come
back and talk to Colonel Sack—let's not play with the yellow rosebuds anymore they depress me and make me
sneeze—don't wonder if Mary can't find the door just tell
her to go to hell—Stop blasphemy why me to know that
evil will that sits up there upon the hill come lay with me—
Don't you're not aware of love and God don't you know that
he's my man can't find a hand so just sucks all day—Hello
Beth—look too far down the road saw a car coming Didn't
say you were going to stop the hop sit down and talk and
bullshit have a beer dance a jig roll over Beethoven we're
bringing my mama home—Did you talk to Bill about how
his shit keeps hitting the fence over by our pool George—
Stop that shit or you'll pay you fucking dicks—No don't
worry they won't care because at least I can't find the dog in
among the cold blue mass running through cold halls look

see jump die can't find out why—don't see Sam in the pack got a knife in his back can't see John or Sue oh shit must get running have a fit—do come in and have some tea Freud was here but he got a cramp and went home back to Trenton to live in the ruins of 1999—Can't see no loving here can't find my poor dear lost my dog and my house what the fuck life's a bitch—You could say that—they don't care when their pants fall over their knees far beyond sunset—And Carolina gold in her piss-yellow hair came up to the bank today—Fucked the meter on the sidewalk and made a deposit—dont care much for honey—Have some pudding instead—Up on the rooftop I sit and stare go to hell you ain't nowhere—Sit among my lily patch—catch a snatch, snatch snatch—Gonna die if she don't call about the brown cannonball Goodnight cat of late of nigh gotta go but I hafta sigh So don't call Peggy a bitch shes just a slut

Mr. Waugh's comments were as hep as my prose: "Well, I am notorious for my dubious taste. But I like this a lot. I'm not willing to go so far as to say it's great art—But it is a high-energy discharge—wild, exuberant, funny, sad in places. You 'mouth really madly' and as such your nonsense is not simply non-sense, if you know what I mean . . . . Anyway it's all wild, woolly and whacked-out." Praying mantis.

Deborah McKay was our other great gift from the gods of unconventional teaching. When she came to Lawrenceville my sophomore year, she was the talk of the student body. She wasn't pretty in the way the two-dimensional Christie Brinkleys and Farah Fawcetts that adorned boys' walls were. She was tall and had a long face with a little mouth and very fine blond hair. But, she had a mysterious, quiet energy that awed and excited many of us. And frightened even more of us. "She's weird," was the comment most associated with her when she debuted. She had each class devise rules for the term. Not a list of prohibitions and requirements—no smoking, hand in papers on time—but a sort of contract.

The first rule for our fourth-form honors English class was "Take Risks." That was hers. Another was "Come into the Class Alone." That meant leave your friends, your parents, your girlfriend and your inhibitions outside. And "Write Something That No One Else in the Universe Could Have Written" was another. The hardest rule demanded, "Be Brilliant." Since she was so cutting-edge, no one really knew what that meant. Guys would spend the whole class trying to say something truly unique and profound. The nicest thing about Ms. McKay was that she never laughed at our attempts.

By the end of one term in her class, we had so thoroughly analyzed Robert Frost's "Birches" that most of us knew it by heart, and we had written four drafts of a term paper. When Andy Spicer asked if he had to hand in a pre-draft before his first official draft—a bit excessive, Andy thought—Ms. McKay replied, "Only if you want the benefit of my infinite wisdom."

Lifting his backpack off the table, Andy said with a huge grin, "That's okay."

She shot back, smiling just as broadly, "Well, fuck you then."

During finals week, after the terrible Kennedy House rout, Nick Roegner came to my room. Nick had won "the Presidency" (as both of us venerably called it). Our friendship, so strong at the beginning of the year after a year in Cromwell, had dried to a residue of cordiality. We spoke when we passed on the stairs. He had his friends: the fourth-form Old Boys and the third-form majority who had crowned him house president. And I had mine: the marginals like Rich Klein (a fourth-form artist) and Steve Wong, with whom I had perfected the politics of exclusion.

So I was surprised when Nick knocked on my door, which even now was always open. He said it had been a tough year and it was too bad that I was not going to be on the council. I told him that was the truth and we smiled nervously, trying to avoid each other's eyes. I said I hoped he would have a good year as president. One of us suggested we split a pizza. After half a large pepperoni and two Cokes, I told Nick that I had hated him during the Campaign.

I thought that he had colluded with a fourth former who disliked me to ensure I would not be elected to the council. Klein had told me that Nick and his fourth-form mentor were traveling the house telling people not to vote for me because I was arrogant and uncool. Nick told me he didn't remember doing that. If his friend had, then he didn't know about it.

I told him I had kept a journal over the last few months, and all my real feelings, the thoughts I couldn't bring myself to say to his face, were smoldering in there. He told me he had kept a journal too.

Surprised and excited, I said, "Hey, do you think we could exchange them?"

With a quizzical smile, he asked, "Ooooo, do you think that's a good idea?" clearly as enticed by the potential pain, but the certain voyeuristic pleasure, as I was.

"Okay," we agreed simultaneously. I flashed a nervous grin as we swapped notebooks. Back in my room, I read slowly, caressing every comma of my friend's private thoughts. He wrote a lot about the cool guys in the fourth form and how the house community was falling apart or uniting. Only occasionally did he refer to the bitterness that was spreading between us like a fungus—how we argued on opposing sides of group disputes; how I was trying to distance myself from the house's most respected members; how I seemed to be treating him with disdain because he was becoming increasingly popular. It was all true.

I read each sentence, then read it again. I couldn't find the seething hatred I had expected. I had written whole passages about how my friend had betrayed me, how it was all racially motivated. If I had been a white boy, naturally, I would have been elected. How hypocritical, I had written, that they call *me* arrogant. No one would have called me arrogant if I too had come from Greenwich and my father was a CEO; then I'd be "confident." Because I was a black boy from Trenton, I had no right to be proud. To them, the very fact that I felt proud was arrogance. I had no right. The bastards.

When I finally finished reading, I gathered myself from the floor and went to his room. "Wow," I said. "That was really interesting."

"Not as interesting as yours," Nick said, looking up at me, pale.

"What do you mean?"

"It was really, really angry."

I laughed. He didn't.

"I know. I wrote what I really felt. And I was fucking pissed. You guys screwed me over."

He said he had no idea I had felt that way. He never suspected that I had seen everything in racial terms, when, in fact, the house's rejection of me reflected how moody I had become, how deliberately I had cut myself off from people and nothing racial, he said.

"Yeah, I don't know, maybe," I replied, noting his sincerity. "I was actually really surprised that you never mentioned a certain racial word in your journal."

"What do you mean?"

"You know, 'nigger' . . . I kept reading for it, expecting to find it."

Staring at me, his mouth dropped open. Then, with disdain, he asked, "You thought *I* would write that. Fuck, Marc, you *don't* know me."

"I'm sorry," I heard myself stupidly apologize.

"That's amazing. I wasn't raised that way," he said, now more offended than dumbfounded.

"Well, look," I said, regaining my footing and my sense of reality. "Most white people would have. That's what they say when they're pissed at a black person. It's like saying, 'Hello' when you meet somebody. It's a conditioned response. It's Pavlovian."

"Bullshit, Marc. *You're* just so racist, you can't believe that everybody else isn't as racist as you are," he said.

Nick invited me up to his house in North Jersey a few weeks later. I took the train to Mattawan Station, where he and his mother picked me up. She was the nicest Lawrenceville parent I knew—tall and beautiful with a slightly aristocratic accent, the model of upper-class poise. She talked to me like a real person, not a scholarship kid or her son's black friend. We even compared backgrounds. She hadn't grown up well-off either.

After a dinner of veal, Mr. and Mrs. Roegner retired to bed while Nick, his older brother John and I went to rent videos. Back in their stone cottage, John suggested cocktails.

Marc, have you ever had a Sleigh Ride?"

"A what?"

"A Sleigh Ride."

Turned out, it was one of his favorite drinks up at the Cape where he tended bar in the summer.

"A sleigh ride was when the whalers would get the harpoon in a whale and it would take them for a ride," John said. "That's what this drink does to you."

John's version that night was a mixture of fruit punch, vodka, rum, triple sec and Cointreau; it was so sweet that I sucked down tall glass after tall glass while we watched *Creep Show*. The bitter feelings of the house election were obliterated in the drunken haze of male bonding. Our voices rose so high that Mrs. Roegner asked us to quiet down.

Soon I discovered my body hanging over Nick's toilet, vomiting. Staggering, John tried to walk me around outside to sober me up.

As I waited in the morning for John and Nick to drive me to the train station, Mrs. Roegner asked if we wanted breakfast. "I imagine not," she said with a smile.

Embarrassed and still reeling, I replied, "Thank you so much for a wonderful weekend, Mrs. Roegner. I'm sorry I vomited in your house."

I thought I was being polite. She laughed and said, "Don't mention it, Marc."

Even as my life with boys from different races and classes was moderating my adolescent passions and my politics, white students—and often teachers—viewed me increasingly as a radical. I thought I was nonthreatening: An honors student active in the Glee Club and the drama society, I hardly had the profile of a Black Panther.

My reputation as a black nationalist was more a source of frustration than pride. I had never courted the label; it just gave people another reason to exclude me. White guys I didn't even know saw me as a troublemaker. Black guys I barely knew considered me an Oreo. The people who were impressed by my defending unpopular views, for the most part, never told me so.

I suppose the popular impression grew from the heated political discussions in the Kennedy common room or at the dinner table. Liberated from the popularity sweepstakes, I was free to speak my mind. As a token Democrat, I had few allies. I'd rant and rave about social injustice, while other boys calmly presented the reasoned, thinking Republican's view. My image wasn't helped by the poems and short stories I published in the *Lit*, which often centered on anger and pride.

That was strange enough in the pages of the hundred-year-old student literary magazine, but even more revolutionary was the political essay I wrote in the fall 1984 issue, my inaugural edition as editor-in-chief. Clearly displayed under the rubric "Opinion," it blasted that summer's Republican National Convention. President Reagan's speech accepting his second nomination to represent his party so enraged me that it prompted an unassigned spontaneous writing. The piece began, "As I sit here watching the Republican National Convention with a slightly sick stomach . . ." and then I vented.

I condemned Jack Kemp's hypocrisy in claiming his solidarity with "the South African black" after the party omitted any mention of American civil rights from its platform. "While the upper-middle and upper-socio-economic classes of our society have benefited from Reagan's policies," I wrote, "more poor people are starving in America's backyard than ever before, minority unemployment is rising at a frightening rate, and the most horrifying thing of all—America is in agreement with the Republican Party!"

Such rhetoric raised the dander of people who fancied themselves my political foes—that is, most everybody. Senior year, the director of the fifth form asked me and John Atwater, the president of the black students association, to say a few words at a hastily called chapel assembly in commemoration of Martin Luther King Day. Some faculty member had decided we should observe the holiday by doing more than just going to class, as had been planned. The headmaster decreed that all students and faculty would attend a half-hour ceremony between lunch and E period.

I sat at the front of the chapel, on the opposite side of the headmaster from Atwater. We were both visibly nervous. I felt like I didn't deserve to be in this sacred space usually reserved for the chaplain or an important school guest. I felt my friends' eyes on me as I tried self-consciously not to look too goofy or too pompous.

After brief remarks, the headmaster motioned me toward the lectern. Smoothing out the wrinkles of my scribbled speech, I looked into a sea of familiar faces, almost all white. Suddenly, I was struck by the importance of the moment. I offered up my own prayer thanking Dr. King, who was more responsible than anyone for my standing there.

"We can come up here today and talk of his accomplishments and his everlasting spirit, and that's all good," I said, listening to my voice lift toward the balcony, then fall away.

It is necessary to remember these things.

But people have a way of saying—So what? How does this apply to me? I can hardly end racism in America, or even in my own dorm, so why even talk about it?

Well, there are a few reasons to talk about racism, and the Black Struggle, which is actually just part of a greater Human struggle for liberty and equality:

The first reason is the simplest. Listen. I stood erect and looked silently into the crowd. I made eye contact with as many people as I could. I let the minutes drift on. The silence became oppressive.

"Silence," I finally said, letting the word hang in the still air.

"Silence. What happens in silence? . . . Nothing."

My Lawrenceville community was listening to me, giving me the opportunity to speak unfiltered and honestly.

No achievement, no advancement, no progress, nothing!

By speaking out for what one believes, and by breaking the silence, in essence by "making freedom ring," you make people remember.

When people don't remember, catastrophes have a way of occurring over and over again.

We must not forget!

The image of the chained, oppressed, beaten slave must be remembered.

The image of the walking skeletons being led to slaughter in Nazi Germany must be remembered.

And the silence must be broken!

In complacency lies the roots of human oppression.

So, we're here today to break the silence—which at the present time is frightening concerning Human freedom.

Another reason to take a few moments to discuss racism and Dr. King's message is that we've got a long way to go. The summit of equality still rises far above the Black American's present position and Humanity's greater struggle is nowhere near an end.

So, you still ask, "What can I do?"

Well, to put it simply you can help end racism by trying to guard against it in your own thoughts, and your own perceptions of others.

Every human being is prejudiced, yet you can make an attempt to rid yourself of this negative, indeed destructive, emotion.

And that's how racism is overcome. Individually—one person at a time. There are many racists sitting among us right now. I am not able to stand up here and say "All the minorities of the world are great. We love you and wish you'd love us too." I can't change prejudiced thoughts with a few words between lunch and E Period.

The only way to overcome prejudice is through individual experience. You have to see, firsthand, that stereotypes are false.

You have to learn for yourself that no group of individuals can be uniformly characterized by certain traits.

Most importantly, you have to see other people, minorities specifically, as individuals!

I am black, a fact of which I am very proud. Yet, it is only one facet of my personality.

And when you approach me, I expect you to realize my color, of course. Yet, when you try to place me into certain categories as a result of that blackness, we have problems.

Recognize people for their difference, yet never limit your view of another because of those differences. Don't define someone in terms of others of his race, define him in terms of himself.

Through recognizing other people as individuals and not stereotypes we cut through the myths and slowly deteriorate racism within ourselves—and that's the only way to do it!!

So, deal with me as an individual, a black individual, but nonetheless an individual.

And when we see each other as individuals and not so much as colors, racism will die. It will be a long time from now. No one sitting here will probably ever know that day of equality, yet one day it will, it must, arrive!

And, to tell the truth, the end of prejudice does concern you, as a matter of fact it depends on you!

Let us all be determined to make his dream a reality!

In six minutes I had finished. In the silence, someone started clapping and Lawrenceville gave me a round of applause.

After the service a few teachers congratulated me, as did fellow students, both black and white. As I headed into the Music House for Glee Club rehearsal, though, one of my friends stopped me and said. "Wow, Marc . . . that was a radical speech you gave today." The look on his face told me he didn't mean radical as in "totally awesome." He was flushed and shaking his head with disbelief. I had self-consciously tried to be tame and respectful, lest I be considered an angry black man, and to deliver a positive message. My classmate said it all sounded like fire and fury to him.

Without a doubt, some of the resentment I caused in my fellow students and some teachers came from their feeling that I should have been grateful just to have the ten-thousand-dollar scholarship to attend Lawrenceville. Some students said as much. And after I started working at *Newsweek* after college, one Lawrenceville parent would write me a letter every time I wrote about racial issues or prep schools. He was the father of an Asian-American kid who attended Lawrenceville shortly after I graduated. He usually complained about minorities whining, but once he actually complained about minorities being minorities: Asians being nerds and blacks and Latinos being hoodlums. He said he had seen "black girls spitting on the sidewalks" at Lawrenceville. "No wonder they could never be true Lawrentians," he wrote.

I spent junior year immersed in classes and clubs; my depression evaporated as unexpectedly and as inexplicably as it had descended freshman year. Finding myself an Old Boy without a title, I had to invent myself. I became a sort of big brother to the third formers in Kennedy, and gained a new gang of buddies. Randall and Dave were best friends, the kind that old books and movies said boarding school was supposed to create. So, even though I was a fourth-form Old Boy, I felt privileged when they invited me along for their weekly Thursday night cheesesteaks at TJ's.

In the middle of spitting straw wrappers at each other, Randall and Dave started to chatter about the "kangaroo court" in Cleve House. When I asked what the kangaroo court was, they thought I was kidding.

"No, what is it? I've *never* heard of it."

"But everybody knows that the rhinies (the new boys) in Cleve are forced to go through kangaroo court . . . at least every third former knows," Dave spoke with a look of fear coupled with disbelief.

"We're lucky that the fourth formers in Kennedy are too stoned to have a KC," Randall laughed.

Then they revealed to me the horrors of the kangaroo court, one picking up where the other left off. They told me rhinies were forced to participate in the KCs, usually after midnight in the basement of the house. One boy had been stripped and covered with Bengay, Pepto-Bismol and Cocoa Puffs. Another had a fire extinguisher discharged up his butt. And some boys were forced to urinate on others.

My fledgling journalistic sensibility was spinning out of control. "This is an outrage. This has to be stopped. Does the headmaster know about this? Does any adult know about this? I've got to write an article for the *Lawrence*. Do you think anyone who's been through this will talk to me?" They shrugged their shoulders. The hazing had reportedly been going on for generations; they thought the administration bowed to tradition.

Armed with the identity of an alleged victim, I walked into Cleve, one of the tightest houses on campus, full of spirit, enthusiasm and unity. I knocked on the kid's door and he invited me in. When I asked him if the kangaroo court really existed, he confirmed everything. A second boy corroborated the first one's account. I still couldn't believe it. This was a provocative story, but I worried for Lawrenceville. What would this do to the school? Then, I thought of the fifteen-year-olds, abused because of some hundred-year-old tradition. At the *Lawrence* office I wrote up a short piece, only five or six terse paragraphs, but frank. I didn't revel in obscene detail, but I stated the damning facts: It occurred regularly in Cleve, at least most of the boys in the house knew about it, and it had been a tradition there long before these boys started doing it. I waxed the back of the typeset article, ready to paste it onto the paper's layout.

Doubts about my story, my sources, myself gnawed at me. I needed more confirmation. I needed to discuss this with more people than just my friends and the editor. I returned to Kennedy that night with the sticky-backed, typeset article and went to bed.

The next morning, after the other students had filed out of fourth-form honors English, I showed the waxed copy to a friend who would be editor of the paper when we juniors took over. He was amazed. As we consulted, our English master, a mainstay at Lawrenceville, said he had no problem with us printing whatever was accurate, but he thought that I should warn Cleve's house-master. I decided to postpone the article for a week so I could talk to the housemaster.

I scheduled an appointment with the housemaster before sports period. I was barely breathing as I walked up the stairs to knock on the door of his apartment. He was the dean of the Circle housemasters and a senior member of the faculty, one of the most revered men on campus. And The Circle, it was always said, was the heart of the school. As I was about to confront him, it occurred to me that maybe I would piss these people off. After all, this was their school, not mine. And if they liked discharging fire extinguishers up each other's butts, if it had been going on since the Battle of Hastings, what business was it of mine? Visions of myself tarred and feathered, running around The Circle, pursued by an angry mob wielding lacrosse sticks clouded my vision.

I thought to run, but just then, the housemaster opened the door and ushered me in with a smile, "Marc, nice to see you."

We sat in the living room as his eyes traced the small waxed piece of paper. I was afraid to peer beneath those gray eyebrows, but I was drawn to his eyes as they passed over the article. Soon he stopped reading and thrust the scrap of paper toward me. "This is a lie. This is impossible. Nothing like this could be going on in the Cleve," he fumed.

"Sir, I am positive that the story is accurate. I have very good sources," I rasped, in a quivering tenor.

He had already regained his composure and was speaking quietly to me. "I ask that you not print this until I can talk to my boys," he said. His natural, generous voice had returned.

"Sir, we have already decided to wait until next week to run the article."

It didn't take long for the news to spread. The same night I got a call from the guy I knew best in Cleve, John Devine, a house officer and one of Lawrenceville's favorite sons. He said there was no reason to run the story, that I was just trying to win journalistic glory for myself.

I asked him, "What about the people's right to know? . . . and that light kills bacteria that thrive in the dark? And what about those abused boys?"

He told me the housemaster had already initiated a full investigation and it was all going to come out. There was no need to print an article that would embarrass the school, the house and the master.

A few days later, I was back in the housemaster's apartment. He confirmed everything I had written. I sat surrounded by his assistant housemasters and the whole Cleve House council. They shared a common cause: to convince me not to print the story. To Lawrenceville's great credit, there was never the threat of censoring the newspaper.

They rehashed the arguments I had already heard—the ones that I had been having with myself. The school's disciplinary system had swung into action. I had already done my duty by bringing this behavior to light, so that the housemaster and the school could deal with it. The boys responsible would be punished. To print the article now would only do harm. Did I have any idea how the press would relish this? They hate wealthy private schools, especially all-boys' schools. They would do anything to smear us. And this article would give them the perfect weapon. Think of Lawrenceville's reputation. And think of all the boys whose parents live in California . . . or Hong Kong . . . and how they will worry needlessly about their child, even if he's not in Cleve. Ask yourself what you'll accomplish by printing this, they implored. I felt like I was the one being disciplined.

I decided not to print it, so the story never ran, a decision I regret today. Looking back, there was no good reason not to run the story. As it happened, the *New York Times* and the CBS *Evening News* ran very small, vague stories about excessive hazing at the Lawrenceville School in New Jersey. I never talked to any reporters. But my decision didn't prevent the hate mail and the threats. Two boys were expelled for hazing, another suspended. Someone slipped a note under my door with the words "Niggers Die" scrawled on it. Another anonymous greeting read, "Nigger Go Home." I received phone calls where some disguised adolescent voice threatened bodily harm. And one night someone pulled the fire alarm in Kennedy and left taped to it the reflection "KKK Kills Niggers."

Damn it, I never even printed the article and I was still persona non grata. I couldn't figure out what I had done wrong, really. The school president, TJ Mark, Kennedy House president from the year before, came by to check on me. He had heard what was going on and wanted to let me know he supported me. TJ was one of the few; some friends stopped hanging around with me so they wouldn't be smeared too. Only my closest ones remained.

Not until I was out of college and living in New York did I understand what unwritten rules I had transgressed. While getting plastered with another Lawrenceville graduate, he turned to me and said, "Man, I hated you. I thought you were a traitor. Everybody did. You had betrayed your brothers."

Drunk and emboldened, I pressed him: "What the hell . . . My brothers, guys who stick lacrosse sticks up weaker guys' butts? What did I do wrong? Besides, those guys never thought of this black boy as their brother for one second of one day of their fucking lives."

"Well, if you look at it that way," he agreed.

At the end of the year, I was reminded that I had not outgrown my need for outside recognition. Kennedy, like many Circle Houses, awarded a prize each year to the fourth former who had contributed the most to the house. It measured scholarship, leadership and personal character and was based on GPA, sports participation, house involvement and extracurricular activities. Though only a mediocre athlete, I was a major booster of house sports and I had the other categories covered as well, so when most everyone told me I was a shoo-in I figured they were right.

Like many Lawrenceville award winners, the recipient received a pewter cup and his name was engraved on a plaque. To us it meant our name would stay behind, and we'd be linked to a virtuous heritage. It never once struck me as corny—the platters, cups, dishes and bowls, the traditions and accolades, or the puffed-up vocabulary of the prep school universe: Dignity, Honor, Good. In fact, it seemed to give meaning to an otherwise specious human existence. My grandmother may have had a truer compass for locating the justification for life, but at the time, I thought the white men who ran Lawrenceville knew more than my grandmother. I was young and stupid.

When I didn't receive the Fourth-Form Prize I was visibly hurt. Sitting in the house dining room as our housemaster gave it to the guy with the highest GPA (I had the second), I tried to smile. I refused to be caught off guard the way I had been when I lost the Rhinie Rep position at the beginning of sophomore year. (Then, I was practically bounding to the front of the room as TJ Mark read Carter Mills's name.) Now, I smiled a joyless grin and congratulated the recipient.

The next day, I was stunned to find myself listening to an assistant housemaster's explanation of why I had lost. I hadn't asked for it. I had only gone in to shoot the shit with him, as a lot of us did. Peter Hunter was on an exchange program from a Scottish public school called Gordonstown and if we dropped round at teatime, he would serve us a spot of tea and a plate of biscuits. Not a bad deal.

Only this time, I received a scolding I wasn't expecting. Mr. Hunter sat me down, and told me that he thought I should know why I had not received the Fourth-Form Prize. "Some of the masters felt that you do the things you do because you want to prove that black people can do things as well as white people." He was serious. "The housemasters decided that that was not in the spirit of the prize."

"What?" I asked faintly. I wanted to holler, "Are you people out of your fucking minds??? I work my butt off to get good grades, I participate in half the clubs on this campus, I counsel and tutor half the third formers in this house—and half the fourth formers in English—to prove to *you* that black people are as good as whites?"

Only I couldn't bring off any substantive reply. I actually thanked him. After leaving his apartment, I realized that when blacks performed below par we risked being tarred as affirmative action candidates, but I had had no idea that if we were good, we'd be painted as racial zealots, out to prove we were better than whites. It was a new slap in the face for me. In later years, I would come to understand that the old "uppity negro" correction had been meted out to me. All my accomplishments had been reduced to fodder in a war of the races.

It was a potentially debilitating wound: to realize that the men whose acceptance and validation I sought through my hard work would never find me worthy. My very efforts to prove I merited membership in this privileged world had made me meritless. For the housemasters, I accomplished my goals not because I was talented or diligent, but because I was an angry black man. Sitting numbly in the room, I was surprised that it felt even worse to have my accomplishments attributed to my skin color than it did my failures. I felt trapped; even if I succeeded, I failed. There was no escape.

And yet, junior year was rich. I was learning to view the occasional racial incident as an exception to my general Lawrenceville experience. It was. The setbacks in Circle House had deflated my ego too. I had learned the difference between friendship and popularity. No, Lawrenceville was not a perfect universe, but it was challenging and exciting, and it was home. I lived life with the ease and confidence of an Old Boy, racing from club to class to meal, solidifying the great friendships I would take with me when I left this place. And having a blast. I even accomplished a goal I had to come to think was beyond reach: I excelled at a sport.

I went out for rugby because it was the only sport I could think of that everyone else hadn't played since they were seven years old. After the JV football fiasco, I figured, it would be a fairer test of whether I could ever be a decent athlete.

I still hated practice. Our coach made us run the whole campus some days. (None of us was surprised at the end of the year when he joined the Marines.) I loved the sport so much that I forgot that we ran for twenty-five-minute halves without a break. I played the loose forward positions, usually number eight, and occasionally prop, which I hated. Taking the hits and advancing the ball, rucking, mauling and the rest, instilled new confidence in me.

Like most Old Boys, by senior year I had made peace with Lawrenceville. I was understanding of its shortcomings, thankful for its blessings. The way I thought I would have felt toward my father in those last months before manhood, if I had had one. Unlike most Old Boys, though, I had no desire to leave the nest. I was a prefect in my old dorm, Cromwell. I headed most of the clubs I had belonged to the year before. It was my crowning year. Not only because I felt that I had earned the respect of teachers and peers, but because I was happy with the self that Lawrenceville and I had fashioned inside this crucible—a classless, raceless self.

The proof, I often thought, was the relationships I had built with my Lower Schoolers as a prefect. My kids were almost all white, with the exception of a few African-American and Asian-American kids, but the counseling and attention I lavished on them was never race-based. Neither were the respect and the occasional hard times they dished out in return.

I coached our house soccer team to the best record in the Lower School league through praise, perspiration and profanity. I read more ninth-grade papers than anyone should ever have to. I held illegal feeds in my room after lights out. In short, I had far more fun than my self-conscious classmates did in Upper, where they generally bitched and whined about the restrictions that Lawrenceville imposed even on seventeen- and eighteen-year-olds and fought the same old battles over relative coolness and popularity. I much preferred nursing homesick thirteen- and fourteen-year-olds. I saw myself in their early months in this paradise, reflected in the frenetic enthusiasm they brought to everything in their new world.

But if an adolescence spent in the pursuit of "accomplishment" culminated senior year, so did my perception of real racism. Not the kind that I had once incorrectly thought attached to the political party one belonged to or the class one came from, but rather a personal, tangible racism that betrayed itself in thought and speech.

One night near the end of senior year, after lights out in the Lower School houses, I paid one of my regular late-night visits to McPherson House, an Upper School dorm behind Cromwell. Ted Chow, a former Kennedy House mate, was giving me his college acceptance update. He had just gotten into Princeton, or was it Harvard? I told him I had finally heard from Stanford and that I would probably go there. A popular white kid, a resident of McPherson, who had overheard our conversation and congratulatory exchange, came up to us and snarled, "I guess you have to be a chink or nigger to get into a good college these days." He said it with the ease and confidence of saying his name, echoing

America's latest vogue justification for racial hatred: minority "privilege."

John Devine had graduated from the Cleve House council to prefect of Perry Ross, upstairs from Cromwell, and we had become close friends. During our year in Lower, I discovered that John was not simply the perfect Lawrentian to which I and everyone else had reduced him, but he was also intelligent and compassionate, two traits that rarely came together in a young prep school student. He agreed with my principles of a society supporting its weakest citizens, but usually disagreed with my impractical bleeding-heart strategies.

That's why I was so hurt the night that I complained to John about the racist comment about chinks, niggers and college. I was looking for outraged affirmation. Instead, first he said to me, "I know that guy. He jokes all the time. It must have been a joke."

I glared incredulously.

He continued, "Well, he couldn't have meant it. I know him. He's not a racist. He's a good guy." Then, his most unbelievable comment: "Marc, I know you," he said, smiling. "You'd be so bummed if racism disappeared tomorrow, you'd have nothing to fight about. And you love fighting."

Holding back tears of anger and hurt, I said, "John, there are so many more worthwhile battles. This is one I would do anything to never have to fight again."

For the most part, I thought I had breached the gap of racial misunderstanding with most of my peers, at least at its most fundamental boundaries. I had argued that not everybody in Trenton was a criminal, and that black people were intelligent and hardworking, even those on welfare (I only told a few of them that I was speaking from personal experience). As for me, I no longer thought all Republicans were evil and insensitive by nature. I knew white people, even rich ones, had problems. Money was just money.

But on my very last day as a student, I learned how vast the cultural divide was that still yawned between me and the 175-year-old school I had come to love.

June 1, 1985 was an ideal spring day in New Jersey. The sun drenched the campus in hues of dark green and blue as seniors in coats and ties rushed around, directing their parents. I had been eighteen years old for just twenty-four hours. The eight African-American seniors gathered on the knoll between the track and the Dining Center for a group picture. We were handsome and proud, and very aware of what this passage would mean for ourselves, for our families and, hopefully, for an entire race of brothers who would never attend anybody's prep school.

Later, on the basketball court in a wing of the Field House, now converted into a backstage for the massing seniors, we pinned on our red carnations. Dizzy with anticipation, I steadied myself by chatting with Mike Luciano—"Luch" as we called him—who had been no more to the manor born than I was. He hailed from an Italian section of Hamilton Township. He was cocky, confident and the best writer that Lawrenceville turned out that year. His poetry was as hard and as powerful as a Harley-Davidson, yet frank and vulnerable. Looking at Mike and me, I thought, *It's not such a bad country after all.* I thought then—and I still do—that despite the pain, much of it attributable to basic adolescence, much of it to race, Lawrenceville was the greatest experience of my life.

As we wound our way around the outer ring of the Field House to the applause of our family and friends, the brass section shook the enormous structure. We couldn't help but smile. Our political differences, our intellectual differences, our athletic differences melted away in brotherly unity. As the headmaster read off the names, I wondered if my mother had made it to the ceremony on time. And how many, if any, of my junior high school teachers had driven from Hamilton. Finally, the headmaster called my name. In a haze, I climbed the few steps to the platform, trying to hold my head high and look down at the same time so I didn't bump into somebody's chair.

As I strode up the aisle, I remembered my first tentative steps onto campus. I remembered getting lost and meeting a hyper Asian boy on the first day. Lawrenceville had given me a sense of the possible. From the first day I walked through those wrought-iron gates, limits had exploded. Later, I would learn that other limits that I had always seen right before me, that seemed so tangible I could reach out and touch them, had also disappeared. Why not live and work in a foreign country? Why not change the world if I felt like it? It was a tribute to the puffed-up words and the grandiloquent speeches that even in 1985 a Lawrenceville education could prepare a poor black boy for an activist future.

I wondered if that was why my mother had sent me there. I wondered if Mrs. Sigafoos, the junior high school principal who recommended prep school, or Mr. Mackenzie, the guidance counselor who suggested Lawrenceville, had known. I reached out to grasp Dr. McClellan's hand, hearing the barely discernible shouts of my family. Clasping my diploma, I said, "Thank you" to the headmaster for his gentle stewardship. (He had been the man who had worked courageously to integrate Lawrenceville in the sixties.) Looking out across the sea of faculty faces sitting just before the podium, I found Ms. McKay, who was beaming, and Mr. Graham, who gave me a thumbs-up. But when I crossed Mr. Megna's face, he was staring straight ahead, coldly peering through me, an ice pick.

Troubled, I walked back to my seat and tried to recapture the

feeling of triumph that had slipped away. Only later did I understand that I had again broken an unwritten tenet of the WASP
code. Seniors did not graduate in cap and gown, but in coat and
tie, and I took this to mean that as long as we were neat and
stylish there would be no need for further formalities. I wore my
white linen pants and a snappy blue Lawrenceville blazer. I rolled
my shirt sleeves over my jacket cuffs, flipped up my shirt collar
and loosened my thin white tie à la *Miami Vice*. I thought it
symbolic, imitating the California cool of my future university,
bridging worlds, past and future. Mr. Megna must have believed
I was disrespecting Lawrenceville, broadcasting one final "up
yours!" Friends told me that parents and teachers were shocked by
my act of political defiance. I thought (incorrectly) I was being
stylish; they thought I was making a Black Power statement. After
the ceremony, a close friend's father asked him, "What was Mabry
trying to prove? Is that the latest in ghetto fashion?"

My dress had set off the kind of culture clash that a tourist can
ignite in a foreign country by not respecting local custom. The
parents' response had been silly, but inevitable. My slight had been
inadvertent and innocent, not unlike my arrival at Lawrenceville
four years earlier. I had come there with no idea what I was getting myself into. I don't think my mother knew either. How
could she?

Writing about the pain and the confrontations now, as well as
the growth and the joy, it's hard to bring it all into focus. I understand that at this point I'm supposed to sum it all up for the reader.
I would like to be James Baldwin and reflect on the impossibility
of memory or some other great Theme, avoiding the question.

Lawrenceville remains one of the happiest journeys I have ever made. There is no denying it caused me much grief. But much of that grief had to do with being me and being a teenager. I would have experienced it wherever I had gone to high school. Moreover, the racial issues and the questions of identity would all have come up in college anyway. Lawrenceville was "prep" school for those as well.

In the end, I credit the school with being more responsible for my success than any other institution (along with Mom, Grandmom, me and the federal government). It taught me how to work hard and how to work smart. How to look people in the eye while extending a firm handshake. How to confront the world with confidence and integrity. And it gave me some early clues for coping in a predominantly white world. I would gladly live my Lawrenceville experience again.

The contradictions of those years are still there: I love the school, I hate the racism. But today the love greatly outweighs the resentment. In the same way the happy times were more frequent than the sad. In the same way the fruits were greater than the frustrations. I love Lawrenceville the way I love my mother and my father (whom I would meet years after leaving the school): unconditionally—never ignoring their faults, but never reducing them to them, either, and always grateful for the gifts they gave me.

CHAPTER 6

BLACK LIBERAL GUILT

I spent the summer between Lawrenceville and Stanford working—all the time. Mostly to keep myself out of the house. Now that I was an adult, I was determined never to suffer the soul-numbing boredom of childhood again. Lori Carmignani had told me that Bamberger's, a local department store where she managed a floor, was hiring. I started as a sales clerk in domestics, hawking kitchen appliances and towels, as soon as school ended.

For the first time since junior high, I was surrounded by middle- and working-class white people—the kind of folks that Lawrenceville students called "townies" or "white trash." They were stunned to find me working next to them; you could count the number of black sales clerks at Bamberger's, part of the Macy's chain, on both hands. There was hardly a black secretary or switchboard operator to be found. Almost all the support staff above janitorial positions was Caucasian, and mostly female. They spoke with the thick nasal accent of Jersey's lower classes. Here was a cornucopia of jobs that didn't require a college education—that barely required a high school diploma—and the only people hired to fill them were white.

At Lawrenceville, I had managed to forget that most white

people were neither rich nor well-educated. But lack of money and education didn't prevent them from being arrogant.

My co-workers had an inherent sense of superiority—not because they had a blistering intellect or a granite work ethic—but simply because they were white. Perhaps their attitude masked deeper feelings of class inferiority, but it somehow made them act as if they were better than any of the black people who came to shop. I could laugh at their "subtle" racism because I didn't take them seriously. Trapped in my own snobbism, I thought they were as inconsequential as they thought I was. That was before I realized the power of the masses.

Working at "Bam's," I rediscovered Middle America: characters whose words and thoughts were unfinished, but real and uncensored too. In casual conversation, my co-workers constantly referred to "them"—and occasionally "you's"—as the root of most American ills. Whether it was crime, taxes or the rainy weekend they spent at *da shore*, to my colleagues black people were somehow to blame. Once it was clear that I was not the thieving kind and everyone knew that I had graduated from "that rich school," I was absolved of the crime of being an African-American. "You're not like other coloreds . . . ya know?" my co-cashier would say, popping her gum.

On weekends, work was frenetic between the long lines and the constant price checks and customer-service crises. On weekdays and nights, though, it was almost as boring as being at home. We folded towels and washcloths for hours, moving from aisle to aisle. At these times, my fellow employees kept me entertained, our inane conversations helping the time pass.

Every spare hour I had from Bamberger's I spent peddling "the world's finest cutlery." Scouring the want ads, I had circled one that promised big bucks, independence and flexible hours. When

I called the telephone number listed, a saccharine woman's voice invited me to an informational session. I bit.

Nearly six feet tall with long brown hair, Susie radiated spirit and enthusiasm—so much that I questioned her mental stability. She led a classroom of trainees—all young white men except for me—through a rousing presentation on the wonders of selling kitchen knives and utensils by "personal reference."

"But, it's not door-to-door!" she cheerfully rebuked an apprentice. "And you had better not sell Cutco door-to-door. You are only allowed to call people whose friends or relatives have given you their name and number." (You can imagine how thrilled most people were that a friend had given their number to a knife-wielding black man.)

We were paid a hefty flat fee—a few thousand dollars—if we did enough "qualified" presentations in a certain amount of time: forty in ten weeks, I think. It sounded easy. But a "qualified" presentation had to be unveiled (1) at someone's home, (2) to someone who had a job, but (3) to someone who knew you personally or had been referred to you by another customer and (4) to someone who was not a relative. If you failed to perform the requisite number of presentations, you received a ten- or fifteen-percent commission for what you sold, period.

My aunt Bettye bought my first knife (as if she had a choice). Then, I spent fruitless days driving to people's houses all over suburban Mercer County, shredding pennies, rope, rubber and bread cubes. Dialing the Old Boy network for the first time, I hit up the parents of all my day-student friends. Out of Lawrenceville loyalty, most of them acquiesced. I was amazed that the system actually worked the way I had heard it would.

I came closer than anyone in our group to getting the necessary number of presentations. Half of my group stopped selling after only a few weeks. I thought it was kind of a slimy deal the way they promised us the moon if only "you worked real, real hard . . . Yea!" Still, Knifeco had its rewards: picking up the phone and asking people all kinds of nosy questions was good preparation for journalism.

....

The next summer—after my first year at college—I worked three jobs. Monday through Thursday I held down my first assignment in professional journalism at the *Trentonian*, one of two local papers. Weekends, I clerked at Bamberger's. Nights, I hustled as a waiter at a Mexican restaurant called Casa Lupita. On Saturday and Sunday, after Bam's closed at six in the evening, I would dart across Route 1 in my coat and tie, skirting cars and jumping the Jersey barrier that divided the highway, toting an ersatz Mexican shirt and a black apron.

Working became an obsession for me. As long as I worked, at my mostly menial jobs, I was free from existential questions like what was I going to do with my life and why wasn't my family progressing up the social ladder with me? Concentrating on the tasks at hand—remembering "two Cozumel combinations and a Rio Grande plate" and sorting mattress pads—freed me from scarier pursuits. I never stopped to think that mechanically putting in my hours would fatten my bank account and propel me even farther up the ladder above my family.

I was the only black waiter at Casa Lupita. It was customary in New Jersey restaurant culture for every busboy to be black or Latino and all the waiters to be white. When I called to ask about the positions advertised in the paper, the manager told me they were hiring busboys and waitstaff. When I arrived for the interview, he told me they were only hiring busboys. During our talk, it emerged, somehow, that I had attended Lawrenceville and was studying at Stanford now. He hired me to be a waiter.

It sickened me that a black man apparently needed a prep school diploma and a year of college to tote platters of nachos. Unstated prejudice, manifested thousands of times a day across many companies and industries, helped explain why so many young black men couldn't land well-paying, unskilled jobs. But I needed the work—Stanford required me to earn two thousand dollars over the summer as part of my financial aid package—and since I *had* the qualifications, I took the job.

Not surprisingly, the other waiters were not Harvard students, but more townies. Most of them were decent, hardworking people; waiting was the toughest job I had ever had. Every night I came home with aching feet and sore arms. Some of my co-workers were racists through and through. The waitress who trained me talked down to me for the first two nights I "trailed" her, despite her four-foot-ten-inch frame. She gave me useful advice like who tipped well. "Groups of women, men doing a business lunch and waiters," she said. You were supposed to be extra solicitous of them. "Rich people, old people and coloreds— no offense—don't."

THAT must be a self-fulfilling prophecy, I thought.

She taught me all she knew. In exchange, all I had to do was perform all her side work. One night the best waiter in the restaurant, a burly Italian-American guy, saw me preparing her sets— the napkin, silverware and glass combinations that everyone had to arrange before they knocked off.

"What the hell are you doing?" he asked me, incredulous. "Did she tell you to do that?"

He yelled for my trainer across the cavernous restaurant. "Hey, this ain't fucking slavery you know." Then they went at it. (One thing working-class white folks and black Americans share is the ability to raise hell.)

Once I started working for myself, I made more money than I had ever earned. Customers liked me and I liked the job. Only twice did I spill a Margarita Grande in someone's lap. All those years at Lawrenceville paid off; some white customers were so surprised that I spoke proper English that they beamed up at me every time I walked past their table.

One family stopped me when I tossed off the obligatory, "Thank you and have a good night."

"Where are you from?" asked the bun-coiffed mom.

"Hamilton," I said, my Lawrenceville-era reflex getting the best of me.

"Oh. We knew you weren't from around here," she said triumphantly. "You didn't sound like you were from Trenton."

"Well, actually," I said, reddening with anger, "I was born in Trenton."

"Really?" she gasped. "What high school did you go to?"

"I'm in college. But I went to Lawrenceville."

"Really . . ." she turned wide-eyed to her husband.

"Where are you in college?"

"Stanford."

"Oh, how nice," she enthused, turning again to Father.

I wanted to smack her. I hated feeling compelled to answer her questions. My every response gave them another reason to write me off as "an exception." I wanted to scream, "Look, I'm black, damn it. I talk this way and I walk this way and I go to college. Get over it!"

It was closing time and my boss was giving me the high sign to move these buffoons out so we could all go home. When I returned to clear the table, I found a five-percent tip. I felt compromised, bought and sold—cheaply. I hated myself for having contained my rage.

At the *Trentonian*, I worked Monday through Thursday, five hours a day. The paper didn't have an internship that year, but I had called in the middle of the summer to see if there was something I could do: open mail, clean wastebaskets, anything. I landed a post as a news assistant, replacing a student who was leaving, yet another working-class white woman. I opened mail for the City Desk, filed AP photos and, most importantly, updated the Community and Religion calendars, a whole page of tiny ads with pastors' names and church services that had to be reviewed every week.

Looking at my stack of *Standard Daily* clips, the gruff-talking, white-haired city editor, Wilson Barto, said, "Kid, you can write a lot of stories that you think are important, but nobody gives a whit about. You screw up an announcement for the women's auxiliary lunch, though, and you're gonna hear about it."

In a few weeks, I'd squeezed five stories out of Wilson.

"What are you doing, kid, trying to be a reporter?" he demanded. I so embodied the American meritocratic ideal that Ken Carolan, our Reagan-conservative columnist, detested by my whole family, wrote a column entitled "Future Newspaperman," praising my work ethic and how far I would go. It made my mother and my grandmother—who read the *Trentonian* every evening in her house-dress and slippers, after pulling on her glasses one arm at a time at the kitchen table—take back all the things they had said about him. I was grateful, but torn. Right-wingers at Lawrenceville had used me anecdotally to refute my own arguments about American inequality too, turning my life against me. But no one had ever done it in print.

My workaholic lifestyle had side effects: I was making more money than I had ever seen. Bamberger's paid minimum wage plus time-and-a-half on Sundays. At Casa Lupita, I earned eight to ten dollars an hour in tips. And the *Trentonian* paid $5.25 an hour.

Meanwhile, my mother drifted in and out of work. Every few weeks she asked me for money. I suggested that I give her a certain amount of cash every week; we could call it rent. She said no; she would never take money from her children. What we earned was ours. She would rather ask me "when she needed help." (We had been off welfare for years.) But she never seemed to ask me when I was in a good mood. And she never seemed to need it, in my judgment, for worthwhile expenses.

Her stubborn refusal to accept my contributions on a regular schedule annoyed me. When life was going smoothly—when no one's car was being repossessed and no one was in trouble at school and she was employed—she acted like some upper-middle-class matriarch. "Oh, no, I would never take my children's money . . ."

Bullshit! I thought. *We are poor black folks. Get a clue. You work on and off when you want to, when you are not being hit by some reckless driver.* (She had suffered three accidents in two years and each time the police faulted the other person.) *This is not* Leave it to Beaver. *I am not Wally. You are not June. Chuckie is not the Beav. If things are going well now, hold your breath, they'll be shitty tomorrow.* I knew sitcoms. I liked sitcoms. And this was no sitcom.

Whenever she hatched yet another scheme to earn money fast or start a new life, my pessimism exploded. All the anger of being talked down to by customers, of feeling like an alien in my white world and increasingly separate from the black one (I never went to White City now; I didn't have time) was unleashed on my mother. But my anxieties whispered of failures to come. Now, life for me was bountiful. My negative outlook was based more on my mother's experiences than my own. It was her dreams I always saw dashed. So I wanted to stunt her expectations before they could grow.

"Why do you always have to bring me down?" she would ask, tears welling in the corners of her eyes. "What made you so bitter so young? . . . Damn."

My mother and I had increasingly been getting on each other's nerves. I had arrived home happy to see her and my brother. They were happy to see me too. She had pampered me for a few days. Then we both grew more and more short-tempered.

"Why don't you go out and do something?" she'd ask in her June Cleaver, we're-a-normal-healthy-happy-family way.

"Why are you dropping that case?" I'd ask.

Every conversation became a debate. "You might think you're better than me, but you're not," she would say. "I'm the parent in this relationship. Don't curse in this house. You respect me."

"Well, you curse. Does that mean you don't respect me?"

"Don't get smart."

"I can't help it. I was born that way," I would snarl.

Money grew between us like a thick thorny hedge, higher every day, until living together became unbearable. Every time she asked for "a loan," we argued. The pattern was always the same; and in the end I always gave her what she wanted. But I was starting to loathe her for her dependency.

Late one afternoon I confessed my dark feelings to my friend Dave from Lawrenceville over the telephone. "I'm beginning to resent my mother. She always complains that she doesn't have any money. That's because she's not working. She's always procrastinating, or quitting jobs because they're too shitty. Why doesn't she go to school? Why doesn't she get some training and do something else? Shit, is it my fault she doesn't stick with any-thing? Why should I have to pay for her failures? It's so frustrat-ing. Why can't she be responsible, like a real parent?"

It was the first time I had ever verbalized the mounting strain.

My words echoed raw through the chilly apartment. Giving money to my mother caused me to feel like I was the parent and she was the child—and, even worse, that the money was mine and not *ours*.

"It's a totally fucked-up white American concept," I said. "That the money a kid earns is his own. In the black tradition, in the Asian tradition, the offspring's accomplishments are the family's reward, since the individual wouldn't be what he was without the family's nurturing in the first place."

"Italians and Irish think that too," Dave said.

"I think I'm becoming a Republican," I said, "a cold, heartless capitalist. If it wasn't for my mother, I wouldn't have gone to Lawrenceville in the first place. But I freak out when she asks me for money.

"The other day she wanted three hundred dollars to get my brother's scooter out of the pound. I know he's just going to get more tickets, not pay them, and it'll go right back!"

Without warning, my mother walked through the door and into the apartment.

"Hi, Mom," I said, nonchalant.

She put the groceries into the refrigerator, then went into the bathroom, the only other room in our efficiency in downtown Trenton. As she passed in front of me, the tracks of her tears caught the light.

"Dave, I'd better call you later . . ."

I wanted to vomit.

"Mom?" I asked plaintively.

She emerged from the bathroom, her arms spread turgidly apart, thick wads of toilet paper at the end of each. She wiped her eyes so violently she could have smeared her pupils across the sheets. "I Am *Not* Your Mother." She spat each word at me. She spoke in a harsh, raspy voice I didn't recognize.

I had assassinated our relationship, committed the ultimate betrayal.

"I'm sorry."

"For what?" she screamed, sobbing between airy gasps, her chest heaving. "For what, Marcus? For me hearing the truth? You know I started to walk in when I heard you on the phone, but something told me to stop. And, my God, what I heard . . . what I heard!" Her eyes rolled until I only saw the whites.

I wanted to reach out to her, but instead I stared at the carpet. She flailed about the room, unable to get me out of her sight. Turning nervously on me, she said, "*You* resent *me*. You resent me. Ain't that a fuckin' blip?"

Lifeless, I forced myself to look into her eyes now—punishment for the pain I had inflicted. "I didn't say that." As if by denying it, I would end the nightmare.

"I guess I don't do anything for you. I just sit around on welfare and take your money. I don't ever go to work," she was growing redder and louder. "I guess I shouldn't resent you. You stole my life," she shrieked, shaking my rib cage. "Maybe I could have made something of myself if I was not doing for you all the time.

"I have had it. I have had enough of children . . . mother, father, sister, brother . . . all you people. I have had enough, goddamn it.

"Ever since you went to Lawrenceville, I've seen the three of us drifting apart. That's fine. You have your thing and your friends. Chuckie does his thing. Well, I'm going to do for me now. Every cocksucker for himself."

I scrunched up under the threadbare comforter I had wrapped around myself.

"Mom . . ."

"No." Her eyes slashed at me. Her sharpened finger skewered me.

Why should she forgive me?

"And you sit up here telling that white boy you resent me?" Her eyes were hollow.

Since I had been home, I had wanted to tell her how much I had missed her, how I longed to make her proud. Only, I couldn't say any of that. It just wouldn't come out, but a stream of snide remarks and retorts flowed effortlessly. I could not stop myself from throttling her, or suppress my cruel judgments of people I didn't know or my haughty attitude for having learned more about the world than most of the people I knew would ever know. I was a perfect elitist ass, arrogant and obnoxious. I watched myself perform as if watching a movie. Every day of vacation, I behaved more and more intolerably.

Meanwhile, my mother was battling her own enduring sense of failure, the result of trying to reconcile a career of "cleaning bedpans" with her aspirations to be something more. She despised every minute of the menial labor, the white people telling her what to do, treating her like a maid instead of a nurse. My success—and my all-too-easy assimilation of prep school values (I had even developed an aversion to man-made fibers)—engendered her resentment. Even without my petulant mood swings and my sophomoric snobbery, to her, I affirmed her failure. She had had all the potential that I did, but she had wasted it through procrastination, indecision and inconsistency. Her punishment was to live with the contradictory feelings of pride over the man I was becoming and self-loathing over the woman she was not.

Only adversity united my mother and me. When I came home for Christmas break during my junior year at Stanford, we had moved back in with my grandmother. (The landlord's niece took our efficiency.) And, as always happened when we had nowhere else to go, my grandmother took us in.

It was a difficult Christmas. While my relationships and my sense of self were solidifying in college, my family was disintegrating, slowly falling into greater disrepair. That Christmas, my mother had little money and less self-confidence. The prospects for my brother's future seemed dim. My grandmother was very sick. I was so shocked by what I found when I came home that I had to write about it, to impose some kind of order on it. In my journal I wrote:*

A round green cardboard sign hangs from a string proclaiming, "We built a proud new feeling," the advertising slogan of the A&P supermarket chain, a souvenir of one of my brother's last jobs. In addition to being a bagger, he has worked at McDonald's, Burger King, a gas station, a garage and a linoleum factory. Now, in the icy clutches of the Northeastern winter, he is unemployed. He will soon be a father. He is 19.

Just a few days ago I was at Stanford, among the palm trees and weighty chores of academe. And all I had wanted to do was get out. I was so tired of tests and papers and homework and play rehearsal and rugby practice and the *Daily.* I had had enough. I joined the rest of the undergrads singing the praises of Christmas Break. No classes, no midterms, no finals . . . and no freshmen! Awesome! I was looking forward to escaping. I never gave a thought to what I was escaping to.

Once I got home to New Jersey, reality returned. My

*Newsweek on Campus *eventually ran an edited version of my journal entry as a "My Turn," their reader-written column, in the Spring 1988 edition.*

dreaded freshmen had been replaced by unemployed relatives; badgering professors by hardworking single mothers;
and cold classrooms by dilapidated bathrooms. The room in
which the "proud new feeling" sign hung contained the
belongings of myself, my mom and my brother. But for
these two weeks, my mother insisted that I sleep in it alone.
She and Charles slept downstairs on couches. The room was
about six feet by twelve feet. With the couch that folded out
into a bed, there was barely any room for the space heater
and the chest of drawers.

Most students who travel between the universes of poverty and affluence during break experience similar conditions, as well as the guilt, the helplessness and, sometimes,
the embarrassment associated with them. Our friends are
willing to listen, but most of them are unable to imagine the
pain of the impoverished lives we see every six months. Each
time I return home, I feel further away from the realities of
poverty in America and more ashamed that they are allowed
to persist. What frightens me most is not that the American
socioeconomic system permits poverty to continue, but that
by participating in that system, I share some of the blame.

Last year I lived in an on-campus apartment with a modern bathroom, kitchen and two bedrooms—just for me and
my roommate. Using money from my summer job, I bought
some expensive prints, a potted palm and some other plants,
making the place look like the more-than-humble abode of
a New York City Yuppie. I gave dinner parties, even a *soirée
française*.

For Higgs (my roommate), a doctor's son, this kind of life
was nothing extraordinary. But my mom was struggling to
provide a life for herself and my brother. She worked as a live-

in practical nurse when she could get a job. But she worried about leaving my brother for long stretches of time. My grandmother was sick now and couldn't help. She was almost blind. My brother was struggling to make it out of high school and my mother wanted to make sure he did. She also wanted to make sure he stayed away from what had become the predominant occupation in our neighborhood: drug dealing.

Living in my grandmother's house this Christmas Break restored all the forgotten, and the never acknowledged, guilt. My friends say that I should not feel guilty: what could I do substantially for my family at this age, they ask. Even though I know that education is the right thing to do, I can't help but think that I have it too good. Why do I deserve security and warmth, while my brother has to cope with unemployment and prejudice?

My sense of helplessness increases each time I return home. As my success leads me farther away for longer periods of time, poverty becomes harder to conceptualize and feels that much more oppressive when I visit with it. The first night of break I lay in our bedroom. It was hard to fall asleep because the springs from the couch stuck through at inconvenient spots. But it would have been impossible to sleep anyway because of the groans coming from my grandmother's room next door. Only in her 60s, she suffers from many chronic diseases and couldn't help but moan, then pray aloud, then moan, then pray aloud. I wept quietly to myself.

At three in the morning the house was shaken. My uncle came home. Big, burly and rowdy, he slammed the door. My grandmother had kicked him out of the house many times. But she always relented and let him come home. Now he stormed his way up the stairs and into her room to take his place, at the foot of her bed. There he slept, without blankets on a bare mattress.

That was the first night. Later in the vacation, a Christmas turkey and ham were stolen from my grandaunt's refrigerator, on Christmas Eve. We thought it was one of my cousins. My mom and I decided not to exchange gifts that year. It just wasn't festive.

A few days after New Year's, I returned to California. The Northeast was soon hit by a blizzard. They were there, and I was here. That was the way it had to be, for now. I haven't forgotten; the ache of knowing their suffering is always there. It has to be kept deep down, or I can't find the logic in studying and partying while people, my people, are being killed by poverty. Ironically, success drove me away from those I most want to help by getting an education.

Somewhere in the midst of all that misery, my family has built within me "a proud new feeling." As I travel between the two worlds it becomes harder to remember just how proud I should be—not just because of where I have come from and where I am going, but because of where they are. The fact that they survive in the world in which they live is something to be very proud of, indeed. It inspires within me a sense of tenacity and accomplishment that I hope every college graduate will some day possess.

CHAPTER 7

BLACKER THAN THOU

Stanford was everything that Lawrenceville was not: coed, trendy, warm and unapologetically modern—almost a century younger. What impressed me most were the palm trees. They grew like skyscrapers in California. They towered above the sandstone arches and red-tiled roofs that wove a canopy between the blue sky and the golden hills.

I chose Stanford for two reasons. I wanted a big name and I wanted to escape what had been a fascinating, but taxing, experiment in eastern WASPdom. And there was a third reason to attend Stanford, even though Yale fit perfectly when I visited: free round-trips to California twice a year as part of my financial aid package. One of the few benefits of being poor.

I had no idea that my time in the idyllic setting would be marred by two acrimonious struggles. The first was an old friend of mine, a fight that had divided the African-American community since integration, since black people could *choose* to live amongst ourselves or safari into the white world. Here, it was a confrontation along "lifestyle" lines. Not gay or straight. Not Yuppie or altruistic. But, how you hung . . . black or white. It was as if the conflicts that had raged inside me at prep school had sprung to life outside of me in college. Each argument, each survival stratagem, had become personified in a different African-American student—each one espousing a competing philosophy of who he or she was, a strategy to cope as the perpetual "other." All of them grouped ultimately, inescapably, into brothers and sisters who hung black and individualists or "Oreos" (depending on your perspective) who hung white.

The second battle was less parochial, but more vicious and with higher stakes. It was a political war, a pedagogical debate and an ideological confrontation all in one that would carve new demarcations across old categories, often pitting liberals against liberals, feminists against feminists, gays against gays. It was a fight that by the time it exploded on the front pages of the national media would be perverted, distorted and simplified into one fatal, neo-Orwellian phrase: political correctness. The phrase would come to signify all that was wrong with postmodern, post-Vietnam, post-ERA, post-Black Power American liberalism: the absence of intellectual rigor; vain declarations of entitlements by "so-called 'aggrieved groups'; a dictatorship of the minority; complete moral turpitude.

Stanford was an exceptional university. Not just because of the high caliber of its faculty and students: any Ivy League college could boast that. Camp Stanford had character.

Not the sober prep school version that produced great men of dignity, honor, and valor, but the humanistic variety that made people intriguing. At its heart was the belief that even if smart people should take life seriously, they shouldn't take themselves seriously. You could see it in the application process. Letters from Columbia and Yale were soaked in a grand air of superiority. Correspondence from Harvard made it sound like they were doing you a favor by letting you apply. Only Stanford seemed comfortable enough in its identity to make you feel welcome even before you got there.

When you arrived, screaming Orientation Volunteers, or OVs, crowded the gates at San Francisco International Airport. Clad in red shirts, they chanted your name as you disembarked from the plane. "John! John! John! John!" Jumping up and down, holding signs saying, "Welcome to The Farm," all these people you had never seen before, who came from God knows where, and whom you had not expected to find, shouted *your* name. They formed human pyramids. They yelled. It was chaos.

On campus, the welcome just grew warmer. Every time my eyes met someone else's, they smiled at me. They were cheery, happy, sunny. It was California, alright. As an easterner, it made me sick. But, as the weeks went on, the infectious, annoying cheer wore down cynicism. I hated that most.

It was a matter of course that any African-American freshman would stop by the BROC (Black Recruitment and Orientation Committee) events during orientation to get introduced to the black community on campus and to find friends. I wanted to avoid getting off on the wrong foot with the black community, since I had decided that a lackadaisical beginning was why I had had only a handful of black friends at Lawrenceville. This time I was determined to make an effort. So a few hours after arriving at my new dorm, I set out for the west side of campus, where the first BROC event was taking place. Stanford's black ethnic theme house, Ujamaa, the center of "the community," was located over there. My dorm being on the east side, it turned out that I was stuck living on the white side of town.

I hiked the twenty-five minutes from Donner House to the tiny Ricker entertainment center on the edge of Lake Lagunita.

Lost along the way, I asked an OV where the lake was. She told me I was standing next to it.

I looked to my left. "You mean this big, dry hole in the ground?"

Brimming with Stanford enthusiasm, she said, "Totally."

One of the first to arrive at the party, I stood next to the punch bowl and waited for other people to drift in. One by one, we introduced ourselves. Where are you from? What dorm are you in? Soon whole groups were trooping in. As the room filled up, I felt like I was the only person who didn't know somebody else. A lot of the people had met at Uj or at the BROC recruitment weekend the spring before. A clique of attractive men and women took the stage. With cool detachment or stylish elegance, they outlined the Black Student Union, the community services and the events that BROC would conduct parallel to the university orientation. Over the next two hours I struck up a few conversations, but none seemed to last very long. The guys were all talking jive and slapping backs like they had known each other all their lives.

I thought back to my first visits home from Lawrenceville and my days of code shifting, when a speaker literally changes dialect to match the language of his listener. I considered trying to throw a little Black English around and shaking hands like a brotha. I thought I had transcended this need to be something I wasn't. Instead, I stood there in a circle of black men, smiling and laughing as if I got it.

I attended one or two other BROC events. But my big brother, Peter, soon left me hanging. He hated coming across campus to the east side. I was on my own. Every time I went to a gathering, I felt like everybody else had been rooming together since the last one. That was pretty much correct, most of them lived on the west side. The last night of orientation, each of the committees put on a dinner and a dance: the general committee, BROC, CLOC, NAOC and AANSOC* (seriously). Each featured its own selection of food and music. I could only attend one.

I chose the general party; I wanted to hang with the friends I was making in my dorm. Big mistake. From that point on, I was no longer a part of "the community." Not because I didn't want to be or because they didn't want me to be; but because it all seemed too difficult, too out of the way, too much of a reach. I had my clubs and they had their world. When I dated an African-American alumna only one year my junior after college, whenever she told anyone from "the community" that she was seeing Marcus Mabry, who also had gone to Stanford, they would ask, "You're going with a white man?" (They had never heard of me so they assumed, if I had gone to Stanford, I must be white.)

My naïve belief that I could survive separate from both the black and the white worlds, but be a part-time boarder in both, exploded in college. From the time I arrived in Palo Alto, it was clear I had to choose. The cost of the choice, whichever choice, was virtual alienation from the other camp. I was more comfortable in the white world. It demanded less role-playing of me, so I chose it. I rationalized what sometimes felt like race betrayal by viewing myself as a cultural and political liaison. I answered nonblack students' questions about black people: our customs, our values, our beliefs . . . our hair. In political debates, I outlined the majority black view.

Ironically, the price I paid was rejection by my supposed constituents. I wanted to believe that they had never wanted to accept me in the first place. Most of them were affluent, the sons and

---

The Chicano and Latino Orientation Committee, the Native American Orientation Committee and the Asian-American New Student Orientation Committee.

daughters of doctors and lawyers from Long Island or DC's Gold Coast. I was a poor kid from Trenton. I didn't know their music, their culture or their history. I resented them for their money, but more importantly, for their claim that only they knew "blackness." Only after college did I learn that most of "them" were role-playing too that first day of BROC orientation. The difference was that these people from all over the country, with divergent interests and beliefs, kept playacting until they created a new cohesive community, while I was content to live in the white one. I wish I had known then that if I had kept going through the motions, I would have belonged too.

My absence among the African-Americans on campus meant that whenever I crossed their paths, I was viewed with pity, at best, or contempt. But either response was only momentary; then I was just ignored.

The only community gathering I dared attend was the annual soul food dinner. I went religiously, the same way backsliders showed up in church at Easter and Christmas. Organized by the Black House (the umbrella black community service organization on campus), it was the only time I got to eat soul food at Stanford. Old back women—I didn't know where they had come from—stood behind huge aluminum pans piled high with fried chicken, collard greens and potato salad. There was the gigantic black pot like the one from my grandmother's house, its surface wreathed in steam, its interior packed with the salty-sweet savor of black-eyed peas.

Freshman year I accompanied Jackie Jackson, my black RA. Jackie didn't hang black either, but she belonged to Delta Sigma Theta and as a Delta she was granted charter membership in the community, even if she did have too many white friends. Anyway, Jacqueline J. Jackson was too formidable a woman to be messed with. She simply did not take it—any of it. She was probably the best role model I could have had, remarkably comfortable with herself, proud and, at the same time, nurturing. I would go to Jackie when I felt alienated or lost on the white side of the world. She would comfort me with a relentless realism. Nobody was going to be concerned with my happiness, black or white, but me. "That's what you had better aim for," she said.

Jackie was on an ROTC scholarship. After graduation and law school she became Captain Jacqueline J. Jackson, US Army JAG Corps. I was not surprised.

Each year after she graduated, the soul food dinner was a potentially traumatic experience for me; I never knew when someone would finger me for not being a part of "the community," the way that other Lower Schooler had at my first BSU meeting at Lawrenceville. When I went with my freshmen as an RA my junior year, my friend Michele McMahon (a white chem major who ran track) knew more attendees than I did.

I bonded with the mostly white men and women in my dorm. There was a marbling of black, Latino and Asian, but the dominant color was white. My best friends freshman year were a saxophone player from Kalispell, Montana; another one from Staten Island; an engineering whiz from Minnesota; a fellow Phil Donahue junkie from Oregon; a farm boy from Watsonville (who talked blacker than I did); and a Republican from Kansas—all white. My best friends also included an Asian-American woman from Iowa City and an Asian-American man from Ames and two African-Americans: Mia Johnson, my first college crush, from Virginia and Chris Dunson from Baltimore. We all laughed together, and we got homesick together (rather, they got homesick; I counseled). We went on midnight runs to Safeway, weekend trips to Chili's and roadtrips to San Francisco. And we all lived in Donner.

None of them seemed to care about race when we were together and neither did I. The person I had grown into at Lawrenceville was fine with them. I had never been so fully accepted—without questions, without prejudice—anywhere. Even our political fights didn't mutate into veiled discussions of black stereotypes like they had at Lawrenceville. In the tolerant environment, I relaxed more than ever before. Inside the dorm, in my circle of friends, I let my guard down. For the first time I was free to be whomever I decided to be.

Only when I was around black people did it bother me that most of my friends were white. Then, the unspoken questions that I saw in the eyes of other black students shamed me: What was wrong with me? Did I think I was white? I wanted to plead, "No. No. It's just that I hang with folks in my dorm. They're great. You should meet them." Instead, I tried to dodge their condemning glances.

It never occurred to me that it was my own guilt reflected in their eyes, my own feeling that I should have more black friends. I didn't choose my friends because of their skin color, but part of me thought it was unhealthy, somehow unnatural, for the closest people in my life to be Caucasian. After all, neither black nor white Americans thought it normal. People of all colors, liberals and conservatives, formed friendships mostly with their own kind. They never gave it a second thought.

I was too young to realize that perhaps my friends and I were just more privileged than the average American when it came to racial understanding, just like we were when it came to education and opportunity. We had the same prejudices as most people, only we gave them less weight. There was more room for appreciating the individual. That individual remained black, white or Asian. The petty prejudices of young adulthood could be overcome, and they were—every night in talks and sappy dorm scenes where we uncovered our fears and our dreams to one another.

I was convinced that the only difference between the white people I befriended and the white American masses was that my friends were willing to accept our differences, political, racial, social or cultural. They were not threatened by them. They were not alienated by them. They were simply open. They could never be black, they could never understand all my anger or all my pride, but they could listen. And even though I had a better grasp of white identity—having grown up in America—I could never truly comprehend their realities either. For instance, when I arrived at Stanford in September 1985, I could not imagine that smart, attractive, affluent white people could feel doubt or dread. At school though, we came as close as we could, my friends and I, to seeing through the eyes of the other. We learned more than we ever thought college could teach us.

I decided to major in international relations—a composite of political science, history and economics—and took a second major in French and English literatures. I entered Stanford with enough Advanced Placement credits from college-level courses in high school to equal a year of study. So I decided to use my fourth year to earn a master's degree—in English since I loved language . . . and I didn't have to produce a dissertation.

The real motivation behind my lofty pretensions was prep school. Not the aspirations that Lawrenceville had planted or the success ethic it had instilled—but the Convocation services. That's where I had first witnessed academic class distinctions. The teachers with advanced degrees wore bell-sleeved robes with luxurious hoods and collars. The masters with only a bachelor's were draped in plain proletarian black; I wanted the velvet collar and the magnificent sleeves.

Extracurricularly, I started out at Stanford trying to be the same man I had been in high school. I played rugby, wrote for the *Daily* and acted in a Ram's Head production of *What the Butler Saw*. At the close of my first trimester, I went home suffering from a severe case of exhaustion.

Stanford was infested with high school newspaper editors, class presidents and extracurricular giants. It seemed every student had a 1400 SAT and a roster of club memberships. Like most of my peers, I dropped my hobbies after fall quarter. We gave up our truckload of passions and started choosing what we really wanted to be in a finite world—having had our first inkling of the greater limitations that awaited our generation after college.

These are the best years of my life, I thought, growing up in California. Prep school had hewn me into rough shape, but Stanford was sanding down the knots and splinters. At the same time, it was teaching me that there was no shame in contentment. Most days cloudless skies greeted me. The months slipped happily by. In class, professors ministered more than they instructed, and classmates were partners rather than competitors. I breathed easy. At first, the thoughtless comfort disturbed me. As an eastern–intellectual sort, I thought that since misery typified the human condition, it should comprise mine too. In California, though, no one believed that in order to improve humankind's lot, you had to suffer it.

I wanted to give something back to Stanford my junior year. As a prefect at Lawrenceville, I had learned how important a good counselor was to people far from home for the first time; so I became a Resident Assistant.

Nestled in a comfortable modern condo with huge picture windows overlooking the Pacific, we were deeply anguished. We had just finished off the pasta dinner that Linda, our Resident Fellow, had prepared. And we were sitting around drinking coffee and herbal tea.

It was the first night of a weekend retreat designed to weave a close-knit and caring dorm staff. Since our house was composed of a hundred freshmen, four RAs lived there, one more than was allocated to mixed-class dorms. Ed and Jenny were seniors and Megan was a fifth-year senior. We received a week of orientation and training before our students arrived. We discussed how to build a harmonious community with young adults from vastly disparate backgrounds, how to create an atmosphere where people shared their opinions and no one felt squelched—including residents whose beliefs included squelching others—and how to counsel students with problems from anorexia to differential equations.

"What do you hope to gain from your year as an RA?" Linda asked. An easy one; we all offered heartfelt replies.

"What prejudices do you have that you will have to overcome in dealing with residents?"

I piped up immediately. "Well, I have a problem with racists."

"Uhh-humm," came the nurturing response from around the circle. Validation. It turned out we all had a problem with racists.

"I have a problem with frat boys," Linda confessed.

Each of us had a group that we had to admit we were prejudiced against. Except Ed. The only white male among the four RAs in Donner House, he was pretty much open to everyone, he said, except maybe the racists.

We took a long time discussing how we would have to overcome our prejudice against racists. If we did not, we all agreed that it would jeopardize our dorm community; it would imperil communication. After all, whom would the racists go to when they had a problem?

We didn't know it, but we were part of the burgeoning epidemic that would soon be cursed from coast to coast by the finest newspapers and magazines in America as "political correctness." If you had told us then that our touchy-feely training would soon be reported as the greatest threat to democracy since the Red Scare and the Cultural Revolution, we would have laughed. Bill "Can I Have A Hug?" Clinton would have been the perfect president of our young "movement." We questioned everything so much that we questioned ourselves and then we questioned our questioning.

If you accepted homosexuals, did you have to accept Ku Klux Klansmen? If you accepted antimale radical lesbians, did you have to accept antifeminist fraternity men? How could you discriminate? If you were not going to judge other cultures, but accept them—indeed, celebrate them—didn't you have to accept their racism, sexism and homophobia? Or was it only the Western varieties that merited criticism? Wasn't that paternalism at its worst?

It was a handicap of the truly PC: if you renounced all your prejudices, you lost the weapons with which to defend your beliefs. PC's detractors, conservative and liberal, did not have that problem. Both were so cocksure, so convinced of their own orthodoxy, that they ignored their internal contradictions and silliness.

RAs were considered so important to the university's mission that we were paid—a pittance, but a salary all the same. We worked for a central bureaucracy known as Residential Education. As the name implied, Res Ed aimed to continue the learning process outside the classroom, through talks, lectures and discussion forums that took advantage of the dorm's intimacy and informality and made education personal and profound.

Profound, sometimes. Personal, always.

In Donner, our best-attended program featured the documentary *Killing Us Softly*. Controversial and graphic, the film addresses the connection between pornography and violence against women. The protagonist is a sort of guardian angel who befriends a young prostitute, then escorts her around to porn stores, live sex shops and other seedy places all over Seattle, showing her how pornography and prostitution destroy women's lives. By the end of the film, of course, the prostitute renounces her past life and starts working to deliver minors from the mean streets.

Jenny had organized the program and when it was over she turned on the lights, her face flushed. Almost all the women in the room and most of the men were still and pale. After a long silence, she began, "Well . . . any thoughts? Comments?" A few men, who had whistled at some parts of the film, smirked, rose and left. If there was going to be deep discussion, they didn't want any part of it. The RAs caught one other's eyes and grimaced. It was always the same people who refused to talk about issues. Perhaps they were annoyed by what had become an almost cliché portrayal of men as loutish oppressors—but, since they refused to talk or dispute the limits of male responsibility and unfair blame, we would never know.

It was normal that touchy-feely learning experiences ended up making people very touchy. Not long after Res Ed was created, opponents attacked it as a liberal conspiracy meant to indoctrinate students when they were most vulnerable: relaxing in their boxers. Students of color complained that their concerns were not addressed; the ethnic theme houses (meant to celebrate American cultural diversity on campus) were ignored. Straight white males, on the other hand, complained that most of the programs exalted every conceivable victim and condemned white men.

Res Ed *was* mind-blowing, in the best sense. I had never seen so many issues of race, gender and identity thrown into the open and wrestled with by such a diversity of people. I learned far more in my dorm than in a year of coursework. True, many discussions eventually revolved around racial differences—and intimidated eighteen-year-old white men who had never heard minorities' perspectives, especially in their living room.

Minorities experienced exactly the opposite reaction. Students who for so long had wanted to talk about issues that mattered to them but could only do it in their 'hoods or barrios suddenly found they had a voice. They had never had the opportunity to share their anger or their ideas with people different from themselves—especially with the white men who would run the country. Now they did. Frustrated, affluent minority kids who had grown up in white suburbs erupted in anger that surprised even themselves.

It was not just that volatile issues ignored in the larger society were unearthed on campus; the very terms of debate were minority friendly. I don't remember when I first heard the phrase "students of color." Immediately, though, I felt its positive effect. Minorities. Nonwhites. Third Worlders. All those labels had been based not on the identity of those described, but on someone else's. Those words did not explain who I *was*, but who I was not.

People of color. That was positive. An identity based not on negation, but on affirmation, a positive.

That was not the way the America beyond the of campus functioned. It was a land where most visible minorities were still targets of resentment, fear or anger—regardless of their college degrees. Whites and nonwhites worked together, even lived together, but rarely, if ever, talked about the divisive issues that worried them. At Stanford we did. There were myriad perspectives that ran counter to what "most Americans" believed. But what was wrong with that? It was a university, after all.

As an RA, I had two pet projects. Since I had made the conscious decision to be Black America's Ambassador to White Folks, I was dedicated to bringing programs on race and ethnicity into the dorm. We saw films on race relations (Ed, a history major, programmed *Eyes on the Prize*). Usually the black students and a half-dozen whites attended. During Black History Month, we had a weekly reading of African-American poets. I posted cartoons from a children's book, *A Beginner's History of Black America*, in the bathroom stalls, changing the series every few days. But mostly, I talked—about my family, growing up, the things that were important to black Americans, the things we still suffered, the hopes we still nourished.

My other goal was encouraging men to communicate. As a group, we never talked. Lawrenceville had taught me how frustrating it was not to be able to share your feelings with other men, and what a Neanderthal you became when machismo was the only way to bond. (Linda called it "testosterone poisoning.") So Ed and I founded a men's discussion group—weeks after Megan and Jenny had already established a woman's group, naturally.

One of our first topics was date rape. It was an unusually well-attended meeting, about twenty guys, and Ed opened the discussion by asking the group what was "date rape"? Most of us had seen this phrase in newspaper headlines—above articles we never read. Ever a journalist, I wanted to know how many of us thought we had committed date rape. I raised my hand first and a few others followed. The discussion turned heated when we addressed specific limits of acceptable behavior.

"If she brings you into her room, gets naked and gets into bed, how can it be rape?" asked one frosh.

"If she doesn't say, 'I want to have sex with you,' and you do, is that rape?" asked another.

"If she says yes, but she's drunk does that count?"

"Suppose *you're* drunk and you do it when she doesn't want to?"

"What are you supposed to do? *Ask?*" demanded a frustrated eighteen-year-old.

"Oh, come on. You know. You *know*," insisted another.

"How do you know?" I asked. "Unless you ask, you don't."

"And suppose she says yes, but lies after and says she didn't?"

We haggled for more than an hour. In the end, we did not agree on how sex becomes date rape, but we all had thought about it, most of us for the first time. When I asked for a second show of hands of people who thought they might have committed date rape, about half the hands went up. It could have been a show of misplaced machismo, but some education had slipped in during our discussion too.

Some dorm residents—mostly white and male—felt that the RAs were preaching liberal dogma. Unfortunately, there was some truth to that. But how could anyone who wanted to increase communication between the races and debate issues of gender and class not be branded a liberal?

That is, until the PC backlash began a short time later and aroused the attention of conservatives as well as liberals. Then, suddenly, all conservatives wanted to talk about were issues of race, gender and class. It was a political epiphany.

⸻

I blasted into the Donner dining room in an uncommon rage, based purely on my racial identity. I instantly found the table where three of my Latina frosh were sitting. Slamming the *Stanford Daily* onto the table, I blared so everyone around us could hear, "What more could they do to tell us they don't want us here?"

I said it at once to no one in particular and to Leticia Valadez, an active member in the Latino student organization, MEChA. I targeted Leti because this time I didn't feel like explaining. I didn't want to calm down. Damn the ambassadorship.

I raged against the divisive atmosphere that reigned over Stanford, which some white students had convinced themselves resulted from the existence of minority student groups. If the minorities didn't segregate themselves then there wouldn't be racism, ran the basic argument. Some whites truly believed that racism was no longer a problem in American society: They had never seen black people barred from Woolworth's counters; they had not witnessed police beating a Latino suspect. They were good people who didn't think of race very often. "And isn't that progress?" they asked ruefully.

It was. The problem was that our mothers and fathers—or their mothers and fathers—had lied to us. Fighting for desegregation in the sixties, they had insisted that we were all the same; once ignorance was eliminated and we all knew one another, racism would evaporate, like the morning dew off the spring grass. Dispelling the racist stereotypes of the past was a key achievement of the civil rights movement. But, in fact, we were all different.

As soon as there were enough Asians, blacks and Latinos on college campuses, we had to admit it. Before ethnicity became the most important difference on campus, religion and class divided "us" from "them." Jews and the middle or working class were considered the minority interlopers. But once the "unmeltable" ethnics came to school, race became the ultimate separator. Once they were inside the high walls, the wrenching tensions of the

America outside did not dry up as had been predicted, rather they came flooding in.

At first, representatives of the downtrodden and excluded were welcomed by liberal academic society, even praised. Then they started to issue demands—demands like reading "their" authors, having their own student organizations and their own housing. They brought the historically black sororities and fraternities from the historically black colleges in the South to white campuses where they had never existed. That was fine until the 1980s. Now, white students felt it had gone too far, spurred on by the national trend to condemn minority "privilege."

"Hell," they observed. "There's no White Student Union; why is there a black one? That's discrimination." The pressure had been building since Alan Bakke challenged affirmative action in 1978, saying what many white folks had been thinking for years. Maybe it was the Zeitgeist of the Reagan era that spawned the biggest backlash ever to minority rights on American campuses. For whatever reasons, though, Americans of color, on and off campus, were fighting to protect gains made less than thirty years before. From progress to retrenchment, it had been a very short honeymoon.

What really disturbed majority students—and soon America— was not that Stanford was a bastion of radical black–Latino–lesbian communism, but the fact that it was so completely different from anything they had known before. Indeed, from anything any of us had known before. It wasn't just the language: "people of color" instead of "minorities" and "women" instead of "girls." But these minority students built their own organizations. They made speeches; they held press conferences. White students did not. All of a sudden, they felt like ... like ... *minorities*.

As a mild-mannered RA, I was disheartened to learn that there was virtually no way for black people to be at once proud and nonthreatening to whites. During the year, probably a tenth of the white men in my dorm thought I was a radical black nationalist— even while I was ostracized from the black community. I realized that if black people just shut up one day, most white folks would simply ignore racial injustices. But—I reasoned—if one black person called attention to our plight, collective or individual, white people would have license to condemn him or her for carping, for launching yet another appeal for special treatment. White people did not oppose equality; they just thought it already existed.

There was no way an African-American could win. Be complacent in the name of peaceful coexistence and neglect your responsibility to educate future opinion makers, politicians and business leaders on the problems of muted minorities. Speak up, and awaken white resentment. My only faith that America could escape a cataclysmic ignorance was rooted in the friendships I had formed with people of all classes and colors (a habit that had begun in earnest at Lawrenceville). But that tranquility contrasted grotesquely with the university's general climate.

The *Daily* reported on page one that the BSU had lost its funding request. Usually I majored in racial understanding—with a minor in my academic courses—but this day I had had enough. Every spring, each student group that wanted a piece of the "associations fee" Stanford students paid had to submit a request. In a plebiscite, students either approved it or rejected it. Every big club on campus asked for a chunk of the pie. Requests were granted routinely for everything from the humor magazine to the astronomy club. This year, the BSU's application was refused.

When minority students had occupied the president's office, the BSU had not been involved. Indeed, it had not even sanctioned the sit-in, which ended in highly publicized arrests. But when the fee request came up, white students did not distinguish between the black students who sat in and the black student organization—it was all the same to them. They decided to punish the BSU for the rambunctious protesters.

It had already been a bad week for race relations. Before the BSU's public censure, a group of fraternity members marched on a freshman house. They were protesting the expulsion of a frosh from university housing. He had been booted off campus because he had gone on a violent rampage through the dorm, trashing hallways and common areas, and he had threatened his gay RA.

Already traumatized by their dormmate's raving vandalism, the other frosh in the dorm panicked one night soon after when they saw masked figures outside their TV room. The disguised men stood silently in the night, wearing hockey, lacrosse and ski masks and holding candles. Some residents began to scream. Others yelled out the window at the shadowy figures. Eventually, they went away, chased off by an RA. But shock waves spread through the campus. Masked men, gathering in the night and carrying fire. For some students it called up haunting images of disturbing events. Not because they thought the hooded figures would torch a cross on the back lawn, but because, emotionally, viscerally, it called up bogeymen from our collective nightmares.

Also around that time, a movement had been founded by seniors to force the university to withdraw its invitation to Robert Maynard, publisher of the *Oakland Tribune*, to make the commencement address. They thought Maynard, the only African-American publisher of a major daily, was not the high-profile, high-caliber speaker Stanford warranted. They signed petitions and began a recall drive.

This all coalesced during that one week in the spring of 1988.

The current events reflected the general discord created by

Stanford's ongoing debate over its Western Culture course. It was becoming so intense that marches and demonstrations for a broader course, one that would include women and writers of color, metastasized into a nationally televised debate between university president Donald Kennedy and Secretary of Education William Bennett.

Before the clash of the titans, the Western Culture debate had simple origins. Students—female and minority mostly, but not solely—had asked why, in the one course required of all Stanford students, were there no female or minority authors? The course consisted of eight three-trimester tracks. Each student chose a sequence: one focused on literature, another technology, another on conflict and change, another philosophy, et cetera. Each track treated its theme from the beginning of human civilization (or at least the Greeks) to modern times. In thousands of years of civilization, there was not a single woman or person of color, or even a non-European, who had written anything worth reading in a freshman survey course at Stanford? Students wanted to know why not.

When I signed up for the philosophy track in September 1985, the course did not include one author or philosopher who was not a white male. I wondered why too. I thought it unimaginable that no nonwhite, nonmale writer merited a few minutes in thirty weeks of classes. Not one. Like the vast majority of students— indeed, the majority of black and minority students—I never once demonstrated for it. Not only because my scholarship could be revoked if I broke a university rule, but because I didn't want to take the personal risk of being arrested or vilified—or the time. I was content to watch others—black, white, Asian, Latino and Native American Indian—fight my battles for me.

Since most students of color were like me, the rebellion against

the attempt by "minorities and radicals" to "end" Western Culture surprised me. A small group of white students formed an
organization to "Save Western Culture." Denouncing the provin-
cialism of minorities, they refused to let Stanford surrender its
superior academic credentials. (Apparently, their fear of a loss of
prestige was justified. In 1988, Stanford changed Western Culture
to Cultures, Ideas and Value (CIV), a broader coarse that included
a track that dealt with non-European writers who became a part
of, or reflected on, Western societies. The next year Stanford's
position plummeted from number one to number six in *US News
& World Report*'s ranking of universities. Although we can't know
for certain, the CIV change—or the perception of it—probably
had a good deal to do with Stanford's fall.)

In the end, CIV was barely different from Western Culture.
When Gerhardt Casper assumed the Stanford presidency in 1992,
moving from the University of Chicago, he was underwhelmed
by the magnitude of the change.

"My impression coming in, largely based on articles in the
popular press, was clearly very skeptical. I have come to the con-
clusion that Stanford really got a bum rap," said Casper, no radical, in a magazine article a year later. "Stanford does more in
teaching civilizations, including Western civilization, than almost
all other American universities . . . the changes that brought so
much publicity were really incremental changes and did not go to
the fundamental structure, to the essence of the reading lists."[*]

Despite the national media hype, Plato and Aristotle were still
at the top of the most-read list of books in CIV. Minorities and
women were sprinkled in where they were germane to the topics
addressed. The long and arduous battle had unjustly damaged
the university's reputation. It resulted in a good change. It was

*Stanford Magazine, Sept. 1993.

not revolutionary. And yet, it had required an inordinate amount of discord.

....

The opponents of "multiculturalism" (curricular PC) were correct in asserting that it had a political component—but even the content of school lunches had a political component in the eighties. Was the existence of a canon of literature in which only the writers of one group were purported to be noteworthy not political? Of course, elites dub their own political stances "objective" and, therefore, apolitical. To this reasoning that there were no non-Europeans or women on the Western Culture reading list was not a political statement, it was an objective acknowledgment of the fact that they simply had not written worthy books. They did not comprise the learned class. To include unworthy writers just for the sake of affirmative action typifies "ethnic cheerleading" and damages the canon and academic standards, say multiculturalism's detractors.

But if the canon was objective, then why did it change from generation to generation? Why didn't every schoolboy in the 1970s know Milton's *Paradise Lost*, when every schoolboy in the thirties had? And why did the seventies' kids consider T. S. Eliot a great mind, while no student read him in the fifties? Moreover, there had been great thinkers who were not white men. Granted, most women and third-world interlopers into Western Culture had not been educated, but some had, and a good number of them in the last century.

The media bought the conservative rhetoric. The PC backlash soon outdistanced the "movement" itself. The press reports continue still, long after ill-conceived speech codes against racial slurs and "hurtful speech" have vanished. The anti-PC vitriol on talk radio and in newsmagazines goes on, long after minorities have been harassed into silence by the "politically correct" label and have become more hesitant to make demands on white institutions— the way whites said they had been silenced by the "racist" label.

For all the alarmist fervor sounding off on the airwaves and in news columns, PC is not a new phenomenon. It existed years before the practitioners of eighties-style political correctness res- urrected the term in self-mocking humor. Rather than being an entire school of thought, "politically correct" in the '60s was an adjective that described disparate, specific political opinions (e.g., desegregation should end or you shouldn't wear fur or the US should get out of Vietnam). In the 1980s, supporters intended to describe a way of looking at the world, at other people, that pushed beyond the thoughtless preconceptions we all operate on every day, like bats use sonar. It was about acknowledging one's own preju- dices and trying to dispel them. It was about questioning authority and orthodoxy. It was, in fact, an attempt to find objectivity.

Its political antecedent was sixties-style liberalism, its academic parent Derrida-style deconstructionism. But it surpassed old- fashioned liberalism—and a lot of the old-fashioned liberals. Declared and confirmed feminists started to denounce what they thought PC was in newspaper op-eds and in elite magazine pieces.

I sat on a panel discussion for the McLaughlin show during which professor Christina Sommer, a self-proclaimed die-hard liberal, said that PC was corroding fragile young minds. As evi- dence, she said that at Wellesley, the term "seminar" had been banned. Now they used the word "ovular" exclusively.

The audience roared with laughter. So did those of us suppos- edly representing PCdom. We had never heard of an "ovular." John McLaughlin, our host, said that the PC called American Indians "Native Americans," but that a survey of "such persons" found that they *want* to be called "American Indians." The audience gasped.

I tried to object, to say, "No, no, I am PC and the PC thing to say, knowing that Native Americans are not 100 percent in favor of either term, is the all-inclusive 'Native American Indian.'"

Of course I couldn't yell loud enough to be heard over our host. Besides, how ridiculous would I have sounded tossing out yet another "approved" label? That was the problem with trying to oppose a point of view that was quickly gaining the weight of orthodoxy. You had to yell, to stomp your feet, to be dramatic to get a word in edgewise. The whole world, it seemed, was crystallizing around the notion that PC was evil. To pierce the massing conventional wisdom, you would have to look like an idiot: a subjective, hysterical, minority radical lacking intellectual rigor. It was a self-fulfilling prophecy.

Realizing that they had hit pay dirt, conservatives rejoiced. Dinesh D'Souza, author of a decidedly unobjective book condemning PC, hit the lecture circuit and his book, *Illiberal Education*, hit the best-seller list. Conservatives convened a seminar in Washington coaching campus leaders from around the country on how to capitalize on the fervor by getting their local and regional press to cover the PC story. Momentum was on their side. The generally accepted opinion among journalists had been that the Young Republicans were a bunch of mama's boys and girls, and that their academic counterparts were too dull for a story. Any story. PC, on the other hand, could be pitched as a freedom of speech piece or a race relations story, or from some other titillating angle.

The obvious defense would have been for the PC to show journalists what they were really about. Only that was impossible. Firstly, the PC legions were already in a reactive posture, trying to dislodge an established—and easily comprehensible—specter. Americans knew dictatorships that had tried to impose "right" by limiting opposing speech or punishing those who disagreed. It was communism. It was fascism. It was Orwell.

Secondly, the opposing arguments were not journalistically sexy. Showing what PC typically was was boring. Blacks, whites and Latinos sitting around a dorm lounge discussing what it felt like to be a member of their group was *not* a story. The fact that Stanford's "black ethnic theme house" was more than fifty percent white was not newsworthy. Straight white males reading Maya Angelou out loud was not hot. On the other hand, racial discord, minorities repressing white men—that was news!

The ultimate obstacle to presenting a united PC front, though, was that there was no united PC movement. Despite media reports to the contrary, there was no nationwide conspiracy to subvert American college campuses, eliminate Plato and Aristotle, or enforce thought control. The tense situations on college campuses—from unconstitutional speech codes to diversity seminars to sit-ins—did not stem from a cabal. What America heard from its campuses was the constructive clang and clash of progress as the most diverse learning communities in the world tried to grapple with issues they had never before faced.

By the end of my Lawrenceville experience, I used to tell the guys I argued with over race or politics, "We aren't going to agree. What you believe is what counts. That'll be society's line, so what difference does my opinion make anyway?"

They hated that. They called it a cop-out. They were right.

But if one thing was becoming clear to me in the PC backlash, it was that much greater racial tolerance and understanding cannot come unless white men (and I mean men) are willing to work for it. Will we move increasingly farther apart, toward political and social confrontation? Or will we accept one another and work, unified, for a more just society? As white men are both the gatekeepers and the majority of the social, academic, political and journalistic elite, our future depends on them, far more than on the minority fringes. Since they are also fearful of losing privilege, feeling increasingly menaced—indeed, discriminated against—it is unlikely they will be very generous. Most white men already feel they have given away the farm. They are not about to throw in the house, the car and the family business too.

As long as white America feels threatened by blacks they will devise elaborate rationales to justify—or deny—the reality that to be black in America is to be a second-class citizen. However rich you are, however well educated, as long as you are black, you are black *first*, in the eyes of most white people.

....

PC's ultimate sin may be that it forged a new weapon to consolidate and inflame white-male resentment. It provided a hook on which to hang the dull but gnawing fear that something had gone dreadfully wrong in the world. It offered a rationale to oppose Lani Guinier's nomination as a second-level justice department official, and a factual basis for the suspicion that affirmative action had given the post you should have received to your black female co-worker.

If I had not been there, I too would have been outraged by the press accounts of what was going on at Stanford. Having lived it, I knew how very inaccurate they were. While communication was often contentious and frustrating for everyone on campus, it was also constant. More people, from all ends of the spectrum, were speaking out than were being shouted down.

At the end of my year as an RA, many of my freshmen thanked

me for opening their eyes to realities they would never have known otherwise, and that they would never forget. They had transformed me as well; for all the hype about shutting off debate, I have never since had such frank exchanges as I did at Stanford. If the whole country were as "politically correct," there would be a lot more Americans talking to one another.

For budgetary, and probably political, reasons, Stanford began dismantling the Residential Education system, seemingly abandoning the goal of stimulating meaningful exchange in its dorms between students who might not normally discuss explosive issues with people of another race or class. The media assault on multicultural curricula waned as new fronts in the war against PC emerged. When an obscure college named Antioch issued a set of insipid guidelines to avoid date rape in 1993, it made international headlines. And *Newsweek* columnist George Will went so far as to blame left-wing political correctness for the rise of neofascism in Europe in the early nineties.

Months after I left Stanford to work for *Newsweek,* the magazine would write the definitive popular press piece on political correctness. On the cover loomed the words "THOUGHT POLICE" in mammoth crumbling granite against a shadowy black background. The subhead read, "Watch what you say." Once I saw the cover mock-up, I pointed out to some senior editors that the cover was not only incorrectly menacing, given the more balanced story inside—but contradictory. Was PC about policing thoughts or policing speech?

Our piece argued that at its worst it was about the latter. At no point did we suggest it was the former. The senior editor in charge of the cover appreciated my observation, but said that that was not reason enough to change the cover at that late hour. (He was too polite to tell me that it was a knockout cover that an editor wouldn't change if he had a week to replace it.) The most I could do was add my modest sidebar, the short contrarian piece often found after the long one that develops the main argument. In my article, I tried to demystify—but especially, decriminalize—political correctness by relating my RA experience.

Of course, I failed to make a dent in the galloping paranoia against PC. Five years after college, an American diplomat in Algiers told me that she used the "political correctness movement" in the US to explain to Algerians that America had something analogous to the Muslim fundamentalist terrorists who were slitting thirty throats a day in their country. I was taken aback.

There are many risks for the black person who chooses the ambassador's role as his or her survival technique in a predominantly white environment—and this was one of the biggest: failure. I had failed to decrease the gaps of misunderstanding and apprehension between the races over PC; this United States diplomat thought the BSU was not beyond taking out her family. However many whites you managed to nudge gently toward understanding this or that aspect of the black condition, you were destined to encounter examples of white ignorance or, worse, indifference. You trudged on, cheerfully giving teach-ins whenever and wherever necessary, in the hope that your little efforts would help tip the scales toward understanding and peace. But it often felt like a mythical struggle you were destined to lose. You rolled the boulder up the mountainside just to find it back at the bottom when you awoke the next day.

The greatest risk for those of us who chose the ambassadorship, though, was self-alienation. Since you never sided dogmatically with either blacks or whites, you often offended both. Whites accused you of being racially oversensitive and blacks accused you of being an Uncle Tom. Black people thought you had too many white friends. Your white friends thought you were obsessed with racial issues. White people thought you were too angry. Black people thought you were not angry enough. Black people found you too willing to compromise. White people found you doctrinaire.

That does not mean the ambassadorship is a poor survival strategy. A great number of African-Americans who live and work in white environments use it or some combination of it and other strategies to give meaning to an often frustrating double life. Moreover, every adaptation strategy has its downsides. "The angry black nationalist" is a sure way to avoid advancement. "The self-hating accomodationist" leads to self-loathing by the time you get to the executive suite—and it doesn't guarantee you'll get there. (These are just two of the infinite varieties in coping techniques.)

I still play the ambassador role. It allows a black person to engage successfully in the professional rat race while preserving his or her righteous anger. It also channels that anger constructively (protesting to whites when injustices arise), rather than venting it on other black people (because they're the only people within striking distance).

Despite the frustrations of trying to balance personal and community agendas (e.g., I want to get ahead at this company versus black people would be avenged for that blatantly offensive slur if I punched my colleague in the eye), as well as trying to balance allegiances to the black race and to the American nation, the ambassadorship—most of all—leaves you open to learning from blacks and whites. It is a role based on dialogue and engagement. I learn from my brother's habit, picked up in the street, of speaking plainly and baldly about justice and power. I learn from my

WASP friends about how to be diplomatic and self-examining. Finally, being an ambassador gives you a reason, or at least an excuse, to form close relationships with individuals of all races (it's unfortunate that in America, we still need one), bonds that, even if they don't end injustice, will help produce a generation of off-spring that is less ignorant of "the Other" and more willing to appreciate difference rather than being fearful of it.

CHAPTER 8

FRANCE AT LAST

SEPTEMBER 1988

I experienced no sense of déjà vu as the plane touched down, just the pallid September sun glaring off the faded tarmac. I hurried out the forward cabin door and pushed my way through passport control. Waiting for my luggage, I spotted a few familiar faces: handsome, fresh, young. Even if I hadn't met them the previous spring, I would have known they were from Stanford. In the beginning of my fourth year of college, I came to Paris to study at the Sorbonne and the Institute of Political Studies, to rediscover the country I had grown to love as an exchange student in 1984, and to escape the monotony of life in America.

JULY 1984

Air France flight 029 from New York to Paris was my first plane ride. Getting on board felt like going to boarding school, an opening to another universe, a chance to reinvent myself. My world had been a tiny wedge of the eastern seaboard, edged by New York City, Philadelphia, Washington and the Jersey shore. Now, thanks to a scholarship through the Experiment in International Living and A Better Chance, I was bound for Nîmes, the gateway to a region called Provence, to live for three weeks with a French family.

I couldn't quite believe I would ever see France—until the plane began to drop from the sky and my head started to throb. My ears were ringing and a thunderous headache enveloped everything in a fog of sinus congestion: The dull gray and white buildings. The strange spacelike towers in the distance. The overcast sky. The traffic jam. I had been expecting the world's most glamorous capital, but it appeared as lusterless as White City. At nine o'clock in the morning it looked like dusk. Struck with dread, I thought, *Could I have come all this way for nothing?*

Our hotel fed my unease. Located in a nondescript part of town, not far from one of the grimy suburban train stations, the barracks-like building boasted none of the pretty windows and rooftops from my French books. The neighborhood, dense with ugly, modern buildings, suffocated under low-lying clouds.

The only happy result of crossing the Atlantic seemed to be my new friends. After just one late-night rap session, we were as chummy as childhood pals. Eight girls and three boys. Rick, Steve and I quickly became the Three Musketeers: two African-American geeks—one who tried to convince white people he was a homeboy (not me; and they believed it)—and a macho Irish-American from Massachusetts. The girls were far more self-possessed, elegant, intelligent, mature—or at least they faked it better than we did.

As I fell asleep at five in the morning, I prayed that the center of town would be different. If Paris was not magical, if Paris was not a whole other reality from the boredom of White City, then we *were* living a sad, sad life—and for what?

We started our second day at Notre Dame. After a few hours pondering the inspiration that had led to the building of this place, we set out for lunch. After an hour of whining, we couldn't find a restaurant that all of us agreed on. I stomped off.

As soon as I crossed the rue de Rivoli, I was intoxicated. I could go wherever I wanted, do whatever I wanted. I was in a foreign country where no one knew me. I was seventeen. I was away from White City. My mother must have felt the same way that summer in Colorado when she was seventeen, with the teen goodwill group.

At the first red-canopied café, the waiter brought me a *poulet-frites*. After my quick lunch, I took my bearings and steered toward the Tuileries. I stood for a long while in the place de la Concorde—ordered, beautiful, antique and chaotic—marveling at its grandeur. The traffic whirled around the ancient monuments, the broad roads sprawling beneath an expansive sky. It felt like time and space converged at this one point.

I marched up the crowded Champs-Elysées with the urbane dismissiveness of a New Yorker, dodging tour groups of Japanese and Germans. Swimming in the glitter of the boulevard and the boutiques, I couldn't help but think it all looked chintzy next to Fifth Avenue. Finally, I came to the Arc de Triomphe. For a moment, I tried to picture the men, about my age, who had soldiered off to die. Crossing the Seine, I drank in the air in greedy gulps—the city as magnificent as I had dreamed, more liberating than I could have imagined. I eyed the boats parked on the quays and the flotillas of tourists passing beneath me. I was as foreign as they were, but somehow I felt I belonged.

From the summit of the Eiffel Tower I took greater Paris into my nostrils. It burned, but it filled me with the lust of possibilities.

I don't know when or where I first acknowledged it. Perhaps it was on the Metro platform where no one avoided my glance. Or in the sea of tourists and Parisians who didn't part as I passed through. Or, maybe, when the woman stopped me on her way into the Metro station to ask the time.

"Pardon, Monsieur, avez-vous l'heure?"

I froze. *Oh my God, a French person is speaking to me,* I thought. For a few seconds, I stared dumbly at my watch. Finally, she grabbed my wrist and turned it toward her.

"Seize heures vingt," she said, as if doing me a favor, then hurried off.

Maybe the feeling had just seeped into my bones through some sort of cultural osmosis—but, at some point I realized that I felt strangely at ease. I felt visible for the first time. The white woman who asked me the hour was only part of my new state. Everywhere, people saw me.

In America, people noticed the color of my skin, then responded accordingly. Shopkeepers kept an eye peeled, slithering over to ask if they could help me once I got too close to the nice ties. On the streets of New York and Philadelphia, pedestrians usually avoided me—or stiffened their backs as they hurried by.

This foreign country was more hospitable than home. On the sidewalk, in stores, in restaurants, people treated me like a human being—sometimes only like an American, but usually like a human being. Merchants, in typical French fashion, ignored me until I came to them. Waiters were no nastier than they were to anybody else. And to the average pedestrian on a Paris street, I was not a threat, blackness was not a mental prompt to beware. Not a single woman clutched her bag as I walked by.

I noticed my breath came more easily. More than a century after the Emancipation Proclamation, I was finally liberated.

After five days in the capital, we set out for Nîmes. I had ridden trains before, to Washington or New York, but Amtrak was like going by dogsled next to the Train à Grande Vitesse. It looked like a missile, orange and sleek, poised next to the platform at the Gare de Lyon.

A handsome young family met me in Nîmes. Bernard, my French father, was only twenty-nine. Maryse, my mother, twenty-eight. And my little sister Julie, fifteen months. They looked like any American family, only trim and healthy. Bernard wore a brightly striped polo knit and olive slacks; Maryse, a pale red summer dress and sandals; and Julie, fluffy blonde curls and an angelic smile—and all I could think was, *Damn, no teenagers!*

In just a matter of days, freedom became a sentence. My family, too hip to drag me around tourist attractions or to impose rules, left me to my own devices. With my American friends scattered around town, the old boredom of earlier summers crept back.

My French parents were too adventurous to understand. Bernard was a fireman and the French equivalent of a real-life action hero. He went on rescue missions to the developing world after natural disasters. He and Maryse had traveled all over the globe, from Russia to Canada. They thought a dynamic young American would love being on his own in the south of France for a summer. If only they could have found one. Except for the occasional group outing, I spent my time walking around Nîmes alone or listening to my parents' sixties-era LPs.

Sensing my spiraling depression, Maryse and Bernard tried to get me out of the house. Bernard invited me to play tennis. We visited the Pont du Gard, a first-century Roman aqueduct. And on Sundays, we ate lunch at Bernard's parents' house and dinner with Maryse's family.

Bernard's mother was a plump lively woman, her Midi accent

as thick as her fleshy arms. After we ate, she'd prop an elbow on the table, straddle the chair in her housedress, and tell a bawdy tale about a neighbor or a relative. I loved to watch her narrate, spitting out olive pits as she went, laughing and waving her hand for punctuation. She reminded me of home. At Maryse's family's house, we played *pétanque*. Maryse's father—thin and wiry—was as uproarious as Bernard's mother. While everyone else raced through their sentences, leaving me lost in a sea of cast-off past particles and stray adjectives (I would eventually realize they were talking about me), he talked slowly and deliberately.

To get me out of my funk, Bernard and Maryse suggested I throw a party. They did all the work, and I invited all my friends. We got drunk over grilled *merguez* and overripe fruit. When the annual Nîmes jazz festival kicked off, my parents took me to see Miles Davis and B.B. King in the town's Roman amphitheater.

I finally grew accustomed to the slow pace of life in the Midi. I became Nimois: I slept late, met friends in town at La Bourse, the bustling café across from the arena, and drank icy *pastis* in the late afternoon. Every meal began with *pastis* or port or whiskey. Then we ate, mostly omelets, fresh vegetables or fish—always washed down with liters of red wine, never white. (Southerners thought white wine was for kids.)

Most nights my family had friends or relatives over and we dined on a wooden picnic table on the open front porch. Dinner always evolved into a seminar on religion or superpower politics or race relations in America. *These people are left of the Democrats*, I thought. They peppered me with questions about the US: how big was it, how warm was it, how generous were the people, how good was the life? My favorite time came when the serious discussions dissolved into the soft Midi night, as we joked and laughed over empty wine bottles and cheese and cognac. My parents' friends taught me dirty words under the stars.

The final two weeks of my *séjour* slipped away and we commenced preparations for the grand farewell party. Everybody had to contribute. Steve planned to make his mother's world-famous three-alarm chili. Nicole and Heather wanted to help cook. I volunteered our kitchen.

As the chili piped away atop the stove, I stepped outside for a breath of hot air. From our front porch, I could see the sky darkening, small white flakes afloat on the wind.

"Oh, my God," I called out in feigned panic, "they've nuked Paris." In the backyard, a thick plume of smoke rose above the fire wall, no higher than my waist. "Fire!" I yelled back into the kitchen.

My friends raced out to comfort my hysteria. "Maybe your neighbor's burning garbage," Steve suggested.

"Is there anyone over there?" I shouted. No answer. We didn't have a neighbor. Next door was an empty lot—an uncultivated, unmowed, vacant lot in France's driest region with its most treacherous wind, le Mistral. We climbed off the stone wall and ran into the house. Nicole dialed the firemen, I rehearsed my French, Steve watered down the back of the house (constructed of stone). Heather, anticipating a Scarlett-like swoon, rushed to the couch.

The firemen couldn't understand. I stammered, "Joo-ssss-efff Daaahhhhhrrrr-boooowwwwww," sounding it out again and again. *If only I had paid more attention in Madame Garros's French IV!* When I told the dispatcher Bernard Piq lived here, he said the firemen were already on the way.

I went out to help Steve water the house. Bare backed, he was living one of the ego fantasies of every small-town high school football star: battling a raging blaze single-handed.

Nicole, ever the fretting mother, asked, "Don't you think you should call your family and let them know their house is burning down?"

As the flames spread, making pretty crackling noises next door, Steve noticed a car parked near the fire wall. The gasoline could ignite and explode. Nicole dashed inside to steer. Just as we shoved the car in front of the house, the fire engine raced up the dirt driveway. They couldn't maneuver the truck near the wall unless we pushed the car back.

Nothing doing, we protested breathlessly.

They drove over the grass and pulled up to the fire break. Their petite French water hoses flooded the empty lot while we looked on like idiotic American teenagers watching a fire in the south of France.

A gaggle of Bernard's family drove up, the third ring of our circus: brothers, sisters, cousins, in-laws. They had been called by his friends in the fire department. I ran to answer the phone. It was Bernard. Trying to be cool and mature, but speaking ever more quickly, I told him what had happened.

Nonplussed, he asked, "Do you want us to come home?"

I don't know. It's your house almost caught fire, I thought. *In my country, we come home.* I put on his brother.

"*C'est pas grave. C'est pas grave*," he kept saying.

In fifteen minutes most of the family and all the firemen were gone; only Bernard's brother and his friend remained. Heather experienced a miraculous recovery and ended up telling the Frenchmen how cute their eyes were. She and Nicole swindled a ride home. I turned off the chili and locked up the house, and Steve and I headed to Nicole's for dinner.

Later that week at the farewell party, there were about twenty pounds too much chili. After the *soirée,* we brought the still-full pot home. We figured we could use it to smother the next brush fire.

The whole group had fallen in love with my family—because Julie was the cutest kid in France and Bernard and Maryse the coolest parents anywhere. At the train station they wore the same crisp outfits they had met me in. I cried and I kissed them good-bye—three pecks each in the south of France. And the TGV pulled out of the station.

SEPTEMBER 1988

France had been my big bang. Returning for my second stint there, I longed to be contemplative, but my parting scene with my grandmother had haunted me through the seven-hour flight. We had hugged for a long while, until tears welled up in my eyes and streamed down her smooth yellow skin.

"It's alright, baby . . . you'll be back. I'll see you again," she had said, pulling me tight against her body. My mother engineered a briefer good-bye, dropping me curbside at JFK. We only had time for a quick "take care" and a tossed off "I love you."

Now, the chronically happy faces of Stanford students assuaged me; they were raining health all over dingy de Gaulle airport, as if nothing gloomy could live in that much sunlight. Our van let me off in a nondescript section of a nondescript arrondissement. Now, a sick sense of déjà vu did swirl in my stomach. The sprawling collection of tall brown and white buildings evoked the projects. On the ninth floor of one of the buildings, an elfin old woman greeted me. She measured about four feet tall and had Asian eyes and a tiny voice. She welcomed me exuberantly into her home. The apartment looked spacious but dark. Nervous, I forgot to put down my luggage. I stood in the entryway, straining every muscle to understand her.

My room, as big as a Stanford double, gleamed. An antique armoire with a mirrored front stood beside a glistening white desk and a tidy little bed. On the desk sat fresh flowers and notebooks.

Madame told me I had to eat something after my long journey. I said I didn't feel hungry. She told me not to talk back, grabbed my arm and pulled me into the kitchen. She sat across the tiny table, watching me eat, asking questions about my hometown, my family, my major. Soon an attractive woman, a little older than me, arrived to collect the toddler who had been roaming the apartment.

Anne-Marie, Madame's daughter, appeared the ideal *parisienne*, pretty, smart and poised. Madame's husband—Monsieur—was a retired French naval doctor, cantankerous and lanky. They had met on a warship in Vietnam, which the French still called "Indochine." Anne-Marie's husband, a dashing bespectacled bourgeois named Hubert, worked as Coca-Cola's marketing director in France. Witty and charming, every time we met, he would ask, "*Et l'amour . . .* ???" with an elongated *oooooouuuuuuur.*

I had a month before classes began. I used the time to eat, drink and dance with the twenty other Stanford students—and to explore Europe. (My Stanford scholarship paid for my studies and some travel.) Everywhere, I discovered myself. Madrid's liveliness made me question my sobriety. London's parks invited me to dream. Spain's barren countryside reflected the isolation of the "life decisions" that confronted me. The Normandy beaches made me feel almost guilty for my leisurely youth.

I learned a lot less once classes started. I took International Relations courses at Sciences-Po and French lit at the Sorbonne. The schools could not have been more different. While the Sorbonne symbolized open-admission French egalitarianism, Sciences-Po represented wealth and privilege—an institution whose graduates often went on to one of the Grandes Ecoles, then to some ministerial post, like president of the Republic. I could barely pay attention in class for all the Hermès scarves and umbrellas that the "Sciences-posers" brought with them, but the teachers were superb and the name was as prestigious as Harvard or Yale.

On the other hand, admitting you were studying letters at the Sorbonne was like saying you were majoring in communications at Stanford, a "Mickey Mouse" major. Most classes were lecture courses, taught in huge amphitheaters. For an American these settings were historic and impressive, but finding them meant negotiating a maze of jeans-and-leather-clad smokers who didn't much care if they got to class or not.

I knew I would never make any friends at Sciences-Po. I lacked the pedigree and the central social precept was: everyone I need to know, I know already. I signed up for a weight-training class at the Sorbonne. In no time, I had a coterie of French friends. I tried to join the rugby team, but after three practices decided winter came too early in Paris.

I spent most of my time studying, eating with friends and my family and talking on the phone with my mother. She reported that one of her siblings had bought my grandmother's house and planned to kick her and my brother out; my mother had not paid rent in months. She had been letting our homeless relatives and some neighborhood hoodlums squat in the house. Her car had been repossessed and she had stopped working. My brother was unemployed too.

Every time I hung up the phone, I looked wiped. My French great-grandmother (my friends and I had named her that since she was older than everyone else's *mère*) would throw a fit.

"She has no right to call you with her worries," she yelled. "You are just a boy."

She couldn't understand. I sent my mother five hundred dollars from the money I had saved the previous summer.

....

Before I could embark on a Christmas break tour of Europe, I had to mail my law school recommendation forms to the US. With their usual sense of timing, the French postal service went on strike the day after I mailed them. To make matters worse, my journalism summer internship applications would be due soon. I was also nervously waiting to receive my LSAT scores.

Madame told me not to worry: we were going to throw a party. She was the most generous person I have ever met. Although she was sixty-something, she brought companionship to "elderly" shut-ins, chaperoning their field trips and listening to their stories. She cared for her grandchildren, who ranged from fifteen months to twenty years old. To them she was counselor, granny and enforcer. On top of it all, she played mother hen to strangers from strange lands; I was her twentieth exchange student!

This little woman, with the slightest paunch and the brightest eyes, was her family's fulcrum. As if to balance the weight of my family's pressure, she babied me, demanding I eat seconds at meals, anticipating my every need. My friends started calling me "*l'enfant gâté,*" the spoiled child. Her dinners were legendary, whether a "simple" hunter's-style braised rabbit or an elaborate Vietnamese delicacy. On the weekends, she fed me for free (Stanford only paid for the weekdays and you were supposed to pay your family extra for weekend meals.) Every day I found fresh flowers on my desk. Since I didn't like coffee, every morning she provided orange juice and fresh croissants.

Over one of her nightly feasts, she had confessed she was a Gaullist. She knew I was a Democrat and, therefore a "leftist," so she waited until we were well acquainted to come out to me. Balling her convictions into her tiny hands, she delivered her political gospel. But France's mainstream "conservative" group, the Rally for the Republic, was more left-wing than the Democratic Party. They supported socialized medicine, cradle-to-grave job security, even state-owned monopolies. They would have been communists in America. Yet, whenever company was present and political discussion commenced, Madame would point in my direction and, in a stage whisper, tell our guests *"Mais, ouiii, monsieur est de gauche!"* (Oh, yes, the gentleman is a leftist!) and clasp her hands together.

Our party was a success. Madame ushered everyone in, pushing them toward the champagne and smoked salmon. Seeing my great-grandparents surrounded by my friends, laughing uproariously, seemed the most natural thing in the world. When my friends left, as enamored by my family as I was, Madame couldn't stop remarking on my friend Gustavo's good looks: "Oooo-lala," she kept repeating, wringing her hands and slapping me on the back.

Soon after our party, with my mother and my applications still on my mind, I set off with my friend Traunza to see the rest of Europe. School would be ending in six months and I still had no idea what I would do after graduation. After visiting Maryse, Bernard, Julie and their new baby, Tre and I "did" Geneva, East and West Berlin, Vienna, Budapest, Athens, Rome, Florence and Venice—in three weeks.

I had never felt so unencumbered. All my attention was focused outward as Europe rushed by. Everything was an issue here except me: the people, their customs, their art, their history, their food, their buildings, their faces, everything. I fell in love with Budapest for its energy and life, Vienna for its elegance and reserve. I hated the chaos of Athens and Rome, but dreamt my way through Florence. In the Hungarian capital, LL Cool J serenaded an outdoor skating rink and Whitney Houston videos played in the metro (and a sumptuous meal of chicken *paperkash,* a delectable wine and an extravagant dessert cost less than eight dollars).

I realized that I could never live within America's borders again and not feel the tug of the world outside. I felt freer in France, and anywhere else, away from the confining, all-consuming American obsession with black and white. Here, I didn't have to choose.

Still, my responsibilities to my family and to my future pursued me. On Christmas night in Vienna, I prayed in a Catholic church that my mother could sense my happiness. I called the *Washington Post* and the *San Jose Mercury News* to find out if they would give me internships; the *Los Angeles Times* was pressuring me to accept or decline their offer. In Berlin, I called to get my LSAT scores. In Florence, Jim Hoagland of the *Post* said yes. In Venice, *Newsweek* offered me a summer job.

Back in Paris, novelty ceded to routine. I spent most of my time holed up at my polished white desk in my bedroom or in the library. Buried in literature, European Community economics and political science, I struggled to understand the precepts of the Negritude movement and to grasp Proust's passion for a pastry. The shared suffering of papers and exam period made me Parisian.

Even in the fog of philosophical French, my worries about my family intruded. I identified with Père Goriot, who feared death not because of what would happen in the hereafter, but because of what would happen to his loved ones in his absence.

On the day that I called to tell my mother I had been accepted to Yale Law School, she told me she had broken her arm in a fight with my brother and had walked two miles through the snow to the hospital. The utilities had been cut off. A relative had charged her with letting drug dealers sell crack out of the house. My news sounded puny.

One of *Newsweek*'s correspondents, Ruth Marshall, suggested I get a job with the magazine. I was flattered—until I realized I had never wanted to work for a newsmagazine. I had interned in *Newsweek*'s Atlanta bureau the summer before. It was an excruciatingly slow work pace; you had to beg editors to run stories *they* had assigned. I politely thanked Ruth for her suggestion.

Three weeks later my mother telephoned to tell me that I had been accepted to Harvard . . . and she had received the subpoena to appear in court. For a week after that she didn't call. I couldn't reach her because the phone had been cut off. I worried that she had been arrested. Finally, Mom called and said she "won" the case, but she had to vacate the house by March 31. I called Ruth to say I'd like to see what *Newsweek* might offer. The day before I left Paris, the chief of correspondents called to say I had meetings scheduled with the editor, the business editor and the chief of research to discuss a possible job. I asked my journal, "Is this what I want?"

I left Paris on the twenty-third of March unable to remember what life had been like elsewhere. France had seeped into my soul—not in the way the light and the food and the language had washed over me as a teenager—but Paris had sunk itself deep into me, into my imagination, my hopes. It had become home, and in doing so, liberated me from the need to have one. Before I lived here, I had longed for a home—one like the one that I imagined Nick had or Dan or Steve—a place where I could go during the holidays and have my mother greet me and my kids at the door, drying her hands on an apron that smelled of pies and stuffing.

The closest thing I had to a childhood family home was about to disappear forever. Besides, I had rejected the notion of White City as home when I decided it was the black hole of aspiration.

Living in Paris—racing for the subway, cramming for exams, missing sleep to pull all-nighters ("*Metro, boulot, dodo,*" the French called the routine: subway, work, sleep)—had rendered the exotic routine.

I had remade Paris and in the process I had been transformed. Those ageless facades and that unapologetic arrogance were no longer strangers to me. French was just English with a head cold. I recognized the dim streetlamps to the point of banal intimacy; home did not have to be a place. America did not have to be a prison any more than White City. I could choose it; I did not have to choose it.

Lawrenceville's promises had come to fruition: I did have the power to remake a universe, wherever, whenever, however I chose. My mother had been right all along.

CHAPTER 9

BUPPIE BUT NOT BROKEN

I hopped a cab from JFK to the Hotel Inter-Continental. Driving through midtown Manhattan, the city threatened to cascade down on me: the buildings, the traffic, the crowds, everything was beyond human scale compared to Paris. I wondered how I could have lived here as a child.

Newsweek really knew how to impress a guy. The bellboy took my shoulder bag and ushered me into a gold-encrusted lobby. Other than the occasional Holiday Inn when I was a kid, I had only stayed in a hotel once, as a *Newsweek* intern. Alone in my room, I stripped off my traveling clothes, slipped into the monogrammed robe and jumped up and down on the lavish bed. After sending my suit out to be dry-cleaned, I ordered room service: fettucine alfredo with baby shrimp and salmon. Basking in the warm, nostalgic glow of American TV, I tried to relax for the next day.

Newsweek really knew how to impress a guy: forty-two thousand dollars to be an associate editor for one year, with an option for me or the magazine to call off the whole deal after that. Dizzy with jet lag, I sat across the desk from Mark Whitaker, the business editor, fighting back a grin. I thought journalists earned twenty thousand dollars a year; the forty-two grand seemed to increase my delirium. It made me wanna holler, "You want to give *me* forty-two thousand dollars a year?! You people must be crazy!"

And they wanted to make things easy: no need to decide on going to law school right away, take a deferment, earn some money, get a life. I could always attend Yale next year. Attempting to look natural, I crossed my legs and said, "The jet lag, you know, and the time difference, I'm all . . . fuzzy," I sounded like Woody Allen. ". . . Can I think it over for a few days?"

Two days later my train pulled into Trenton station under a freezing rain. My aunt Janie, my grandmother's sister, picked me up. After six months of horror stories, I dreaded what I might find at "home": the house filled with oversized rats and my mother and my brother withered away? I had not seen Janie in years, and the sight of her—the most sophisticated of the three sisters, with a quiet strength born of maintaining a chilly distance from people around her—invested me with confidence. I was made of the same stuff.

My family looked fine. I set about convincing my mother to follow through on her plan to move to Florida. My brother didn't want to go, but I said there was nothing for her in White City. Emboldened by the tangible knowledge—for the first time—that I would really escape this dismal place, I told my mother she must leave forever. I was liberated and I wanted to emancipate her too. For days, she avoided me, complaining I was pressuring her. I persisted, exploiting the face time I had left before I flew to California, never to live in this house again.

She left New Jersey a week after I did.

For my mother's forty-fourth birthday, I gave her an all-expenses-paid trip from Florida to California for my graduation from Stanford. She had come out once before, at Thanksgiving my freshman year. Then, she slept at my aunt and uncle's house on the Presidio army base. This time, she stayed in my on-campus apartment. I felt a little ashamed that I couldn't put her up in a hotel. But it was fun sharing my apartment with her. I felt like she was living the college experience that she had always deserved.

We talked late into the night about how far we had come together—it was because of her that I had made it, I said—and about what the future might hold for us. We talked about her anger over the fact that my father had not been there through any of it. I consoled her and suppressed my resentment at the man I had met only a few years earlier and still hoped to have a relationship with. My brother was already working and soon I would be too.

"It's time for me to pay attention to me now," my mother said. I prayed she would.

As soon as the International Relations ceremony broke up, I pulled my mother to the registrar's window at Old Union, as she tried to hold on to the big white hat that she had bought for the occasion. We were so giddy we were almost jogging. I was dying to see what a master's degree looked like. My white velvet hood, trimmed in red and black satin, flew out behind me.

As the student-clerk stuck a calligraphed page into a faux-leather binder, he smiled and said, "Congratulations."

Delirious, I shook his hand and said, "Thank you."

Outside, we grabbed a student and asked him take a picture of us, me holding my bachelor's degree, Mom holding the master's, Hoover Tower in the background. I told her that the master's was hers. Aping the old white men I had seen all day, I stood before my mother and made the impromptu presentation: "For all the work you have done toward this degree," I intoned, handing it to her with a firm handshake. She was crying. She said she couldn't accept the diploma until she had her own place to live, her own apartment or house, where it could be properly displayed.

Five years later, it would still be sitting next to the lesser degree on a bookshelf in my apartment overlooking the Seine.

....

It was 1989 and we were living large. From the balcony of our Upper East Side high-rise, the midtown skyline sprawled at our feet; at this angle, the neon *Newsweek* sign hung directly below the lighted top of the Empire State Building. My roommate, a college buddy (Mark, the "Republican from Kansas"), worked on Wall Street as an investment banker, and I wrote for *Newsweek*. We were both twenty-two, our household income skirted six figures.

Every morning, I rolled sleepily to the health club in our building and exercised for an hour and a half. After a fresh-squeezed orange juice and a piece of fruit, I hustled to the Lexington Avenue train, riding three stops to Fiftieth Street. Every Friday night, our late night at *Newsweek*, staffers ate at a fancy midtown restaurant, another luxury I had never known before. And on weekends, I got discount tickets to plays, went to the movies, discovered tony restaurants or hung at home and watched TV.

And yet, I refused to accept the worst. I adamantly denied that I was a yuppie. I insisted to engineer friends who earned less than I did that journalism was a public-service job. And I couldn't be a buppie—one of those spoiled rich kids I had hated at Stanford: upper-middle-class African-Americans who disdained anybody who didn't wear the right designer or drive the right car (read: the rest of us). I would go off at the mere suggestion. I had always looked down on *them*. First, as a poor kid, because I had worked for what I had. And second, because as a preppie snob Lawrenceville had taught me graces that the nouveau riche noir could never master. They were too material to appreciate intellect or originality.

I didn't accept my yuppiedom until my mother and my brother visited my apartment and told me I had no choice: I was buppie. Buppie, but not proud. My family still lived in poverty. I gave my mother money now and then, and eventually she moved in with me. But for now, the old guilt came surging back.

When I arrived in New York two days after graduation, I wondered if I could do the job. I had practiced journalism during a few summers but had no idea how to do it every day, day in and day out. What had I set myself up for? I figured I wanted a job that could flow seamlessly from work to life to play. I imagined something fascinating, ever-changing, challenging. I thought journalism would do, especially since *Newsweek* had offered me a job and all. But I held on to my Yale deferment—just in case.

Newsweek was reputed to be less snooty and self-important than *Time*: younger, more brash, more liberal. Perhaps more importantly, the business section was a study in diversity: both Whitaker and the head researcher were black. Despite my almost absolute faith in integration and my history of "hanging white" in college, working in a department where both managers were black gave me an immediate sense of security.

Having a mentor guaranteed growth. Dianne McDonald, the head researcher, sternly admonished me about everything from misspellings in my copy to my habit, once I settled in, of walking around in stocking feet.

"Larry always does it," I protested.

"You are *not* Larry, she said.

Whitaker shredded my copy, told me how a proper *Newsweek* story would have been organized, then sent me back to rewrite it. He rarely smiled. Every time I sat in the chair opposite his desk, I felt the sweat gather on my back.

The business department was far more than a ghetto, though; it was a functional family—by *Newsweek* standards, anyway. It was the only section where the senior editor, writers and researchers would go to dinner together on Friday nights. I instantly assumed the role of promising little brother: rambunctious, temperamental, self-conscious, eager. The four other writers and the researchers provided ideas, criticism, guidance and hazing.

The trick to writing a *Newsweek* article was to make the piece read effortlessly, describe an event and relate it to the universe around it while propelling the reader forward. Words and images figured as prominently as facts and stats. A global network of correspondents allowed a writer in New York to present firsthand accounts of news from continents away. On weeks when I reported and wrote a story without information from the bureaus, I spent three days interviewing and researching, and two days composing. I kneaded through the information, turned it on its head and finally dressed it in vivid prose. We had the time to give news the luxury of language. It was like TV for intellectuals.

Enthralled, I glided through the first months at 444 Madison Avenue. Then, in March 1990, we ran a cover story called "Rap Rage." I started reading it innocently on a Tuesday morning as I boarded the No. 4 train at Eighty-Sixth Street. When I exited at Fiftieth my face burned. By the time I reached Madison Avenue, I was furious. I marched into my editor's office. Mark was the business editor and this was an arts cover, but I didn't know where else to turn.

"Have you read this?" I asked, quoting the sections I had

underlined in red ink: "Let's talk about 'attitude' . . . as in, you'd better not be bringing any attitude around here, boy, and, when that bitch gave me some attitude, I cut her good . . .

Rap's most visible contribution has been the disinterment of the word nigger . . . bombastic, self-aggrandizing and yet as scary as sudden footsteps in the dark . . . taken sex out of teenage culture, substituting brutal fantasies of penetration and destruction."

The embodiment of all this danger was cover boy Tone-Lōc, composer of rap's most playful ditties, like "Wild Thing." But the article had next to nothing to do with Tone-Lōc. Looking up from my limp magazine, I asked, "How can we ignore the majority of the hottest music in the country, examine the rawest lyrics of two groups (Public Enemy and NWA) and then pass it off as representative? We never even explain what rap is."

I told him the story made me ashamed to work at *Newsweek*. He suggested I express myself if I felt so strongly. Almost unthinkingly—maybe, only unthinkingly—I fired off a memo to the editors.

To their credit, they responded quickly. I met with the Wallenda (the title given to the highest echelon of editors at *Newsweek*) who had top-edited the magazine and the senior editor who had supervised the cover story. I put on my most rational and objective face—an "angry black man" would be less effective. I wasn't even sure what I was trying to affect. The damage was already done. (For years afterward *Newsweek* reporters and writers would have to answer for the piece every time they talked to a rap artist or producer.)

The Wallenda told me how disconcerting he had found my memo. The senior editor nodded her agreement. We all looked very grave. He asked me what exactly I had found offensive about the article. I unfurled the list, careful to quote only the factually inaccurate passages. When taken together, they misrepresented the music. They suggested an insensitivity, even prejudice, against young African-American men. I assured them that I didn't think anyone connected with the piece had racist intentions. I said it twice.

The Wallenda summed up my comments, "So, if there had been a sentence stating that this was not all rap music, just one variant, that would have corrected the story?" His comment was reductive, to say the least, but I conceded. "Yes, that sentence, defining the subject of the article, would have made all the difference."

In fairness, someone probably would have inserted the necessary sentence if the writers, editors and Wallendas who normally wrote music stories had not been on vacation. But the acting editor-in-chief decided to do the story anyway. The "Rap Rage" author, one of *Newsweek*'s best, had never actually listened to rap music. He told me he had been given a stack of lyrics on Friday night and was told to write the cover story. The only black *Newsweek*er who had worked on the piece, a twenty-year veteran correspondent and the Atlanta bureau chief, had demanded his name be removed when he saw the final piece. Yet, no alarm bells had sounded for the editors in New York.

We all shook hands, smiled and adjourned. But *Newsweek* was publicly flogged for weeks in music and press columns around the country for a narrow-minded article. In the future, the magazine would be more careful, vetting such stories through African-American reporters. When we produced a cover on the black family, *Newsweek* flew the Atlanta bureau chief and a black Washington correspondent, both of whom had worked on the project, to New York so they could participate in the editing. Some white staffers—who had far less control over their final copy—charged political correctness and hypersensitivity to minority anger.

The real problem was not the composition of articles, but the composition of the staff. In a writing crew of about seventy when I started, *Newsweek* had only two black writers (including me). My boss in the business section was the only African-American editor, and there were no Asian or Latino writers or editors. The correspondent field looked more diverse: four out of about forty domestic correspondents were black. There were no blacks overseas or among the Wallendas. Traditionally, in the same way that newspapers reflected the local white ethnic makeup of the city they covered (Irish, Italian), newsmagazines had been notorious bastions of Ivy League WASPdom. Management said it was attempting to recruit minorities. They always said that: they couldn't attract blacks to the magazine, and once they did, they couldn't convince them to stay.

We had such a minority shortage that when rioting broke out in Crown Heights, Brooklyn, between Lubavitcher Jews and blacks (a relatively small story for a national publication), I was flown to New York from Washington, where I'd been working. When rioting erupted in Los Angeles in the spring of 1992, I was imported from DC along with two other African-American correspondents, one from Atlanta and one from Detroit. I was happy to cover a big story, but frustrated that these were the only big stories I got to cover. Crown Heights and Los Angeles were disturbing reminders of why blacks had been admitted to American newsrooms in the first place: to report the bloody conflagrations of the late 1960s. Twenty years later, it seemed little had changed at the newsmagazines, anyway.

Despite *Newsweek*'s declared desire to hire more minorities, by mid-1994 there were fewer black reporters, editors and writers than when I arrived in 1989. There was an African-American in the foreign correspondent corps (me) and my former business editor was now a Wallenda, but there were only two black reporters in our domestic bureaus, one African-American writer and no black senior editors. There was one Latino and one Asian-American reporter.

I do not advocate numerical quotas (the above inventory notwithstanding), but it is difficult to understand how any analytical, general-interest newsmagazine cannot accomplish a goal that it says is a top priority: hiring a more ethnically diverse body of journalists. Women have done relatively well at *Newsweek*; they comprise almost half the players at every level of the magazine. Hauling correspondents to New York to edit special projects would not be necessary if at every stage of the journalistic enterprise there were more diverse participation.

In recent years, the only African-American hires above the level of researcher had been contributing editors, who are not considered staff. Then, in 1994, a series of unfortunate coincidences occurred and *Newsweek* got serious.

First—and most important, according to several editors—Washington Post Company CEO Donald Graham told *Newsweek*'s top editors that we *had* to hire and promote more qualified minorities. Graham, who had been heading the *Post* for many years, added *Newsweek* to his responsibilities in 1993 when he also became chairman of the board. Suddenly he got a close-up look at the world of newsmagazines and was scandalized by the dearth of people of color (the *Post*, like most large dailies, was far more diverse). What had been a hollow commitment, according to many editors, became a priority.

Second, a younger generation of editors, who had come of age when blacks were present in newspaper newsrooms—and who

had black colleagues—enthusiastically supported Graham's directive. Mark Whitaker (who had hired me), the only African-
American manager at the magazine, had made it clear when he
was promoted to Wallenda that *Newsweek* had a serious problem.
New chief of correspondents Ann McDaniel began recruiting
promising researchers and reporters. The business editor and the
lifestyle editor (both of whom had worked at dailies) stole promi-
nent journalists from their former publications. (Newspapers had
produced a critical mass that *Newsweek* could tap.)

The new commitment came too late to save the magazine one
young, talented African-American reporter. At about the same
time that Graham's directive on minority hiring went out, Farai
Chideya, a Washington correspondent, left *Newsweek* for MTV
News. The chief reason for her departure was what she felt was a
lack of mentoring of young reporters at the magazine (a problem
for whites as well as people of color). In a confidential memo to
the Wallendas, she cataloged a long list of problems at *Newsweek*,
dividing them into problems for young reporters and problems for
minority reporters. It is important to note that Chideya was (and
is) a friend of mine.

In her year and a half as a reporter, she was hardworking and
industrious and supplied *Newsweek* with a hip perspective that was
otherwise lacking. The magazine had succeeded in identifying
her promise. Still, despite her letting it be known that she aspired
to be a writer in New York, the fact that she had not performed
satisfactorily during a month-long writing tryout meant the editors were not going to try to elevate her writing to *Newsweek*
standards. Frustrated with a job she did not find very interesting
in a city she did not like, she left for a job that more suited her
style—and was located in New York—when the opportunity
arose. But we could have done more to keep her, for instance,

making her a New York correspondent responsible for arts and society stories. Universally, as far as I can figure, her resignation was seen as the magazine's failure to cultivate not just African-Americans but young talent, period. Significantly, it was viewed that way by editors most of all.

That represented, I hope, a positive change.* The magazine needed one. While discussing a black contributing editor's piece with a friend from Stanford I had received a harsh reminder of the racial realities that persisted even at *Newsweek* in the 1990s. The article reported that some white newspaper editors told unqualified white male applicants that they could not hire them because the next opening had to be filled by a minority or a woman. "That's what the *Newsweek* bureau chief I interviewed with told me," my friend volunteered.

"What?" I asked, incredulous.

"He said, 'If you were black, we would hire you in a minute . . .'"

I had not believed the article. It simply didn't ring true. White editors all over the country telling unqualified candidates that they would not be hired because the next post had to go to a minority . . . *in order to spare their egos?* Editors specialized in crushing egos, not coddling them. To me it seemed more like a ploy to escape responsibility for dinging the applicants; it was easier than telling the truth.

Naturally, it incited resentment of minorities in white males who were told (falsely) that they were being bypassed in order to fill quotas—when, in truth, they were not qualified. I insisted to my friend, "But when you interviewed, there were no jobs available in that bureau." Not only was my friend underqualified, but

---

When I left Newsweek in July 2007, the magazine's only African-American senior editor, there were no Wallendas of color; no black, Latino or Asian-American senior editors; two black correspondents and three black writers.

the number of blacks in that office had not increased at all in the years since his interview.

The anecdote highlighted a bitter hypocrisy of the news business: in spite of the stated intentions of editors, journalists of color are simply not being hired in significant numbers. The truth is that we remain an exotic ornament rather than an integral part of most American news organizations—despite being an integral part of American news.

At newsmagazines, in particular (where the record of hiring and promoting minorities is more dismal than at large newspapers), the Old Boy/Old Girl network supplied a tremendous number of the people we interviewed and, eventually, hired. Since the majority of our staff is white and most of the people they know are white, most new openings are filled by whites. The only way to alter the dynamic is through a concerted, sustained effort to get talented minorities through the door for interviews in the first place. Whether individual prejudice, institutional racism or benign neglect explains the lack of effort doesn't really matter. It affects the way we look at the world every day and helps to increase the communication gulf between us all.

....

After a year and a half writing for the business section, I was offered a job in *Newsweek*'s Washington bureau. The bureau chief asked for me by name. Had I been less cynical, I would have been flattered. Instead, I worried that the chief needed a black body. None of Washington's twenty reporters were African-American, and the last one had defected to *Time*. How could I leave New York for a famously competitive place where I might represent nothing more than a quota?

But images of me interviewing the president danced in my

head. If I wanted to work overseas—and I desperately did—I would eventually have to transit through Washington. I signed on.

I stopped boxing my books to ask the then-chief of correspondents when I would receive my moving bonus. He explained that *Newsweek* didn't distribute "curtain money" for temporary moves.

Bug-eyed as Buckwheat, I inquired, "*Temporary* move?" I checked with my editor. Like me, he had thought my move was a standard three-year or so stint.

The Washington bureau chief responded to my panicky phone call with his usual candor, saying that since he had to keep his staff numbers stable, my move might only be a one-year "exchange" with a correspondent he was sending to New York. "I should have told you about that," he added.

Can you say, "bad career move"? I thought to myself.

When I arrived on the eve of the Gulf War, Washington was busily gearing up and journalists were drunk with expectation. A few colleagues made time to buy me lunch. Some wanted to chart my aspirations, some to plumb the content of my character, others craved the latest New York gossip. Some simply wanted to welcome me. The Washington corps proved more terrestrial than I had anticipated. At the same time, behind a collegial simpatico, real warmth or camaraderie rarely surfaced. I missed the business department, which had more young people and more singles. Since it was one-third the size of Washington, where correspondents kept mostly to their own work, business had been far more cohesive.

I rented an apartment in Adams Morgan, the closest thing I could find to New York: the Village, the Upper West Side, Clinton and Chelsea, all in one.

Writing files—the primary occupation of a correspondent— proved more pedestrian than writing articles. The goal was to report as much information as possible, probing all sides of an issue, then regurgitate it in an orderly fashion—just like college.

Every Thursday night the office ordered in mediocre food. (Official Washington pretty much viewed nourishment as just another annoying hurdle to career advancement.) A procrastinating bachelor, I'd often find myself alone in the bureau after our regrettable repast. Having completed three days of reporting, I would begin writing my over-expansive file. Breaking only to catch *The Simpsons* and *90210*, I'd plow dizzily through the notebooks scattered about my cubbyhole office, pulling quotes from interviews with government officials and academics, statistics from books and magazines and supporting data from conference papers and graduate theses. When I had sent my dossier to New York by modem, I would stand on our balcony in the heavy early morning air, the sun often having stained the sky behind the Washington Monument in pale dawn colors. I had the greatest job anyone my age—anyone any age—could have hoped for. And I knew it.

Exhausted and exhilarated, I'd leave the bureau, half a block from the White House. I learned early on that for a black man, even an aspiring international correspondent, it was very difficult to find a cab in DC between sunset and sunrise. If I neglected to call a car beforehand, I walked home.

The capital was a frightful study in American race relations. Skin color was a reasonable indicator of the tasks one performed, despite Washington having the second largest black middle class of any American city. Blacks seemed to mostly collect the garbage and clean the city; at best, they comprised its bureaucracy. Whites mainly wore suits and ran the country. White women often avoided black men on the sidewalk, however we dressed. Once, after leaving a White House interview with National Security

Advisor Brent Scowcroft, I stepped off the curb at K Street where cars were stopped at a red light. I was still swollen with self-importance when I heard a cascade of automatic door locks as I crossed the intersection. Merely seeing me, a black man in a suit, who had just left the White House after an interview with the president's most powerful advisor on national security, was a reminder to the white drivers that they had to be wary of crime.

The only upside of working in DC was collaborating with superlative journalists. I learned far more reporting in Washington than I had writing in New York. Correspondents performed the real work of journalism: they cultivated sources, unearthed stories, interviewed people who refused to talk. They gathered the facts that made the writing more than just pretty prose.

To my surprise, I also discovered a second *Newsweek* mentor in Washington—the bureau chief. Six months into my tour, he transferred me from the Labor Department to number two at State. The chance to report on a major beat, even in the second tier (Asia, Latin America and the Caribbean), excited my greatest ambitions, and I stepped closer to an overseas post.

Initially, he had been as suspicious of me as I was of him. Before I accepted his offer to move to DC, having worked only a year and a half in New York, I asked *Newsweek* to fly me to Washington. The bureau chief obliged; he even had me to his house for dinner. But afterward he told colleagues that my persistent questions about what the bureau had to offer *me* were the height of youthful arrogance. I think he assumed it related to being black— an affirmative action case with an attitude. In fact, it bore much more directly to my prep school heritage, one of the many experiences Evan Thomas and I shared.

We both had attended elite universities. He had gone to law

school; I had almost gone. While neither of us trusted the other's objectivity—merely because of race and class—both of us respected the other's professionalism. Together, we explored the deficiencies of black leadership and the unstated fear of black men (years before Jesse Jackson admitted his own). We fought, sparred and challenged each other. We compromised. I learned to criticize the black community fairly, without giving in to the facile critiques in vogue in the early nineties. I think he did too.

Only once did I lose a debate outright. I walked into Evan's office with a sheet of computer paper. "I think we should do a story on DC statehood," I said, floating it onto his desk.

"No," he said, floating it back without looking at it.

"Why not?" I asked, prepared for resistance.

He gave me all the clichéd reasons DC should not be a state: too small, too few residents, conflicts of interest between federal and local governments. After each argument, I gave the equally well-worn rebuttal that purported to refute it.

Finally, he said, "DC is so mismanaged, the government is so fucked up . . ."

"And if those were criteria, we would have a lot fewer states," I said. (The second requirement for a *Newsweek* story—after "pictures"—was tension, and this one had that.)

He said, "OK. If you think you can make it work, give it a try."

But my enthusiasm was spent. "No, that's OK."

Unfortunately, I had defeated myself before the bout even began. I had convinced myself he wouldn't buy the story—and if he did, he wouldn't enthusiastically push to get it in the magazine. I had actually entered his office a loser—because I believed that almost any white male journalist held a trump card, actually two, when it came to news judgment: he was white and he was male, two of the principal bases for "objectivity" in American journalism. (This applied especially to stories that could be construed as "black stories," like DC statehood.) Journalists of color were often solicited only for "perspective," or ass covering.

To some degree, news organizations were justified in their perception—as evidenced by African-American journalists' particular sense of dread each time our publications turned their sights on blacks. "Oh, my God, what are we going to say now?" *Newsweek* staffers asked each other when a black story was scheduled. Calculating a reaction to the piece was the truest test of political acumen. Pipe up too early and get pegged as an oversensitive minority. Say nothing and risk heaven knew what horrible pronouncements appearing in a national weekly.

Many journalists of color feel they have a sort of missionary role to play. Our dilemma is often one of wanting to educate white Americans on minority issues and perspectives, but at the same time not be relegated to covering only racial stories. For me, it echoed back to my time at Lawrenceville and Stanford. As I had then, at *Newsweek* I felt two conflicting impulses: one, to blend in and enjoy the challenges and rewards all journalists crave; the other, to set myself apart and assume the taxing role of educator. In the end, I believed the latter to be an obligation—at least for me—at a mainstream publication. Black man's burden. It invested me with a larger sense of purpose than wanting to receive a paycheck and get my name in the magazine. It was also a way to alleviate the survivor's guilt of escaping poverty, while so many people around me were stuck in it. It is not easy for editors to deal with these conflicting desires—the same reporter who will complain about being assigned a black story one week may bitch about not being consulted on one the next. But, with patience and communication, I think most editors and reporters can find a mutually beneficial, flexible compromise. (My bureau chief and I would.)

But while blacks had to consciously balance journalistic objectivity and their racial identification, it was assumed white men did not. Their perspectives supposedly set the standards of objectivity. (There were exceptions: When a white reporter's brother worked in the White House, for instance, he was unfairly assumed to be in the tank whenever he had something positive to say about Bill Clinton.) But, being doubted for your affiliations or those of your relatives is not the same as being suspect because of your identity. For the most part, white men were "journalists," we were "black journalists" or "women journalists" or "gay journalists." The danger of being labeled kept ambitious minorities and women from confronting all but the most egregious examples of prejudice.

My first fall in Washington, I was planning to accept my friend Fabrice's offer to tour Gabon. Fabrice was a French friend from my year as an exchange student in Paris. He had grown up in Africa. He also suggested, as if it were the most natural thing in the world, that we spend two weeks in South Africa after my week in Gabon. I was surprised.

"Can a black man and a white man travel around that country together, legally? Can any black American stomach 'visiting' such an evil place?"

I conducted a poll; I asked African-American friends if it was race betrayal to spend money in aparatheid South Africa. I asked Jewish colleagues if they would have toured Hitler's Germany in 1933.

Since South Africa was undergoing a radical transformation, these moments would never be lived again. I had reported on Mandela's visit to the US just the year before, after 27 years in prison, and had seen him electrify a group of black schoolkids and adults, people I had thought too disillusioned to have heroes. He kindled the kind of hope in their eyes that I had seen only in movies. My trepidation turned to fascination. I had to see.

Driving from Jan Smuts airport, Johannesburg glittered like any Western metropolis. Towering, sprawling, rich. On the streets of South Africa, black people and white people walked side by side. They went to work. They went to the movies. They shopped. And, at the end of the day, they formed long bus lines to go home. Black people took orders behind the counters of fast-food restaurants, hauled the trash, swept the halls and cleaned the gutters. Most of the people who walked the streets in suits and ties were white. White women avoided me on the sidewalk.

The similarities should not have surprised me: two vast nations carved out of a hostile wilderness, two great Christian peoples subduing an inhospitable land and a pagan race that aggressed them, two manifest destinies. Standing inside the Voortrekker Monument, tracing the contours of panel after panel of bas reliefs showing Zulu savages ravaging white frontierswomen and killing Afrikaner children, the trace of Native American in my own blood, inherited from Georgia Cherokees, cried out. I turned away in shame, not for the South Africans' necessary lie, but for my own nation's myths and genocides.

From the moment we touched down, Fabrice and I argued about the South African situation. For most of a week we fought, from Johannesburg to the jacaranda-scented suburbs of Pretoria, from Durban to Cape Town.

Having grown up in Gabon, Fabrice found South Africa enchanting. "I never knew there was a country this rich in black Africa," he said admiringly. "If only we could replicate this on the whole continent . . ."

True, it was one of the most beautiful countries I had ever seen. The landscape was as diverse as America's and large patches of it lay untouched. Yet, wherever we stood, however crystal clear the water or humbling the vista, I was conscious of the millions of dispossessed we didn't see.

"You can't eat democracy," Fabrice observed at one point.

"What good is life if you're not free?" I asked. "Have you never heard 'Give me liberty or give me death?'"

"Well, most of Africa is getting death," he retorted, accusing me of being a naïve American. "Like all those Peace Corps volunteers that try to judge whites who live in Africa. They don't know Africa. We know Africa."

I called him a racist colonizer. His relationship with his Gabonese workers had disgusted me. In Lambaréné, especially, the employees at the beverage factory he supervised behaved like children to his *patron*. Men three times his age, elderly women— all treated him as if he had the power to bestow immortality. I knew better than to expect an idyllic motherland in Africa, but I had no idea how bleak it would be. Black people, it turned out, were free nowhere, not even in our own land. It looked like our friendship would be yet another casualty of apartheid. We agreed to stop arguing; instead, we stopped talking.

Wherever we encountered South Africans, white or black, they would pummel me with questions. Blacks thought I hailed from paradise.

"Are all black people rich in America?" a housewife inquired over tea in her tin and cardboard "house" in Soweto.

"Do you know Michael Jordan? Michael Jackson? Mike Tyson?" an adolescent boy asked eagerly in a burger joint in downtown Johannesburg.

White people interrogated me too. They figured that somehow my presence meant a reprieve from their status as international pariahs. Sitting in a motel in the rural town of Beaufort Wes, deep in the middle of South Africa, I watched the Rugby World Cup with white Afrikaners while the owner plied me with free beer. My drinking partners were stunned to find out that I had played rugby in high school and college. They told me how South Africa had been misjudged by the world and misrepresented by the media. We didn't understand that blacks there were not educated like blacks in America. In many countries, it seemed white people preached "our" blacks are worse than "your" blacks.

Throughout our trek, whites turned to me and asked, "What do *you* think of South Africa?" They actually expected me to say it was a spectacularly beautiful country. I obliged, then said it was too bad not all its citizens were free. Only once, crossing a "border" at three in the morning between the Ciskei homeland and South Africa, did I respond, "I think it is a very sad place. It breaks my heart. May I have my passport back?"

Our two days stranded in mostly Afrikaner Beaufort Wes (we were there because Fabrice had driven off the road in the middle of the night) managed to affect my friend's perception of South Africa. A flock of poor black children followed him everywhere he went, their tiny arms extended, begging for food or money. They never approached me. None of them spoke English.

"This country makes me sick," he said as we boarded the bus

for Johannesburg. "Even in Gabon, the people are not reduced to this. They have their pride."

. . . .

Immediately after I returned from South Africa, Secretary of State Jim Baker embarked on a diplomatic mission to Asia. My bureau chief thought I should accompany him. My first foreign assignment. There was little work, since I had no sources in Tokyo, Beijing or Seoul, and the State Department spoon-fed us what they wanted us to know. No one did much reporting; the newspaper correspondents filed on what Washington told us. The rest of the time we traveled on "shop ops," shopping opportunities, to find the best bargains in whatever city we were visiting. In South Korea, one correspondent had two suits tailored in an afternoon for half the price he would have paid at home. In Beijing, I loaded up on silks for my mother and my girlfriend and a down coat for my brother.

The trips I made overseas, including an excursion to Cuba, convinced the editors that I had a genuine interest in foreign news. Just after the Clinton Inaugural in January 1993, they transferred me to the Paris bureau. Colleagues I had never met and who had rarely read my files were certain that it was because I was black. I had no doubt that being a "rare commodity" had helped me get the assignment, but that rarity included strong reporting and writing ability, as well as the promise of future growth—not just being black. But for some colleagues, I was merely an affirmative action baby headed to France.

When I was hired, it had been the same story. Even before I arrived for the interviews, rumors circulated that I was getting the job because I was black. One white male fact checker complained openly to his boss that he should get the job. Did he know

I had a master's degree? Did he know I spoke fluent French? Did he know that I had been a wire editor at the *Daily* and a reporter for the *Boston Globe*? Did he have any idea what my qualifications were? Did he know me? No. And he had started at *Newsweek* with far less experience. No one had ever called into question my credentials like that in college or at Lawrenceville.

It had already become a mantra in my fledgling professional life. "Because you're black . . ." they would start; then they would go on to explain how I had received the promotion because I belonged to this privileged race. One of my Washington colleagues was honest enough to tell me that he thought himself "at least as qualified" for Paris as I was. But, as a liberal, he told me, he supported my getting the job instead of him. It was the price of creating an equal society—and he accepted it. I told him I didn't think he was as qualified as I was, but I agreed that if he were one of the rare minorities at the magazine he would have had a better chance of getting promoted. Even though there were more blacks who stalled at *Newsweek* than advanced.

A white editor had told another black correspondent once, "We all resent Marcus." I thought he was kidding, but the reporter insisted that he was serious, speculating that the editors resented having to give me great jobs, even though I was young. They felt blackmailed by the fact that I could find a job somewhere else relatively easily. My friend said as long as white editors "resented" me I would never rise to a high position at a mainstream publication, however talented I was. I disagreed. He said I was dreaming.

Standing in my bureau chief's office on a crisp January day, we explored the challenges and rewards that Paris would offer. Overly sentimental, I wanted to thank him for all he had taught me—not just newsmagazine politics, at which he was a true master, but the fundamentals of good journalism: the value of persistence, the importance of clear analysis. I wanted to tell him I was happy we had overcome our differences, to confess how much I had feared him, how I had steeled myself for disappointment and how reaffirming it had been to gain his respect. I wanted to tell him I was better for the experience.

The closest I came was "I can't tell you how much I've learned. Despite," I spoke in an uneven cadence, "some . . . initial . . . misgivings, I think we worked well together—and I just wanted to thank you."

Unfailingly cool, Evan acknowledged I was valued and liked.

We discussed the hostility I had already sensed on the part of some white male co-workers. He assured me that that was the price one paid for being successful and black. Of course I knew that. My grandmother had told me long before.

Yet, on a visit back to DC once I was living in Paris, my mentor explained that most people realized I was in Paris because I deserved it.

"You would be overseas if you weren't black," he said. "You might not be in Paris, but you would be somewhere." It was as if he had forgotten the long months of machinations over my future. He knew better than anyone why I was in Paris: because another editor didn't want a novice in a one-person bureau overseas (white or a person of color).

Shakespeare said "there is nothing either good or bad but thinking makes it so." He should have said nothing is true or false—but white folks thinking things make them so. It is not that white people are stronger willed or have a greater effect on the universe, but in America they constitute an overwhelming majority, so their perceptions matter in a way that nothing else does, including facts. It is now politically correct for Caucasian Americans to feel they have a worse lot in life than minorities—despite studies, statistics and plain old common sense. When *Newsweek* surveyed white men for a cover titled "White Male Paranoia," 29 percent thought that white men had a worse chance than nonwhites and women of being accepted to university. Twenty-four percent thought that they had less chance of getting a union job and 23 percent thought they were at a relative disadvantage for gaining political appointments.[*] A 1992 People for the American Way report found that 49 percent of white fifteen- to twenty-four-year-olds thought it more likely that "qualified whites lose out on scholarships, jobs, and promotions because minorities get special preference" than that qualified minorities are denied those opportunities because of racial prejudice.[†]

Before being assigned to Paris, I had fought for the Johannesburg bureau. The editors had rebuffed me. But Evan seemed to have forgotten all the melodrama and had rewritten history to read that I received a cushy post because I was a black. Even a mentor who respected my work, who had been instrumental in engineering my foreign assignment, could not explain my career path without implicating black privilege. It was telling: white people assumed that their black colleagues, however talented, were beneficiaries of affirmative action. For them, it was a certainty of American corporate life, usually left unspoken.

Like my colleague who thought he should have been moving to Paris instead of me, my former boss was inadvertently pointing out a genuine dilemma of affirmative action: the legitimate resentment of some white men who are qualified for jobs, but lose out to minorities or women who are less qualified. It happened. There was no reason to deny it—at least not a good one. And no one could fault the angry white guy for his resentment. But, such instances of

---

[*]*March 29, 1993.*
[†]*"Young and Guilty by Stereotype,"* Holly Sklar, Z Magazine, *July/August 1993.*

reverse discrimination are few and far between—if they were as common as garden-variety prejudice, institutional racism and Old Boy networks, the ranks of corporate America would boast more than a handful of token women and minorities. Wouldn't they?

Nonetheless, the lion's share of Americans are absolutely convinced that reverse discrimination outweighs racism: 46 percent versus 23 percent, according to a 1995 *Newsweek* poll.* As long as even one qualified white male was passed over for a minority, he would be bitter—and the legions of other white men, actually less qualified than the person of color to whom they had lost the promotion, would use affirmative action as an excuse to explain their shortcomings. (It was an inversion of minorities using racism for the same purpose.) Any managed unfairness, however noble the goal, was bound to incur the wrath of the newly "disadvantaged." Even if affirmative action were based on class rather than race, as pundits like Stephen Carter, William Julius Wilson and others recommend, the majority would still rebel—and eventually end the attempt to correct for past discrimination.

America seems trapped at an impasse: We cannot grant disadvantaged minorities opportunity—say, helping poor kids from White City go to great universities—without arousing the anger of members of the majority. The cascading backlash has already begun. We are probably destined to remain a desert of inequality with a handful of minorities, most affluent to begin with, admitted to rare oases of opportunity. This reality should not lead African-Americans to relinquish our individual or collective goals. Instead, it should fortify our determination. This struggle is our history. It is also our present.

---

*"*Affirmative Action: Race & Rage*," Newsweek, *April 3, 1995.*

I was flying from Paris to Naples, Italy, to cover a dog-and-pony show aboard the *USS Roosevelt*. The editors in New York knew the trip would prove uneventful but thought that we should suck up to the navy in case the US actually did intervene in the Bosnian war. I went gladly, ending a trip to Algeria, which was wracked by civil war, earlier than planned. I knew this was the chief of correspondents' way of giving me a break after the frustrations of arriving in Paris and being unable to shoehorn a story into either the domestic or international edition for a month.

I almost missed takeoff, sprinting the distance from passport control to my gate. It wasn't the first time I reached my seat in business class and had an amazed white woman stare at me as I asked her to move over so I could get to my seat. Ashen-faced, she squashed herself so far into her seat it must have hurt. Smug, sweaty and offended, I peered out the window as we pulled away from the terminal.

I loved takeoff. If I managed to stay awake while the plane taxied gently over the runway—usually I drifted off—I would say a prayer thanking the Lord for the privilege of flight when so many didn't have it and asking him to keep us in the palm of his hand until we came to rest again on solid ground. Amen. Then, swoosh . . .

By the time the flight attendant took second drink orders, I had once again assumed my Good-Negro persona, no longer hating my neighbor for her ignorance or her suffocating, if expensive, perfume. I was reconciled, well balanced. I asked the flight attendant for an orange juice. Impressed by my three phrases of French, and since I was reading a *Newsweek*, my neighbor smiled as I took my glass from the tray.

"You speak French marvelously," she said. "Are you of mixed ancestry?"

The question.

"Thank you very much," I said. "No, I studied in high school and in college; most of my teachers were native speakers," I continued, as I often did, and unveiled my life to a white person who thought it strange that a creature like me existed. "I also studied for six months in Paris at university."

"Oh, that's wonderful," she glowed. "What a great opportunity. How did you get here? Was it an exchange program?"

Briefing most white people I met was an enormous pain in the ass, but I lived by the credo "If I don't, who will?"—especially in international business class. As a foreign correspondent, I felt I was even more of a racial ambassador than I had been in college.

"I went to Stanford . . . from a lower-class family . . ." I always added that just after the language and degree disclosure, lest my listener think I issued from the real-life Huxtables and was the son of a doctor or lawyer. Now, they would have to admit I started out black and poor. I wanted to volunteer that I had grown up on welfare, food stamps, free lunch and summer jobs programs . . . and that racism was a bigger impediment than poverty and that I wasn't the only smart boy in my neighborhood . . . that I was just one of the lucky few who got out . . . and that it sucked to be a black man in America . . . and there were thousands just like me rotting in prisons or under gravestones because they didn't have my mother and my grandmother and scholarships and teachers and hope and faith and arrogance . . .

Instead, I smiled back at her beaming face and said, "Yes, America truly is a remarkable country."

....

The Metro zoomed through the Palais Royal/Musée du Louvre station. A high-toned whistle sounded and the doors swooshed shut, banging me back to reality. I was looking at Sam, my mouth open, my jaw slack.

"What? . . . You don't *un-der-stand?*"

"No," my best friend said, with bracing assurance. "What's your point?"

I crushed the pages in my right hand. "What don't you understand?" Heat slowly mounted toward my temples, tension gripping my head. I wanted to be reasonable, logical, intelligent.

"Well, Harvard is a private institution and it has a right to admit whomever it wants. It's their prerogative."

Attempting to sound objective, I said painstakingly, "What I am saying is that yes, they are two different things . . . one is preferential treatment based on race, the other is preferential treatment based on your parents' academic affiliation.

"What I am saying—and what I believe the author of this article is trying to say—is that America is irate, up in arms, red in the face over the former, but couldn't care less about the latter. Call the former affirmative action and the latter elitism.

"What the author—and I," I was losing my battle with myself to keep my temper, "are saying is that there is only one explanation for that apparent discrepancy."

I was going to blow.

"America is racist. It is a racist country where no one cares about preferential admission for children of alumni, but everyone protests half as many places going to niggers and spics."

I had blown—sank from objective reasoned discourse to berating, ranting, raving, victimized finger pointing. Still, I pressed onward. Sam failed to understand one of the basic issues of our times, one of the fundamental realities of my life: white people's opposition to affirmative action had a lot less to do with fairness than it did with race. They were virulently opposed to it, not because their Johnny would be deprived of a Stanford education, but because they thought that their race was losing out to the dark horses. It was about power and access.

We emerged from Pont-Marie station into the chilly Paris night, Sam already apologetic. "I'm not supporting either feeling—that either type of preferential treatment is bad. I don't care that they're pissed off," he smirked. "That's their problem." "They" were the white folks who had not gone to Harvard or Stanford. Sam had naturally included me in the "us" versus "them" calculus. To him I was part of the elite. But my mind had already transformed me and Sam into warriors from separate and unequal camps. After all, Samuel Tribble Crews VI, descendent of the first Englishmen to settle the New World, could shrug off the hatred of the teeming white masses. But for me, even walking across a centuries-old bridge beneath the lights of Paris, they were present and oppressive. Reflecting on Sam's at-once elitist and naïve dismissal, I had to laugh. He really didn't understand.

The quote that had sparked our argument was: "the many children of color who succeed educationally despite the obstacles are often portrayed upon entering college as subpar beneficiaries of 'reverse discrimination.' Meanwhile, without stigma (or bestseller 'exposés'), there is de facto affirmative action for White and wealthier alumni offspring who don't otherwise meet the college's 'standards' despite their more privileged childhood. A *Boston Globe* (September 18, 1991) article on so-called 'legacy admissions' noted that the acceptance rate for all Harvard applicants, class of 1992, was 15.6 percent while for children of alumni, 35.2 percent. As the article put it, 'far from being more qualified, or even equally qualified, the average admitted legacy at Harvard between 1981 and 1988 was significantly *less* qualified than the average nonlegacy.' "*

White class tension—seldom examined, rarely acknowledged—paled in comparison to white racism: Caucasians who had not attended Harvard were less bothered by the children of alumni getting a break than they were if black children got one. It was a constant in the American social equation: even poor white folks on the bottom of the economic ladder could at least consider themselves better than black people. As long as they believed they could rise above their birth, they did not revolt against privilege—indeed, most Americans did not believe classes existed. The middle class sustained itself on the conviction that one day they would be rich, if only they worked hard enough; with the exception of a relatively few populist movements, they did not challenge elitist privilege because, firstly, they denied it, and secondly, they wanted to keep it in place, so that when they "made it," they could benefit from it.

Black kids going to Harvard upset those delicately maintained myths of race and class. If significant numbers of African-Americans became more prosperous than whites, racial superiority—a myth that had kept poor whites despising blacks more than they did rich whites for three hundred years—might become unhinged. Poor and middle-class whites might start to see everyone with money as the enemy, whatever their color. That would jeopardize the entire system of denial. Luckily, as the article showed, racism remained far more pervasive than class resentment, and very few minorities were going to Harvard (less than eight percent of the student body was black).

I had read the article aloud, anticipating a reflexive *amen* from Sam. Black nationalists—and most other black folks—said true

* *Sklar, 1993.*

friendship with whites was impossible. Sitting with the person with whom I had shared every secret of my life—and most of the laughs since university—this was one of the humiliating moments when I feared they were right.

During our travels in Europe, race kept coming back at us like a boomerang. Standing beside him on Mount Ugall, studying the Bay of San Sebastian, I had felt alone and distant. The shallow inlet looked like a saucer of blue milk likely to float over its sand rim with the slightest jar. It had started to pour rain during our ascent and was only now letting up. I tried to stem my anger and self-pity—to remember why we were friends—but every time I looked at him, the rage crept up the back of my throat. His arrogance, his certainty, his promise all mocked me. From the beginning of our trip he had been haughty and presumptuous. Was it the master's degree in engineering or living in a house of men who'd attended Andover—or was it simply that post-collegiate Sam was self-absorbed?

No matter what line of reasoning I pursued, I always returned to the same loathsome racist equation: he was a white man—with all the egotistical fringe benefits. He could walk into a room and command immediate respect—or at least not start from a negative and have to prove himself. As long as he walked with the self-assured gait and the bright eyes of the educated, he would never be questioned or rejected. Or so it seemed to me.

Sam didn't feel he was taking liberties by insisting he have his way, whether deciding which path to trace back to our pension or plowing through a throng of locals. He had pocketed some Spanish coins from my study before we left and thought so little about it that he only mentioned it when I commented that I thought I had had more.

"I took most of the big denominations," he chuckled. His sense of entitlement was astounding—and completely instinctive. Looking into his laughing face, I wanted to dash him on the rocks below, where the Atlantic surged violently.

"By what right?" I asked, taking on the arcane language of his forefathers.

I wanted him to answer, "Because I'm a white man." And he had at times, in the protection of warm moments of friendship and humor, but to do so in the course of a fight would have been an unbearable admission, for both of us.

"I don't know," he shrugged.

Sensing a legitimate cover to penalize him for all his arrogance, I upbraided him. It wasn't the first time. While marveling at Moorish and Islamic achievements in Spain—in Granada, Seville and Cordoba—I had already inflicted my rekindled ethnic pride on him. Like a dagger, I'd thrown it at him, the only white person present.

Sam and I had been best friends since I was his RA at Stanford. He was one of the most mature eighteen-year-olds I had ever met and one of the most tolerant people I ever knew. He was instinctively racially aware. He quickly became part of my circle of favorite frosh, and soon he was counseling me. He was more free of prejudice than I was. Ironically, our rare disputes over racial issues—and my thoughts that fall in Europe—were more a reflection of my frustrations and prejudices than they were of any insensitivity on his part.

The fight about the affirmative action article was a perfect example. Sam had not disagreed with me. Our argument was not over a difference of opinion. It was over his less than quick understanding of what the quote I read aloud implied. He didn't get it as soon as I wanted him to—as soon as I needed him to—to make me feel that I was right, and all the voices, black and white, that whispered constantly in my head that we should not be friends, our racial differences were too great, were wrong. His crime was that he didn't follow my vague logic. My furious reaction grew from the anger I felt generally toward white male privilege, not toward Sam. He just paid the price.

As the TGV whipped me through the French countryside back toward Paris, I escaped into Maya Angelou, reading the account of her graduation ceremony from Lafayette County Training School, where the proud assembly is shamed when an uninvited white man strolls into their midst and destroys the magic that had, for a moment, allowed them to forget that they were poor black folks living in Stamps, Arkansas.

I had been puzzling over the dilemma of how to communicate my privileged generation's racial angst. Our pain was not rooted in exclusion from the best schools or jobs anymore. I never called "po' white trash" children "Miz," or had to avoid white women's gazes. How, then, could I complain of racial injustice today as a young African-American?

As always, Auntie Maya had the answer. All those black people at the graduation had been brought down not by an ethnic slur, but by the white man reminding them, in as many words, that their diplomas were worthless, their achievement empty. On the face of it, the man announced an investment in their school: he would pave sports grounds, get new equipment for the home economics and wood shop classes. If Angelou were writing then, her readers might have asked, "How could investments in your school make anyone unhappy? Are black people crazy?" But the implicit message had been "You people are bucks and maids, hewers of wood and drawers of water." There was no question of becoming more. For the young black woman of the nineties, the corollary would run: You can go to Harvard and get a great entry-level job on Wall Street, but you can never be a chief executive, whatever your qualifications. You can never be a player. The dictum had not changed: remember, you progress at our discretion, thanks to our goodwill.

As I reached the passage where the valedictorian leads the auditorium in a grace-giving rendition of "Lift Every Voice and Sing," I cried. I used to sing that song in dark moments at school or at home. So did my mother. In Europe, I had all but forgotten it.

....

At my favorite bistro on the Isle Saint Louis, I sipped the kir that our hostess had brought and remembered to breathe. I looked across the table.

"How does it make you feel when I go off like that?" I asked Sam. I was trying to sound gregarious, but I was also genuinely curious. Friends reacted differently to what Lawrenceville classmates had called my "outbursts."

"Do you wish I would shut up? Do you see where I'm coming from? Do you see where I'm coming from *and* wish I'd shut up?"

After a slight pause, Sam murmured, "Responsible . . . I feel responsible. Not for the people who get pissed over racial preference—but for my ignorance, for not understanding. And for the unfairness."

He did not speak with the facile and fake empathy and shame of white liberal guilt. Sam was not some sixties white boy feeling that he was to *blame* for America's injustices. For the most part, our generation has grown beyond that superficial solidarity—for better and for worse. (For better because most affluent white folks no longer assume a reflexive paternalism when confronted with a black person who is worse off than they are. They don't take the no-brainer route of summoning a momentary guilt to convince themselves of their righteousness and then hurry on their way. For worse because our generation's healthy skepticism, when faced with a bad-off brother, can run to the opposite extreme, denying sympathy and wholly blaming the victim.)

I had won, but not on the grounds I had wanted. I sought an objective, rational agreement that there must be some explanation for why Americans despised racial preference but not nepotism. Instead, I had trumped him with the tattered race card. It was fair but it brought an unsatisfying victory.

Living in Paris, I disremembered that old frustration of being a black American in a white America, a hybrid—of being in perpetual negation when trying to communicate with white folks. Where they could see or hear you only in reverse because our views of the world—like whether an act was "racist"—were so different. It was like living inside a mirror. When you moved left, they saw you move right. There was no way to escape this backward universe, or to convey to your observer that he was looking at a mirror image. From his or her perspective it was the right one; how could there be any other? That's why so many African-Americans, even successful ones, grouped together: to see the world from the same side of the mirror. That way, the universe looked almost whole.

I had gladly unlearned what it was like to live in a world where the social issues were personal, where the hatreds and antagonisms affected, even afflicted, me . . . where I was the enemy. I had allowed a dusty amnesia to settle gracefully over the bitter discussions about race at Stanford and Lawrenceville and *Newsweek*.

Sam followed his confession with a plea. "I want to stay aware, but how do I?" It was a practical question, not a political one.

"You are aware," I said, understanding exactly what he meant. "Dude, you're a white guy who was working eighty hours a week trying to get a graduate degree in mechanical engineering. You lived with three other white male engineers from Stanford. However sensitive you are, you aren't black. What are you supposed to do, go home each day and take a moment of silence to think about racism?"

There was pity and frustration in my voice. I would love each American to go home at the end of the workday or after school and take a moment to think of the pain and indignity caused by thoughtless prejudice. At the same time, I knew it was impossible. My answer left us both unsatisfied.

Into the silence, Sam recounted a Kwaanza dinner at school. An African-American speaker had preached that whites, especially liberals, could do nothing to improve the lot of black people; "I couldn't believe she was right. But, she was so bitter, so sure."

I told him she was telling her black audience not to wait on white folks; we had to fight our own war of liberation. She was right. Community solidarity was natural. Twenty years from now Sam would be more comfortable with any white male Stanford grad that came looking for a job—he'd see a younger version of himself—than with any black woman. He didn't deny it. It didn't make him a bad person. It made him human.

We sat over our duck in raspberry sauce, not eating. "I don't think things will ever change," I said.

"Never?" he asked, searching my eyes.

"Well, not for the next fifty or hundred years or so. I think we've plateaued. We're backsliding now."

"But look at how much things have improved in the last fifty years, the last hundred."

"Things have changed materially, but not spiritually. You and I can be friends, something unimaginable for Maya Angelou's grandmother, but I feel as shackled as she did. It's just the way things are, and always will be." Then, I reaffirmed the side agreement that made our friendship possible—our friendship which contained in it the seeds for a better future than the one I evoked, the future I truly dreamed of but dared not describe out loud for fear of killing it by exposing it to the air; "That said, I don't think we can progress without white people's help. We can't do it alone."

Having rediscovered our complicity, Sam said lowly, "Being white, I just can't imagine what it must be like."

Smiling broadly and letting myself indulge in the forbidden fantasy that I had banished since Lawrenceville, I looked past Sam and into the Parisian night. "It must be amazing . . . being white. It must be like taking the coldest shower in the world, then stepping out to have a cool bracing wind dry your skin—into a bright day, where anything is possible."

"Yeah, I guess," Sam said, bemused, as unable to connect with my vision of his reality as he was to my vision of my own. He was—and is—my best friend because everything *but* race unites us, and race is not enough to separate us.

We took another sip of the Alsatian pinot noir.

"Hmmm." I let the liquid burn the back of my throat. "How are your parents?"

CHAPTER 10

I AM MY BROTHER'S KEEPER

BOSTON, AUGUST 1987

There are few moments in a man's life more important than the moment he meets his father, I thought sarcastically as I drove toward Logan Airport. I had been working in Boston that summer as a reporting intern at the *Boston Globe*. Luckily, my editor had assigned me a story that required a company car, which allowed me to pick up my mother.

Mom seemed chipper, despite the obvious stress we were both under. As I sped toward the New England Blood Center, we made small talk, each trying to comfort the other. I dropped her off in front of the building and found a parking space farther down Beacon. Soon we were seated in the lobby, my mother flipping through a magazine.

"I wonder if he'll bring *her*," she said with disgust.

"Who?" I asked, even though I knew.

"His *wife*." She didn't even look up.

"Mom, let's try to be cool about this. I know it's hard for you, but soon it'll be over."

"Hey, I'm fine," she said, pushing the magazine away. "I said that, now I'm through with it. It's gone," she waved off the phrase.

"Good."

A handsomely dressed couple strolled through the glass doors. "Hello, Jerilynn," said the man, his mellifluous baritone lapping against the walls. My mother had assumed a dark scowl, her don't-fuck-with-me look. I tossed her a silent plea.

"Is she getting a blood test too?" Mom sneered.

"Mom, please."

"You must be Marcus," the broad-shouldered man said as he reached for my hand. I shook his firmly, the way Lawrenceville had taught me to.

"Oh, Maurice, he has your eyes," his wife gushed. "Oh, it's so good to finally meet you." I wasn't sure if I preferred my mother's hostility or her feigned politesse.

My mother moved to the chair next to mine. We sat in uncomfortable silence, the man trying to look natural, his wife with the fake bougie smile plastered on her lips. Finally, she asked if I knew where they could buy a Harvard sweatshirt for their oldest daughter; she was applying.

Where can you get a Harvard *sweatshirt?* I thought. "You mean while you're here in *Boston*?" I answered, trying to sound polite and distant.

The nurse, an attractive black woman, finally appeared. "Mr. Hall, Ms. Mabry, it'll be just a few minutes more. Can I bring you something?"

"I'll take some water, dear," my mother said, overly snooty.

"Sure," said the nurse, scurrying away like a rodent before a rising storm.

"Marcus, can I see you outside?" I heard the broad-shouldered man ask.

"Why?" my mother asked, her challenge bringing me to my senses.

"I'll be right back," I told her.

He followed me toward the bustling street. I wanted to turn around and look into his eyes, to see what I saw there. Were they my eyes? At the same time, I felt the need to stare straight ahead, to prove my self-sufficiency. Outside, I would try to meet his gaze with the cold journalistic distance that robbed both subject and object of their humanity.

....

It was my fault that we had congregated in Boston. Earlier that summer my mother had gone on vacation in Florida and on a whim had driven through her old neighborhood in West Palm Beach. She stopped on Seventh Street and celebrated a teary reunion with Margaret Hall, my father's mother. Now slightly stooped with age and her children's problems, Margaret Bernice still had poise and a pretty-girl sparkle to her eyes.

My mother called me on a Saturday afternoon to deliver the good news: she had a picture of my father posing in his judge's robes with my grandmother. Struck with fear, I murmured, "What?"

"Isn't that wonderful? It was so good to see Margaret. She looked so good, Marcus! West Palm Beach is so different now." My mother bubbled over. "You'll finally see how much you look like your father. People always said you looked like me and I'd say, 'Well, you should see his father . . .'" I had heard it all before.

"Mom, what are you talking about? Why would I want a picture of my father—a man I have never known, who's never taken responsibility for me? It's like I used to tell those guys at

Lawrenceville who put up centerfolds. 'Why would you want a picture of the *one* thing you cannot have in an all-boys boarding school, just to remind yourself that you're deprived?' What makes you think I want a picture of that man?" I stopped abruptly, winded. My venomous reaction had surprised me.

"Oh, my son, my son," she whimpered. "I would never do anything to hurt you, certainly nothing concerning this bastard. He's not worth it. Oh, my son, I'm so sorry."

"Mom," I said, softly and slowly. "I'm sorry. Don't cry. I'm not hurt. I don't know what came over me." Regaining control, I said, "I thought I had dealt with this fatherless childhood thing."

"I'll throw this picture away. I'll burn it. Whatever you want. You don't ever have to see it."

"No, I want to see it." Retreating into clinical language, I said, "Clearly I have some unresolved feelings. Mom, do you have my grandmother's phone number? I think we should settle this."

I spoke so deliberately my mother complied without consideration. "Whatever you want to do, son, I support you. I love you."

"I love you too." We talked as though I were going off to some primordial rite of passage from which I would return, for better or worse, a man.

When I called, a sweet woman's voice answered the phone. When I said who I was, she enthused, "Oh, hello! I'm so happy to hear your voice."

I wanted to be polite, but I had a mission.

"It's nice to hear yours, as well," I said. "I was just calling to get Maurice Hall's phone number."

She gave it to me. "I always knew you were my grandson. But once Maurice married . . . well," resignation echoed through the static, "there was another family, another life and I had to shut my mouth."

I thanked her for her kind words, said good-bye and hung up.

Without pausing, I dialed the number she had given me; "Maurice Hall, please."

"This is he," came the booming response.

"My name is Marcus Mabry. I'm Jerilynn Mabry's son."

Without any hesitation, he said, "Yes, I know who you are. How are you, young man?"

I told him I had decided that I wanted to meet my father. He said there had always been a paternity question in his mind.

"I am aware of that," I said. "I would like to resolve those questions, in the interest of everyone concerned."

"Your mother has always been unwilling to have a blood test."

"She is willing now," I said.

"Very well. I'll pay for it."

The journalist was negotiating with the lawyer. I told him I lived in Boston. He said he would fly there. Later I recounted the conversation to my mother, word for word. She sounded at once frightened and relieved. She worried about what new pain I would suffer by knowing this man. At the same time, she had prayed for our meeting every night of every year since I was born. She did not stop at that point to ask what she risked losing by my meeting my father.

After I hung up the phone, I asked my friend Theresa, who was visiting, "Guess who I just talked to."

"Some source?" she ventured.

"Nope, my father."

"*Oooo*, creepy," she shivered.

The building belched us into the hot Boston summer. Standing a few feet away from me—close enough for bonding, far enough to avoid intimacy—the broad-shouldered man began, "Marcus, I just wanted to tell you that your mother and I once loved each other very much, as much as two teenagers could love anyone. Whatever happens, I want you to know that you can always call me when you need anything." He spoke with an impenetrable self-confidence, which would have been assuring if it didn't contain his conviction that I was just another poor black boy raised by a single mother on welfare and in dire need of a male role model.

But I knew better. I wondered what the man standing in front of me would do when it turned out that he couldn't play Father Flanagan to my Bowery Boy. When life didn't imitate the play he had constructed, what would Maurice Hall—president of his local NAACP chapter, community leader, founder of his own law firm—do when he became just another irresponsible black man?

Back in the cool building, the nurse asked us to follow her. My mother and I went into one room, my "putative father" into another. Now Mom fired off the comments she had been suppressing. Relieved to be away from the power couple, we laughed together. Watching my mother on the shiny metal table, compact and alone, a needle stuck in one arm, I remembered how much I admired her. I was probably destined to always have contradictory feelings toward her—frustration at her not fulfilling her potential, pride in her strength, awe at her endless optimism and her ability to dream. I hoped she would go to school or get a nursing degree. But if she never did—and if I was giving her "loans" until I died—in the end it didn't matter. She was my heart. I'd love her always.

WEST PALM BEACH,
DECEMBER 1987

I had never been to Florida. As a prejudiced northerner, I didn't particularly look forward to it. But my mother was planning to move there, so I drove her from New Jersey. When we finally arrived at Margaret's house, Mom joked to everyone, "Y'all know that movie, *Throw Momma from the Train*? Well, my son wanted to throw Momma from the car on the way down here."

"You weren't that bad," I said sheepishly, hugging her. (For a second, I saw myself digging my brown arms so tight around her puffy body that we would merge and I'd never let go.)

She embraced my grandmother and my two aunts. After my mother sampled the black pots simmering on the stove and dished out criticism, she and the other women played "What ever happened to ... ?" Although these people were strangers to me—even though I saw my nose here, my lips there, and my belly everywhere—to her they were kin.

It was just after Christmas. The festive little house could have been my other grandmother's, the way it used to be. They appeared to be as poor as we were, though they were middle-class with college degrees: teachers, bankers, and guidance counselors. They spoke more properly than my family, but not as properly as I did, except my cousin Stacia. She sounded as white as I did. She was my instant soul mate.

Margaret invited me back to her little bedroom. Newspapers and children's work sheets littered the bed and floor. She sat down on one end of the bed and motioned me to the other.

"Well," she said airily and expansively, with the tender invitation of a second-grade teacher, which she was, "... well." She laid her wrinkled hand on mine. "It sure is nice to see you, Marcus Mabry. I have prayed for this day for twenty years. You see the Lord does answer prayers." Tears trickled down her cheeks. She wiped them away without commentary. She clasped me tight to her and I began to cry too.

Then, she dusted off old albums and introduced me to my history. She made excuses for her son, for what had happened in his life, how he had grown up without his father, how she had raised her children without touching them often enough. "But, the Lord answers our prayers. It's gonna be okay, son. It's gonna be fine," and she smiled at me—like all the women in my life, formidable.

My mother intruded with a yelp, "What are you doing to my child, Margaret Bernice?"

"Oh, I'm stealing him away," my grandmother laughed, touching both hands emphatically to my knee. My mother stood in the doorway and stared at us, then ducked into the bathroom.

When my father and his wife arrived, they took me outside and apologized for having denied my existence for a couple of decades. They said the lab results had shocked them. So the scene in Boston had been pure vaudeville, I thought, remembering my stepmother's fawning, "Maurice, he has *your* eyes."

As my father and I went out together, my mother joked, "You bring back my son. Don't try to take him somewhere and leave him."

"Oh, Tillie, stop," my aunt Gloria said, shamed by my mother's boldness. "Maurice is gonna do right by Marcus."

I heard that expression all week long: Maurice would do right by me. What did it mean? My father's sisters, nieces, brothers-in-law, even his mother were sure that he would "do right by me" now that his error had been pointed out.

My mother saw this logic as a sick joke. As much as she carried a deep-seated love for Maurice Hall, she nurtured no illusions about his character. For her, that verdict had been rendered long ago. Yes, she had refused a blood test when he demanded one twelve years before (she said she would not put me through the pain of a needle "for him"), but he had not insisted, happy to let me disappear from his life. Like millions of men, he had done nothing. My mother knew he was not the person his family idolized, but she didn't try to tell them—or me.

We drove to a restaurant where I sat across the table from my newly confirmed father, facing Riveria Beach and the black Atlantic. I asked him what kind of man he thought he was. He was honest enough to say he didn't know. My appearance had turned his life inside out. Listening to the waves crash, I felt for him. I hated myself for it, but I couldn't help but see myself as a teenage boy accused of making a baby. What would I have done?

"The one question I've wanted to ask you for twenty years," I said, looking straight into my margarita, "is how could a man— how could you—have a piece of yourself out there, somewhere, and not know whether it's alive or dead, sick or healthy? How could you do that?" Glancing up, I searched his eyes for the answer he might not be able to pronounce. I discerned nothing. Was that a reflection of confusion, or lawyerly guile?

"I'd like to know too," he said, chuckling. "I ask myself that question all the time, every day. I can't answer it, at least not satisfactorily."

In spite of the lack of answers, it felt wonderful to sit there with him: two men drinking (he had a soda). I wanted to loathe him, to punish him, but I wanted to win his approval, too, to hear him congratulate me, "Well done, son." I sat there admiring him—impressed by his intelligence, his humor and his wit—and hoping he was impressed by mine.

....

Over the next few years, my father and I tried to build a relationship—or I did. I called him; he rarely telephoned me. I wrote; he never did. He offered to pay the hotel and gas bills from my trip to Florida; Citibank almost canceled my credit card, waiting for his check. His family started to apologize for his not "doing right by me."

"I just don't understand," my grandmother and cousins moaned.

"Give him time, Marcus," advised my aunt Gloria, trying to convince herself as much as me. Even his wife had told me that first day at Margaret's house, "He has a hard time showing love, but he cares about you." Then, she had smiled.

While I navigated a one-way street toward reconciliation, a lawyer friend at Stanford who had been the teaching assistant for an International Relations course I took asked if I wanted his help. Talking idly over a burrito in White Plaza one day, I had told him about meeting my father.

"You mean this guy was a successful attorney, while you were growing up on welfare?" Richard asked. "Marcus, this is a fucking outrage."

"Tell me about it."

"I'm sure you have a cause of action against him," he began. "I don't know if you want to sue. Certainly your mother is entitled to something for the shitty life she led, trying to raise you."

"Definitely," I said.

"Do you want money from this guy—at least for your mother— or do you want a relationship?" he asked, framing the question

like a choice between vanilla frozen yogurt and chocolate maca-
damia nut. "If you take him to court it'll probably put a damper
on any father-son picnics you were planning."

I smiled and picked at my guacamole. "On the one hand, I
want a father. On the other, I think it's amazing that even now,
he doesn't have to take any responsibility."

"Let me do some research for you. Then you can decide if you
want to pursue a claim or not," Richard suggested.

We met a few weeks later.

"I'm really sorry, but your father's a judge and you don't have
any money. And Florida law is designed to protect rich old men
from cases like yours. Even if you could find a lawyer willing to
take on a judge for a percentage of your settlement—if you win
one—your father has the *defense of laches*—basically, your mother
waited too long to pursue her claim."

The justice system spared me having to make a choice.

I wanted a father. I wanted him to embrace me and show me
off. The first time he gave me a tour of West Palm Beach, he usually introduced me as Tillie's son or didn't introduce me at all. On
a weekend visit to his law firm, he guided me through the partners' offices. In one, I spied a captain's chair—I recognized the
form immediately: shiny black lacquer over a wide seat and an
elegant spindly back, a staple of preppie memorabilia. Then, the
school seal, emblazoned on the back, leapt out at me. *Virtus Semper
Viridis.* My mouth dropped open. Lawrenceville. Stepping inside
the office, I ran my index finger over the golden seal. My heart
stirred with images of Lawrenceville. It shamed me to feel linked
to this lawyer I had never met and a stranger to the man in the
doorway.

I told Maurice our relationship was not progressing as I had
hoped. "I am not a black woman, willing to give and give, and

get nothing in return." The black women in my life had all done that. My mother, my grandmother, even my new grandmother loved unconditionally. I needed a little quid pro quo.

When I had made the call that summer afternoon in Boston, I thought I would simply satisfy a lingering, unacknowledged curiosity. At most, I would find the man my mother compared me to all my life, my father. At least, the matter would be settled and I could move on with my life.

For months after our Chrismastime reunions, I tried unsuccessfully to build the relationship. I went to West Palm Beach to visit, but I slept at my grandmother's house. (I assumed it would be too awkward to stay with my father, his wife and their three daughters.) He came by to pick me up and take me out to eat or to the movies. Now that I knew him, he felt even more absent to me. It was Margaret Hall who helped me appreciate the family I had grown up with, constantly complimenting my mother and grandmother for the fine job they had done raising me. Before I had gone to Florida that first time, Grandmom had told me, "Son, you know you already have a family that loves you very much and that wants the world for you. Whatever happens with Maurice Hall, you *got* a family."

When my father proved unwilling to construct a relationship, I felt abandoned again—and this time, he knew what he was missing.

"You can try hard enough for the both of us," he joked.

For long months we didn't talk. I vowed not to call or write until he did. After six months, one April day, I answered my office phone to a rousing, "Hey, young fella." (Only forty-two years old, my father had a thing for saying "young fella.")

"...Hello," I stumbled.

We talked for fifteen or twenty inane minutes, but they were some of the most glorious minutes I had ever spent. He had called me without warning or motive. Ironically, I had been in the middle of polishing a *Newsweek* piece about us, a sidebar to a cover story called "Deadbeat Dads." I was telling the world about us, without mentioning Maurice's name.

He called again the next week, as my article wound through the editing process. Again, we chatted about nothing in particular. I couldn't break into our bonding to confess that I planned to denounce him to the world.

The Sunday before millions of *Newsweek*s hit newsstands, I called my grandmother and read the story to her. I asked her if she thought I should warn my father. She told me not to worry. "He can read it tomorrow," she said.

I telephoned him the next morning and told him about the piece. I read him the cover title. He seemed calm, giving a slight chuckle and an "Oh, my God . . . " He asked me to fax him the story. Even before he read the article, he said he was happy I had published it: He was tired of hiding from the truths in his life. He had separated from his wife. Now I understood the recent phone calls.

He telephoned half an hour later. "It's very good. I showed it to everyone in the office." He said he could quibble about some of the facts but overall he agreed with it—and he liked my prose. He asked if he could write a response to it. I said *Newsweek* would love that; I would love that.

Suddenly my father made a greater effort to forge a relationship. He visited me in DC and New York before I left for Paris. When I moved to Europe, we talked less frequently. (I learned he planned to remarry when I received the invitation in the mail, the day before the wedding.)

But believing that he wanted a relationship now, I was

comfortable with our sustained silences—even though I wondered if I would ever reconcile my respect for my father, whom I had to defend to my friends, and my outrage toward men like him, especially black men. That millions of men could escape without paying child support was an injustice at least three-fold: against the child, the mother and the taxpayers who footed the bill.

I compared my father to my brother—and my brother came out ahead. Charles had gotten his high school sweetheart pregnant too and fathered a child out of wedlock. He earned barely more than minimum wage, but he had always helped his daughter, if not in child support, in gifts and cash to her mother.

Even in our most intimate moments, when my father and I laughed about the travails of life in the white professional world or pondered questions of love and friendship, when our twin voices became one over the satellite signals, the contradictions remained: I wanted him to be an ever greater part of my life, but I resented the pain he had caused me and, especially, my mother. He had been one of the authors of her suffering. As much as I admired him, I thought he could never be the father, or the man, my brother was.

Today I try not to make comparisons. There is little to be gained. I love Maurice Hall and somehow (I can't really explain how) I feel we've been linked since I was born: growing together, feeling the same things. Maybe it's because our lives have been so parallel: fatherless childhoods, strong mothers, professional careers. But I think it's more. Maybe when you're the progeny of two people who loved each other so much, both of them become as much a part of your spirit as they are of your genes. Maybe not. In the end, who cares, my father is my father and that's enough to gain my unconditional love.

WASHINGTON, SEPTEMBER 1991

The call surprised me. Charles had only telephoned me twice in our lives: once to complain about that article I had written for *Newsweek on Campus* after Christmas break—I had disclosed that he was a single parent and worked minimum-wage jobs—and once to request a loan. Despite my pleas over spring break, he never sought older-brotherly advice and counsel. I had failed as an eldest sibling and as the man of the house. He had seen me as little more than a limousine liberal, temporarily slumming.

We had started as opposites, then grown apart. As kids, he played the wild one, the athletic one, the Scorpio. I played "the professor," the geek, the Gemini. At his second birthday party he stuck his hand into his cake, splattering the gleaming white perfection, and *I* had cried.

My mother had done her best to raise us without a husband: dating men who treated us well, registering Charles for Little League, buying me trombone lessons. She left work to taxi him to football and baseball practice. She delayed paying rent so she could cover the fee on my instrument. But even a mother willing to hock her last possession for track shoes couldn't be a father. And we both wanted one badly, even if we never admitted it.

Once when we were kids, preparing for one of our annual trips to South Jersey to visit our grandmother Connie Mabry, my mom mused about the prefatory phone conversations with my stepfather. "I hope Charles doesn't think we're getting back together," she said as she made our breakfast. The thought clearly enticed her, and it excited us too. The idea of having a father. A man to hang out with, to talk to—even to be punished by. Standing in Grandmom's kitchen, my brother and I made kissy sounds. I hoisted him on my shoulders and we ran around the table singing, "Could it be I'm falling in love . . . with ya, baaaabyyyyy . . ."

Though we never complained about missing our fathers, we brandished them mercilessly when we fought.

"That's why your father abandoned you," I'd jab.

"At least I know who my father is," he'd swing.

"I know who my father is, dummy," I'd weave.

"Well, at least I've seen my father," he'd sucker punch.

"So, your father loves me more than he loves you." KO.

But usually we kept to our separate worlds. I had my encyclopedias and my grandmother. He had his sports and his friends. Then, during adolescence, we diverged further. I studied and talked studies. He played football and talked football. When I went to prep school, any hope of a real relationship evaporated. He became a certifiable b-boy, I became a certifiable white boy. I was Marc Mabry; he was C. Money. He wrote his own raps; he performed the beat box. He wore a baseball cap, Adidas with fat laces and a sheepskin jacket. His posse trailed behind him like he was John Wayne.

In school, learning disabilities dogged his best efforts. He worked his way out of the "special" classes into the standard curriculum, but he hated academics. He studied because my mother threatened, cajoled, insulted and bribed him.

But in the street, he was the shit. His sly smile—the reason my mother dubbed him "a devil" at two years old—earned him admiration from older guys and romance from the girls. He was a Romeo, light-skinned with a cherubic face and a small but athletic body. And he was tough. On the football field, he took knocks and tackles and kept getting back up. I was proud of his pull in our neighborhood, though I could never tell him.

When my mother had been impressed by his progress in school, she bought him a car for his seventeenth birthday. She said she'd buy anything if it could keep him in school and out of trouble. When I objected, she insisted, "I *want* to do this. This is my money." She reached the pinnacle of parenthood the day he swaggered down the aisle to receive his diploma.

But once he graduated, Charles couldn't find a job. He studied carpentry at vocational school, but then his Ford GT broke down. My mother tried to reorganize her cases so she could chauffer him to school and pick him up, but she couldn't manage it. He had to stop going.

He took the only jobs he could find within walking distance or on a bus route from home. He worked as a mechanic's assistant in an auto body shop until they laid him off. He worked at Burger King, but even after he gained seniority, his supervisor refused to move him off the part-time night schedule. He went across the street to McDonald's until he got sick and they fired him for being out. He spent months looking for a job, but couldn't find one he could walk or ride to. In the meantime, he performed yard work in Trenton and White City.

I had told him he could call me anytime he needed me. Suddenly, he was answering my need to be needed, placing me before my principles. He had had a fight with the friend whose house he shared. He was out of work. He wanted to leave Trenton, to come live with me in Washington.

I asked the first question that came to mind. "How long do you want to stay?"

I had visions of him in jail or on a slab at the morgue because I had slammed the door in his face. At the same time, I feared for myself, for my freedom—that my past would scare away my future. And what about my roommate? Nick Roegner was an old friend; he was also white and rich. Suppose my brother never left?

I made it clear that I would only help him lay a foundation for his independence.

That was all he wanted.

I wired train fare to Trenton.

My grandmother tells stories of Charles tagging behind me as a baby, calling me "bruzza" before he could pronounce *brother*. But until now he had hardly played a part in my life, outside my prayers. I only thought of him in the daytime when I saw a young black man on a street corner in handcuffs or working at McDonald's. I wondered why I had been spared from the statistics and he had not. When we met at holidays, a chasm yawned between us—we made halting small talk and avoided each other's eyes.

When he first arrived in Washington, I hardly recognized the chastened young man before me. Where was the brash, overconfident "Chaz" I had always secretly envied? His meekness and discomfort embarrassed me.

Chuck and Nick quickly became friends. They sat up at night drinking (Nick, Foster's Lager from Australia and Chuck, Red Bull Malt Liquor) and smoking cigarettes in Nick's bedroom. But my brother and I talked to each other with the strained politeness of strangers: "You will be sleeping on the futon in my bedroom. This is the bathroom that we use. This is Nick's bathroom. Now, the refrigerator is divided . . ." I sounded like June Cleaver hosting Ice-T.

Once we settled him into the apartment—he had brought only a dark green garbage bag filled with clothes—I started bringing home the office's discarded papers so he could scan the want ads. While my brother sat in front of the TV, cajoling me to go out and buy beer, the newspapers piled up. I didn't push.

Lying in bed one fall night, clutching the covers to my tired body, I tried to put *Newsweek* out of my mind and go to sleep. My brother had other ideas.

"Hey, Marc?" (He was the only person outside of Lawrenceville who called me that.)

"Yeah?" I moaned.

"You remember," he talked so slowly I would urge the syllables forward in my mind while he lingered over them, "when we were little?"

"Yeah . . . " I whined.

"Remember when we used to play *S.W.A.T.*?"

"I was the black lieutenant . . . " It just slipped out.

The images of playacting with my brother and my uncles flickered across the ceiling. My fat uncle Bobby, the oldest, always made himself the leader. I was number two and my brother and my uncle Ronny were the gun-wielding tough guys, rolling around the living room floor or bursting out the backdoor into the yard.

"I was Street," my brother said. I could hear his smile.

"Remember *Lost in Space*?" I asked.

"Yeah," he said, regaling me with an anecdote from one of the episodes.

"Remember the time you snapped when we were living in New York? You broke that brush, veins popped out of your head. You said really slow," his voice trembled, "'I am going to kill you.' Boy, I was scared. I ran into the bathroom and locked the door. When Mom asked why had you broke the brush, you was in a daze and said, like you had just woke up from a dream, 'I don't know my own strength.'" He cackled.

My brother was a master storyteller. His most heartening yarns starred my grandmother, but his most powerful stories concerned death, especially his friends'. One of his friends was killed when an eighteen-wheeler crossed the center line and mowed into his car. Another flew out the rear window in a crash, shredding his face before he died. John Pishonio, his best white friend, died speeding in his Iroc-Z. Chuck couldn't believe he had died until he looked into his face, pale and heavy, in his casket. He didn't let anyone see him cry, but every day for three years, he thought about John Pishonio, stiff and wooden in his casket.

He refused to attend the funerals of our uncles, aunts and cousins.

....

I tried to be a good liberal, but after a few weeks, I could't take it any more: my brother had to get a job.

At first, I applied gentle persuasion; "Chuck, why don't you scan these papers and see what's out there?"

When that approach failed, I got angry: "A job ain't gonna come up and bite you on the ass. Shit, get motivated, man!"

He blamed his malaise on DC. He didn't know how to use the Metro or which suburbs were close by. He complained about missing his daughter, his friends and White City. He'd spent the night before he left Trenton drinking with buddies, grown men who rarely showed their emotions dissin' and frontin' and crying. He had gone to the station alone the next morning, letting the first two trains depart before he forced himself to board the third one.

He dwelt on the glorious past. While his obsession with it frustrated me, I admired his ability to cherish the good things that had made us happy when we were young. I had to be sarcastic and bitter; he could be forgiving and ironic. Eventually, I came to understand our different bonds with White City: he was *from* there; I had just lived there.

Once he had mustered the determination to look for a job—thanks to my browbeating and Nick's more brotherly encouragement—he quickly landed one at a fast-food restaurant and soon got a second. He worked sixty-hour weeks, more if he could wrangle extra time. He traveled an hour by Metro and bus to these two low-paying jobs in the suburbs. (It took more than an hour's wages to pay for transportation.) I grew angry thinking about how his resolve could serve him well in a real job. But at least we were at home with one another; he started to call me "Brother."

Chuck lived with me for a year, moving with me when I bought a condo in DuPont Circle. At last, we became friends as well as brothers.

But after a year, we gradually began to wear on each other. His rave reviews at work made him increasingly cocky. He resented my authority. I resented his dependency. *Newsweek* cut short our deepening mutual annoyance by sending me overseas.

Chuck couldn't afford to rent my DuPont Circle condo. He had to find his own place. He held down two jobs and both fast-food restaurants valued him immensely, but his confidence still faltered. When I told him in the fall of 1992 that I would be leaving in January to move to Paris, he said simply, "Hey, you gotta do what you gotta do," and shrugged his shoulders. But he looked wounded.

He had never had to look for a place to live. He scoured the DC newspapers and quickly found that the free *City Paper* had the most choices in his price range; he had to take a room in someone's house or find a roommate. Unwilling to live with a stranger, he chose to rent a room.

After weeks of searching, he despaired. He had telephoned and gone to look at rentals, but they never panned out. One night, while I sat deeply enthralled in *Murphy Brown*, he dialed number after number, rejected each time.

"They're all taken," he said from the dining table behind me, exasperated.

"What?" I was only half listening.

"Man, that's the third apartment I called about tonight that was already rented!" he sighed.

"Three in one night?"

"Yeah," he said, wiping his hand down his face. He was still wearing the greasy uniform from his twelve-hour shift.

"Let me try," I said, raising myself from the futon.

"What!" He pushed back from the table where his newspaper, pen and pad lay neatly next to the phone. He was annoyed. "What are you doing, Marcus? The lady said the room was rented."

"I know. I just want to see something."

I pressed redial. A pleasant, light voice glowed at the other end.

"Hi," I said. "I'm calling in reference to the ad in today's *Post*."

"Well, it's a very nice, very large room. It's fifteen by fifteen with great light. Fabulous feature followed fabulous feature.

"So, it's still available?" I asked.

"Oh, yes."

"And it's only $375? Is that correct? (This was an incredible steal in DC!)

"Yes, we want to rent it right away," she chirped. "Would you like to come over and see it?"

I made an appointment. "Thank *you*," I gushed and hung up. The color had drained from my brother's face. He sat speechless, his arms folded. I shook my head, trying to give him solace. (This was in the days before caller ID was widespread.)

"White people are so fucking racist," I said.

"I don't understand . . . " Chuck started. "Why would she tell me the room was rented . . . "

"Because you 'sound black.' I don't."

"Damn," my brother said, defeated. "I don't believe that."

He decided to restrict his search to the black neighborhoods of inner DC, a longer commute to work, but at least he would have a roof over his head. Within days, he'd leased a room in an elderly black woman's house. (Even she seemed hesitant until she spoke to his Stanford-credentialed brother.)

A year and three months after he had moved into my apartment, homeless and unemployed, my brother furnished his place with a bed, a TV and an aquarium, and stocked his kitchen. He also had a bank account. As surely as I had saved him, he had saved me, reminding me that the true measure of my success was not in the applause of strangers, white or black, but in the strength of my family.

WHITE CITY, THANKSGIVING 1992

Before leaving for Paris, I decided to spend my last holiday "at home." As Chuck and I drove up the turnpike, the smell of the turkey and the raucous laughter at my grandmother's house—a world that no longer existed—swelled my head.

Cowering in my cousin Beverly's small, tidy living room, I tried to look comfortable. I wanted to lay down, to run away—to be back in DC. My family's reality had become alien: A grown cousin and an uncle worked as grocery store stock boys. My best-paid cousin had been laid off from a factory job. Most of the men hadn't held steady work in months, and some—in their late thirties—still lived with their mothers. Surveying the crowd, I didn't see much cause for giving thanks.

Tired of feeling sorry for myself, I retreated to the front porch where the men were drinking, mostly from forty-ounce brown bottles. I wanted to show I could hang with the fellas. And I wondered if I could. I grabbed a stool. To my surprise, they were discussing politics. My cousin Glenn argued that Ross Perot had been good for the democratic process because he shook up the Democrats and the Republicans. "He made the parties deal with the real deal," Glenn said.

My cousin Danny countered that Perot was a distraction; "Just because you know how to run a business, doesn't mean you know how to run a country."

"Amen," seconded my uncle David. They moved on to world affairs.

Listening to them debate the news I covered, my despair turned to pride. Then, pride turned to anger. Why were these men, capable of so much, doing so little?

The women all had jobs as nurse's aides or secretaries. My aunt was on her way to completing a bachelor's degree. The chain of responsibility in our family passed from the older women to the younger ones, like my cousin Beverly.

When I came in from the porch, she told me she wanted Tiffany, her daughter and my first cousin, to see Lawrenceville. For months we had talked about me introducing Tiff, a promising eighth grader, to L'ville, though she seemed ambivalent. Her friends were going to Hamilton High and she felt she would be just fine going there too. But Beverly convinced me that I should put off my return trip for a few hours and take Tiff to Lawrence-ville. I would take two of her girlfriends too.

It was four o'clock and dusk was already falling. I worried the grass wouldn't look green enough. I wanted everything to be at its peak, for Tiffany to fall in love with Lawrenceville the way I had.

After we drove around The Circle and the new girls' houses, we stopped at the Field House. My charges gasped. I remembered the way I had felt when I saw it for the first time. The building looked big enough from outside, but inside! The girls almost ran from the indoor track, to the tennis courts, to the volleyball courts, to the basketball courts. They watched boys warm up in the hockey rink. They peeked through locked doors at the Olympic-size pool. They read the sports off the captains' boards: hockey, lacrosse, crew.

We ran into Mr. Maxwell, one of the black teachers, at Mem Hall. The girls marveled at the math and computer center. Tiffany was most impressed when Mr. Graham gave me the keys to the science building and told me to take the girls on a tour. As we left the dark campus, I prayed that Beverly and I had planted a seed in Tiffany's mind that she would never be able to dig out.

PARIS, MAY 1993

Outside my living room window, the *Bateaux Mouche* glided along the Seine. As the boat navigated the turn around the eastern tip of the Ile Saint Louis, its floodlights bounced off the crystal chande-lier, drizzling shiny whites, yellows, purples and reds around the walls before disappearing through the trees and leaving me in darkness.

I had been a Paris correspondent since the end of January. My mother had just finished a two-week visit. I had said good-bye at Orly Airport that morning, then breathed a long sigh and headed for the office. I recognized the feeling. It was freedom, the same freedom I had felt that day when I set off up the Champs-Elysées on my own, the same freedom I felt when I moved into a bare new apartment: the blankness of opportunity.

Living in Paris as an adult, that personal freedom was almost tangible. But the rarer freedom—the racial freedom that I had felt ten years earlier as a high school student—was dying. Prejudice still weighed far less in France than in America, but the French were muttering increasingly about "the Arabs . . . the blacks . . ." Sometimes, a cabbie would not pick me up or would ask where I wanted to go before he unlocked the rear door. Once, while looking for a friend's apartment on a Sunday night, pastry box in hand, I approached a building as a couple exited. The man stood in the portal long enough to ensure that the door shut behind him, yanking it for good measure.

"What's your number?" I asked the man in French.

"Who are you looking for?"

Hearing his real question—and already an hour late for dinner—I found the word I had been searching for: "Address . . . address . . . What's your address?"

His girlfriend safely in the street, he insisted, "Who are you looking for?"

Tired of the game, I yelled, "Enough! All I want to know is the address of this building."

"Five," his companion volunteered, edging toward the curb.

"Thank you," I spat. "Would nine be up this way?" I pointed with the cake box.

"Yes," she said, as Prince Valiant stared at me, immovable.

"Thank you. Good evening." I hammered each word and headed up the narrow street with a loud "Whew."

Witnessing the French's increasingly inhospitable attitude toward Africans, I took pains to distort my accent. I had been proud of the voice that native teachers at Lawrenceville had implanted, the accent that Frenchmen could never place; they usually thought I was from Guadeloupe or Martinique, Caribbean islands that are a part of France. To avoid being treated here as a black man would be in America, I aped the dialect of an American in Paris, squashing my crisp consonants and flattening my rounded vowels, stretching out the short *aaaa* sound for as long as possible and smashing the airy *rrr*.

As a teenager and then a college student, I had mistaken relative tolerance to be an absence of racism. I was wrong then, and in covering France as a journalist, I chronicled rising prejudice. First came the landslide victory by the conservative coalition in March 1993, which gave them an unprecedented eighty percent of parliamentary seats. Then came the ever more draconian laws limiting the rights of immigrants and even their French-born children. Under the guise of eliminating illegal immigration, the government restricted whom French citizens could marry. Racial violence—mostly against North Africans, France's black men—increased markedly, in tandem with the government provisions.

Living abroad, it was impossible to ignore that bigotry was the rule worldwide. American racism was only a particular breed of a universal species. The relief from racism that France offered the African-American, particularly the African-American male, was necessarily unsatisfactory. The issues that my education and my privilege had made it my obligation to address were not on this side of the Atlantic. France could no more be my refuge than it could be my home.

PARIS, MAY 1994

I was on my way to a dinner party at the American embassy, hosted by the ambassador herself, Pamela Harriman, in honor of Katherine Graham, chairman of the Washington Post Company (which owned *Newsweek*), when the telephone rang.

My cousin Stacia cut short my breathless exuberance. "Marcus . . ." she said in a hushed voice.

"Yes," my response came almost involuntarily.

"Uncle Maurice has been shot."

I fell back into my chair.

"Marcus?"

I pictured my father felled by some crackhead as he got out of his Lincoln Town Car.

Stacia was saying that it had happened during a deposition a few hours earlier. In the middle of an interview, the plaintiff drew a nine-millimeter semiautomatic and emptied it on my father, his client and the co-defense attorney. Both of the other victims were dead, and so was the thirty-year-old attorney's unborn child.

The next day, when I walked into the intensive care unit at Broward General, Maurice was sitting upright wearing a blue baseball cap, a plastic tube looping from one nostril. He looked as strong as he had when I had last seen him, a year and a half ago. He smiled broadly and his eyes sparkled with awareness—the only real difference from the time I saw him last was his awkward forward slouch.

I dragged my luggage into the room, smiled and said hello to my new stepmother. I moved toward my father, but my mind was immobile, idled by the sounds and smells of the dark artificial space, the innards of some horrible machine. Was I experiencing the dread of realizing that the one invincible person in my life was mortal? Wasn't that what the children of heart attack victims said after seeing Dad hooked up to a respirator? I thought it ironic I could know that fear, never having known the illusion.

I had pictured myself running to him and throwing my arms around his bearish frame. I would cry out, "We've wasted so much time. Let's phone each other every week and write once a month. Let's send cards on birthdays and exchange presents at Christmas and Father's Day."

Only the Kodak moment that had played in my head during the eight-hour flight never came. I did call my father "Dad" for the first time—I thought it best to stop saving up steps for later. But the unbreachable space that had separated my father and me still stood between us, cold, clammy and silent, now increased by the eerie feel of the ICU.

Over the next ten days I stayed with my grandmother and visited my father periodically, a reenactment of the old ritual I hated. His condition steadily improved. The doctors called it a miracle. I had imagined I would see him every day, but he said I should take time for myself. Part of me selfishly resented being shunned, but I knew he needed his rest. Every time someone stopped by, he put on the brave face of a community leader and church deacon—joking, laughing, gossiping, even backslapping. His denial of his pain and fatigue recalled some stoic Boston Brahmin. By the end of any visit, though, he always nodded off.

I usually stopped in with my grandmother or one of my aunts. The pattern was always the same when there were no other visitors. I would ask how he was feeling. Susan, my stepmother, would detail the latest. As we stood around the room or sat on his bed or in chairs, the conversation turned to what was happening at home, in my life, in the media circus surrounding the shooting. Inevitably, we would all end up laughing softly, politely, at some barely amusing anecdote—between bemoaning the evil circumstances that made America Dodge City and celebrating the heavenly ones that had spared my father.

Sitting on the edge of his bed, I felt like his son. Even if what passed between us was stilted and incomplete, it was enough. Everyone gave me the best position, as if it were only natural. I could feel the warmth of my father's leg. I had never been able to touch him before, other than the quick hug American men share. We held hands and dared to look into each other's eyes, trying to overpower the hollow melancholy.

We never discussed how the shooting had made us more aware that our relationship could be cut even shorter—the doctor called the bullet to my father's stomach and intestines a "fatal wound." I only saw a trace of emotion when my grandmother told him that his assailant had shot his ex-wife ten years earlier. My aunt said the Lord sure had blessed my father, and suddenly he began to whimper like a child. His face screwed up and his lower lip quivered. His chest began to heave and the tears came. My grandmother moved closer to his bedside and clasped his head to her breast. He wept into her body like it was a sponge. I wanted to turn away, but I watched.

The day I left Florida I wrote Dad a note, because a minor complication had forced him back under the knife. It spoke of my pride and my hope that I could be as strong if ever I had to be. Later, he told me how happy he had been that I had come, how he wished we could have spent more time together, how much he still regretted the lost years. I said only the years ahead of us mattered, but I couldn't predict when we would next get to see each other.

Ten days after I returned to Paris, I boarded another flight for America. Charles had had a massive heart attack. One of his roommates called to tell me at three in the morning. I phoned my mother and she took the train from New York to Washington.

I flew into Dulles the next day to relieve her—and my brother, who was tired of her lectures on his weight, his diet and his cigarettes. He told me the story of the weekend before his heart attack, when he had spent Father's Day with his daughter.

"Grandmom gave her money. Cholly gave her money. Janice. I said, 'Baby you're loaded. You gonna take *me* out to lunch?'" He laughed. "I was just playin', you know." Then he sat there, staring at the distant wall. The scene reminded me of our time together in Washington. He talked about his daughter, Tiffani, how she needed him, how her mother's squalid house was no place for *his* daughter to grow up.

I took up residence at his bedside. As I tapped the keys of my laptop, he filled out his Medicaid application. He had worked, stressed and eaten his way to a coronary. Two jobs had led him there. He had left Roy Rogers after the store manager had promised to promote him, even given him manuals and test guides, but had never actually given him the tests. Even with a completely clogged artery and an IV in his arm, Charles could only think about returning to his new job at Jiffy Lube. Of course he had no health insurance; he had been at the job less than a month. And as a member of the working poor, he might not qualify for Medicaid.

As my twenty-five-year-old brother drifted off to sleep, I wondered how he could ever change his habits. He ate, drank and smoked too much. Looking at his jaundiced round body, my old resentment of America rose again, dark and smoldering like a coal fire. My brother's life, even more than my mother's, informed my view of the cruel and dangerous society that left the bottom to rot.

....

On an earlier visit to Washington from Paris, I had met Charles and Nick at a popular Yuppie restaurant, the California Cheese-cake Factory. After the three of us stuffed ourselves, Chuck went to the bathroom. Through the haze of a food coma, Nick and I eventually noticed that he had not returned. I spied him in a heated exchange with two managers and felt immediately queasy.

I asked if I could help. One of the men said my brother had been harassing some female customers. My brother disagreed, seeming close to telling these gentlemen where they could get off. They seemed on the verge of kicking him out. I pictured a DC police black-and-white and my brother in a jail cell with murderers—all for talking to a white woman. Black men had been killed for less.

Back at our table, Charles explained that he had caught the eye of two young ladies. They looked depressed and he asked if they wanted him to cheer them up. They replied that he could try. He talked to them for a while and they laughed together.

The hostess who called the managers did not dispute this much, but she said the women had grown tired of my brother and wanted him to leave the table. They never told Charles that, but the hostess could see they were getting uncomfortable. She said the women thanked her when she called him from the table on a ruse to admire his gold rings.

I didn't understand why the managers had gotten involved once my brother was discussing the merits of male jewelry with the hostess. But one of the two men approached him and said, "Sir, may we escort you back to your seat?" (Every black man knows when "May I help you" really means "Don't try to pocket that Dior tie because I'm watching your black ass.")

And my brother answered the only way he knew how: "No, you may not."

At that point, my brother's 'hood machismo mixed with the preppie pomposity that had rubbed off from living with Nick and me. "I'm a paying customer in this restaurant," he said, indignant.

I am here with my brother who works for Newsweek *in Paris and his friend*, he thought.

I am delivering the fair-haired damsels from the marauding black hordes, the young white man probably thought.

Listening to Chuck's story, I pieced together the probable sequence of events. No doubt, the young women did enjoy his company; my brother can be funny and electric. They probably grew tired of him and started to worry he would never leave. If the planet had been peopled by women, the incident would have ended there, but men will be boys. That a difference in the way b-boys and white boys court could have landed my brother in jail, or worse, shot a spasm of fear through me. I didn't want these characters to think they could threaten to expel every black man they didn't like.

With my brother and Nick gone, I asked the more reasonable of the duo what had happened. He sketched the chain of events and said, "No big deal."

Just as the roiled waters calmed, the younger, cockier manager came over and said, "Your brother caused trouble. He had to go."

We sank into the quintessentially American game of "Can I get your name?" He came back with a card.

"Is this yours or the other manager's?" I asked. It turned out that the card belonged to neither of them; the actual manager was out that night.

"So if I had written to someone, referring to this man, I would have looked foolish, huh? What are *your* names?"

He asked for my card. I took care to say as I wrote another number on it, "This is the Washington bureau's number, if you would like to call me there. I'm here until the end of the week."

I told him this ugly evening could have been avoided with a little understanding and, perhaps, a little less prejudice. He said he didn't like my implication. I said I didn't like his attitude. Arriving at this general consensus, I walked down the stairs toward the exit.

The "manager" followed me. I turned abruptly, "Are you kicking *me* out of the restaurant now? I haven't talked to any white women."

I forced myself to sit down at the first-floor bar and sip a coffee, black.

········

My brother worked harder than most people I knew. He could be a carpenter; he had the work ethic and, from what I understood, the talent, but he had no union contacts. When it came to other jobs, because he didn't speak with a Yuppie accent, interviewers wrote him off as soon as he opened his mouth. He never received the chance to prove himself, and he probably never would. The legions who loathed big government and "welfare fathers" would not cry for him when he worked himself to an early death. They didn't even acknowledge his existence.

Not one to fret about the fragility of human life, Chuck acted the fool instead, bitching to his nurses about the food and feeling confined. Only in our first minutes alone, as he recounted his frightful drive to the emergency room and almost losing consciousness, did he let slip, "Man, I didn't think I was gonna make it."

When my brother fights back tears, he stares straight ahead, as immobile as an eagle peering across boundless space at some distant prey, and gradually he becomes stone. We sat there silently together. The world outside ceased to be. Now we negated its existence. I thought about how I had almost not come to Washington. I had been finally overcoming the jet lag from my last trip and finding the rhythm to write. The most beautiful summer days in history were draped over Paris, long, silky and fragrant. Every night the setting sun turned the sky blood red and turquoise between the trees of the Ile Saint Louis. But when my brother needed me, I came.

Sitting in a hospital room in Gaithersburg, Maryland, nothing mattered but us, our family ties, our love for each other and our strength. He braved the crazed brothers armed with semiautomatic weapons on the streets of DC. I ran the gauntlet of the jealous ones who didn't like Oreos who talked white—and both of us faced the assault of white vindictiveness: Chuck as he persevered against diabolic odds and belied the racial myths that were the alibis for inequality, me because I dared aspire to the measure of "their" success.

Even after coming so close to Death he could smell His breath, Charles was massive and immovable. His posture, rigid and upright, reminded me of the rewards of surviving this life as black men—certainty, courage and self-respect—every day of breathing a triumph.

EPILOGUE

I have learned many things since I first sat down to write this book; some of them have to do with the subjects treated here, some of them don't. Many of them came out of the writing; even more of them came out of the reading. My mother's typically unsubtle response to reading an early draft was: "Well, I guess I'm just the biggest welfare bitch that ever lived." My grandmother requested that I remove all members of the family from the book. My father didn't return a phone call for a month. And my best friend, Sam, thought I drew such a radically insensitive caricature of him that he didn't know what he would tell his mother when she asked, "When does Marcus's book come out?"

I never expected that writing a memoir would be easy; but I didn't expect the fallout to be so lethal, either. While I think—perhaps naïvely—that love and time have already begun to heal the wounds that my telling our stories has opened for those closest to me, the most important revelation that came to me in writing the book may not be healable—it may not even be a wound. But I think it is.

In the first draft of the book, I wrote for many pages about my argument with Sam over the magazine article. I never said a positive thing about him or explained why he was "my best friend." (My mother, my father, my grandmother cannot make this complaint, but they can make equally valid ones about how what I left out was hurtful to them.)

In talking to my father about what he called my "vision," it struck me that what echoes through the pages of *White Bucks* is an abounding stoicism, even pessimism. For instance, having read this book, you might not know that most of my friends are white. I have implied it. But I rarely show it. Most moments of black-white interaction are either tension-filled or negative. (Of course, most of the black-black interactions are less than merry.)

I would like to blame my penchant for negative reporting on my training as a journalist. Good news is no news. When one of my readers asked me, "You make Sam sound pretty horrible. Why is he—or was he—your best friend?" My first response was, how do you explain why someone is your best friend—without sounding mushy and saccharine? How could I relate the thousands of happy moments I had shared with friends, when race didn't seem to matter, though those moments outnumbered the times when race created tension one hundred to one?

I cannot blame journalism solely for my negative news bias. I brought it with me to the job—adding my own cynicism to a profession that had plenty already. My pessimism was a survival mechanism that I brought with me from my childhood. My outwardly expressed lack of faith that America would be better tomorrow, particularly when it came to race relations, had insulated me from disappointment. As a kid, I used the cocoon of demanding little from the world and my family as a protection against getting my hopes squashed in a world so unpredictable and unforgiving. Then, when I set out to integrate the white world, I used the pessimism (or is it the realism?) that my neighbors and my relatives had given me, that white people did not like us (the proof was ample) to guard against unanticipated prejudices. In writing my story, every anecdote of prejudice confirmed rang ten times louder than moments of tolerance.

My best reader pointed out that I was funnier in person than my writer's voice. The book is a little bitter and a lot self-absorbed, he complained. The philosophy I penned is more bitter than the views I espoused in everyday life. This difference is explainable. The book is condensed, compact, brutal, ordered, cold. It is divested of the ambiguity that can come from a trembling voice or the self-doubt that someone talking to you can see in your eyes. It is all true. It is not all the truth.

It may be the final price that I pay for my ambassadorship: rationalizing my place as a black man in a largely white world. While I can live comfortably in this world 90 percent of the time and comfortably enough in the 'hood when I keep my buppie mouth shut 80 percent of the time, I can never write a happy ode to integration. You see, I think the price for living a life that is happily integrated is not being able to put it wholly into words. Instead of the happy part of one's life coming out, it's the suppressed concentrate of anger that gets distilled into black on white, print on paper.

I had to seal that anger away, mostly, to be able to live in a white world. At the same time, I had to convince myself that tomorrow would be better, so that the daily disappointments would not dissuade me from keeping on keeping on. If I had expected warm fellowship from whites and brotherly understanding from all African-Americans, the disapproval of both would have sent me back long ago. Where to, I do not know. There is no other place for me but here, in this in-between universe.

So even while my own life experience taught me that we can live and love and learn harmoniously together—black and white— my brain told me otherwise. I came to live Martin Luther King's dream (as close as you can today), but my brain was operating on early Malcolm autopilot. Like my grandmother, I have achieved more than I expected. Only I am still to some extent imprisoned in the cage of low expectations in which I have chained the world—even while I pray that my integrated world (can you call it that when so few African-Americans are permitted into the circle in which I live and work?) will one day be the rule.

It's an old existentialist trick: work for a brighter day, convinced it will never come. Ironically, when it does come (for you, if not the world), the anger that it has not come for everyone prevents you from communicating the happiness it has given you.

I have to think that this anger is a human—even a humane— response to continuing injustice. I believe that the larger realities of the difficulties between blacks and whites are more important than my small successes. At the same time, my successes are a beginning. And that is what *White Bucks* does not say strongly enough.

I do not want to join the corps of racial pessimists who litter America. I am not one of them. I believe we can achieve equality and peace. But it will be one relationship at a time. We must proceed with our eyes wide open, knowing that race *does* matter. Our perspectives will often differ, black from white. But acknowledging that is a starting point to understanding, not a reason for despair. And we must proceed not out of some need to be accepted by a community of strangers, white or black, but out of self-love and pride, and the desire to understand those different perspectives. We have nothing to lose but our ignorance.

Dr. King said that as long as one man is not free we are all slaves. I would like to think that is why my book is angrier than I am. I live a life based on my best hopes, hoping still for a more harmonious tomorrow. But when I write, it's my worst fears—and the pessimism that has led to a successful, integrated life—that roil the pages.

It is, in fact, an extremely happy place, as earthly places go, this place where I live at twenty-seven years old. I am surrounded by friends who love me. I work with smart people who respect me. I have a strong family that shelters and protects me. My friends come in all colors, shapes, sizes and nationalities. I would like to write about this happiness. . . . Maybe next time.

AFTERWORD

The last twelve years have been eventful and, for the most part, enormously blessed. I turned 30, then 40, and in between I wrote another biography, this one of Condoleezza Rice. I moved from Paris to Johannesburg and then back to New York, and after nineteen years left *Newsweek* for the *New York Times*.

While I was writing the first edition of *White Bucks*, living the freedom that I felt in Paris, I was also feeling my way toward coming out. I was not prepared at that time to write about being gay and black, so I didn't. When I came out to my mother, she, typically, surprised me. "Well, I've always been a lesbian," she said. (She laid on top of another girl, with their clothes on, in the fourth grade.) She has been tremendously loving and supportive. I'd expect nothing less from her.

My grandmother, Merle Thomas, was loving and supportive too, though she was sure "that white boys' school" had made me gay. My father, Maurice Hall, with whom I have a strong relationship today, though I wish we saw more of each other, has been supportive too. As has my grandmother Margaret.

Twelve years ago I wrote, "the true measure of my success was not in the applause of strangers—white or black—but in the strength of my family." If that is true then my success is incomplete. My mom is doing fine, working to fulfill a dream of living in Harlem, though her various injuries have landed her on permanent disability. My dear grandmom passed away in 2000, less than a year after I returned to the United States from seven years as a foreign correspondent. The Thanksgiving before she died, I insisted to my family that we take her from her nursing home to her old house for the holiday. It was her last Thanksgiving, and I'm so thankful that I brought her home to spend it with me.

I still miss her terribly.

My brother is not doing well. He's had many more heart attacks and is struggling to win the fight for his life.

My niece Tiffani is in college, the first person on her mother's side to go—and the first to graduate high school.

Sam is still my best friend.

After returning to the States, I settled down in New York with a loving partner. My partner, Chris, and I are discussing growing our family.

And yesterday I was sworn in as a member of the Lawrenceville School board of trustees. In my brief remarks afterward, in a building that did not exist when I was a student, I stood before the headmaster (a woman, in a school that is now coed), my old headmaster, my fellow trustees and senior school administrators, and pointed out the window to my left, toward The Circle. I told the story of Connie Mabry, my step-grandmother, who managed the all-black waitstaff at Griswold House. I noted that my standing before them that day, just two generations later, a trustee of this great school, said a lot about Lawrenceville.

It said a lot about America too.

October 5, 2007
New York City

ABOUT THE AUTHOR

A native of Trenton, New Jersey, Marcus Mabry attended public elementary schools in Hamilton Township before graduating from The Lawrenceville School with distinction. He received undergraduate and graduate degrees in French and English literatures and International Relations from Stanford University. A veteran journalist, he is the recipient of numerous journalism awards. He is an editor at the *New York Times*. He wrote *White Bucks and Black-Eyed Peas* while serving as a correspondent in Paris for *Newsweek*, where he spent 19 years as a writer, a foreign correspondent, an editor and the chief of correspondents. He has also written for *Foreign Affairs*, *Foreign Policy*, the *New Republic*, *Emerge*, *Savoy* and *Black Collegiate* magazines, among others, and has served as a commentator for CNN, MSNBC and Fox *News*.

Mabry is also the author of the definitive biography of secretary of state Condoleezza Rice, *Twice As Good: Condoleezza Rice and Her Path to Power*. He is a member of the Board of Governors of the Overseas Press Club and a member of the Council on Foreign Relations. He is chairman emeritus of the Albert G. Oliver Program, which sends gifted black and Latino public school students to private school, and is a trustee of the Lawrenceville School.

He lives in New York City with his partner.

INDEX

M